RESOURCES
FOR
WRITING
WITH A PURPOSE

RESOURCES FOR WRITING WITH A PURPOSE

Experiments and Readings

Brock Dethier
University of New Hampshire

HOUGHTON MIFFLIN COMPANY   Boston

Dallas   Geneva, Illinois   Palo Alto   Princeton, New Jersey

Printed in the U.S.A.

ISBN: 0-395-43221-9

ABCDEFGHIJ-B-9543210/8987

Text Credits

W. H. Auden, "Work, Labor, Play" From A CERTAIN WORLD: A COMMONPLACE BOOK by W. H. Auden. Copyright © 1970 by W. H. Auden. Reprinted by permission of Viking Penguin, Inc.

Donald Barthelme, "Report" Reprinted by permission of International Creative Management. First published in The New Yorker. © 1967 by Donald Barthelme.

Gary S. Becker, "Why Shouldn't College Be A Smart Investment?" "Reprinted from September 8, 1986 issue of *Business Week* by special permission, © 1986 by McGraw-Hill, Inc."

Caroline Bird, "Where College Fails Us" Copyright 1975. Used by permission of the author.

Sissela Bok, "To Lie or Not to Lie? – The Doctor's Dilemma" "Copyright © 1978 by The New York Times Company. Reprinted by permission."

Lorna Dee Cervantes, "Refugee Ship" Copyright 1975. Reprinted by permission of University of Pittsburgh Press and the author.

Barry Commoner, "An Inherently Dangerous Technology" From THE POLITICS OF ENERGY by Barry Commoner. Copyright © 1976 by Barry Commoner. Reprinted by permission of Alfred A. Knopf, Inc.

Wayne A. Cornelius, "When the Door Is Closed to Illegal Aliens, Who Pays? "Copyright © 1977 by The New York Times Company. Reprinted by permission."

Norman Cousins, "The Right to Die" "© 1975 Saturday Review Magazine. Reprinted by permission."

Edwin Diamond, "Twelve Days of Terror! The Three Mile Island Story" Excerpt from *Sign-Off: The Last Days of Television*, MIT Press. Copyright 1982 by the Massachusetts Institute of Technology.

Peter Drucker, "The Basic Skill" Excerpt from "How to Be an Employee" by Peter Drucker, which first appeared in *Fortune* magazine, from the book PEOPLE AND PERFORMANCE: THE BEST OF PETER DRUCKER ON MANAGEMENT. Copyright 1952 by Peter Drucker. Reprinted by permission of Harper & Row Publishers Inc.

"Education Has Been Neglected Long Enough" "Reprinted from February 2, 1987 issue of *Business Week* by special permission, © 1987 by McGraw-Hill, Inc."

Daniel Egger, "West Germany Pours Hot Milk" *The Nation* magazine/The Nation Company Inc., copyright 1987, used by permission.

Norman Ellenberger's "Tell it Like It is: We have to Make Money" *The Center Magazine*, Vol XV No 1, January/February 1982, pp. 21–22. Reprinted by permission of The Robert Maynard Hutchins Center for the Study of Democratic Institutions.

Susan Fraker, "Why Women Aren't Getting to the Top," *Fortune*, used by permission.

Samuel G. Freedman, "Live Aid and the Woodstock Nation" "Copyright © 1985 by The New York Times Company. Reprinted by permission."

Georgakas and Rubenstein, "Interview with Jane Fonda" Dan Georgakas and Lenny Rubenstein, "Interview with Jane Fonda," from "I Prefer Films That Strengthen People," *Cinéaste*, used by permission.

Continued on the next page.

Continued on the next page.

CONTENTS

PART TWO / READINGS   57

(The numbers of the experiments that refer to each reading appear in parentheses following its title.)

PREFACE

This book serves a double purpose: it is both a student source book for *Writing with a Purpose*, Ninth Edition, by Joseph F. Trimmer and James M. McCrimmon, and an independent collection of readings and writing experiments that can serve as the core material for a writing class. The concept and organization of this book are unusual. It is neither a rhetoric with readings included as models nor a reader with study questions at the end of each selection. It is a collection of readings linked to experiments in using the writing process. The two halves of the book complement each other but can be used independently. And the whole is addressed to students, with student interests in mind.

Although I trust that experienced writers and teachers will be able to pick up this book and use it almost immediately, the sections "How to Use the Readings" and "How to Use the Experiments" include numerous suggestions for making the best use of *Resources*. The experiments are flexible and the descriptions of them brief, consistent with my belief that the writing teacher and student should adapt techniques and approaches for their particular needs rather than follow rigidly defined steps. I use the term *experiments* because these are techniques for students to "try out" or "essay forth" with. My hope is that students will be successful with many different experiments, finding them so useful that they adopt them into their writing process repertoires.

I would be glad to see this book serve many different purposes within writing programs, but I hope everyone who uses it will approach it with a sense of the playfulness, the joy, and the excitement of discovery that should be part of writing and reading.

ACKNOWLEDGEMENTS

I owe a tremendous debt to my friend and colleague, Donald M. Murray. Don's genius in the field of composition is matched only by his generosity in sharing his ideas with others. Everyone now working in composition has benefited from Don's contributions to the study of the writing process and from his contant battle to win for writers and writing teachers the respect they deserve in the academic world. I have borrowed a number of techniques directly from him, and his thinking underlies virtually all of my work; I hope this book as a whole reflects something of his writing philosophy.

Like any other writing teacher, I can trace the classroom activities I now call "mine" to a number of sources, some of which I would like to acknowledge here. Through their books, articles, demonstrations, or suggestions, the following people provided the basis for the experiments listed: Richard M. Coe and Kris Gutierrez, experiment 2; William Evans, experiment 6; Peter Elbow, experiment 7; Janet Schofield, experiment 9; Mary Munter, experiment 10; Richard E. Young, Alton L. Becker, and Kenneth L. Pike, experiment 21; Marya W. Holcombe and Judith K. Stein, experiment 22; Andrew Merton, experiment 26; Melody Graulich, experiment 31; Peter Elbow, experiment 34; Bruce Ballenger, experiment 71; and Don M. Murray, experiments 18, 28, 29, 33, 37, 40, 41, and 42.

I am grateful to the editors at Houghton Mifflin for creating this project and providing guidance throughout. I wish to thank Jenny Nelson for her expert advice in choosing the reading selections in the section "Women and Film." Finally, I would like to acknowledge the unflagging support of my wife, Melody Graulich — but that's a book in itself.

HOW TO
USE THE
EXPERIMENTS

These experiments complement the exercises in *Writing with a Purpose*, Ninth Edition, by Joseph F. Trimmer and James M. McCrimmon, but none of them depends on that text. The experiments can be profitably linked in any number of ways, and at the end of most experiments I have suggested others that would be logical next steps through the writing process. But the experiments are independent and not repetitive; therefore you can use them in whatever way fits best into the other writing and classroom work you're doing.

Except for those in the last section, "Special Assignments," the experiments follow the writing process, from ways of getting ideas and finding the tools that work best for you to exercises in planning, drafting, and revising. They reflect my belief that writers should try to make their work easier and that one way to reduce the pain and anxiety of writing is to experiment until you find your own easiest path from idea to finished product.

Each experiment is both a means and an end in itself. Each focuses on certain aspects of writing and reading, expanding the writer's choices, building the writer's understanding. But most also yield a solid piece of writing in which you have the opportunity to expand and explore your thoughts and feelings on your subject.

You can approach the experiment in three ways:

■ *In Order.* Although they do not in themselves constitute a complete writing course, these experiments completed in order could provide a strong backbone for a writing program. The ordering of a particular series of experiments may be arbitrary, but overall the experiments follow a logical progression through processes that lead up to a finished piece of writing.

■ *By Section.* Working straight through the experiments does have disadvantages — the progression through the process may seem slow, and you may have to hand in a "finished" paper long before you get done with the planning experiments. Therefore, you may want to appraoch the experiments by section, doing a few in the first section, then moving on to try some in the second, third, and fourth sections before returning to repeat the cycle. This approach requires a more careful choice from among the experiments than does the first, but it more closely mirrors a real writing process, during which most writers take a limited number of steps before typing a draft. If you have a paper due Monday, try one of these sequences: 7, 9, 29, 38, 54, and 56 or 6, 17, 28, 31, 33, 34, and 63 or go directly to 30.

■ *By Chapter Headings.* The cross-references on page xix provide connections between the experiments and the fourteen chapters in *Writing with a Purpose*, Ninth Edition. The cross-references allow users of that text to choose experiments appropriate to the chapter under study. They give others the ability to find quickly ways to practice the skills associated with the fourteen self-explanatory chapter headings.

In the instructions for each experiment you'll find suggestions for readings to use in conjunction with the experiment and for experiments to try next. Very often you can use the experimental techniques on your own evolving drafts as well as on the readings indicated. Whenever possible I have tried to suggest ways of using the experiment on its own or of linking it to other ones.

HOW TO
USE THE
READINGS

To be considered for the reader section of this book, the selections had to be well-written, interesting, and related to one of the ten themes: Music — Bridging Cultures; Women and Film; Vietnam — It's Not Over Yet; A Nation of Immigrants; Nuclear Threats and Accidents; Medicine, Ethics, and the Law; Going into Business; The Work Ethic Today; Paying for an Education; What Is a Good Education? If you're using these readings as part of a writing class, consider approaching them in one of these three ways.

■ *Use the readings with the experiments.* If you're working with *Writing with a Purpose* or a program that follows the same order and organization, this would be the most logical approach. Most of the experiments ask you to read one or more selections, giving you a choice from a number of possible readings. Every selection is referred to at least twice during the course of the experiments. Therefore, if you do most of the experiments, you should have a chance to read all the selections. After each title in the table of contents, you will find the numbers of the experiments that refer to that particular reading.

■ *Read them in thematic units.* If you're more interested in thematic connections between the readings than in using the readings in the writing process, you may want to approach the selections section by section. Each section includes a variety of genres — ranging from poetry to interviews to personal essays — from a variety of perspectives. Each provides material for debates, for sparking your own writing, and for learning about writing by analyzing successes. You could write a brief research paper on one of the ten themes using only the information in the readings, or you could use that information as the starting point for a more substantial research effort. Even if you aren't assigned to read the selections, browse through pieces in sections whose titles interest you.

■ *Read them independently.* Because almost all the readings are independent of others, you don't *need* to impose any organization on your selection of readings. Your teacher may suggest that you read particular articles so you can see how an author uses a certain technique or provides the reader with context. You may choose a selection in hopes that it will suggest to you essay topics of your own. You can view many of the selections as models, and you can read some as adversaries in a debate about a subject you care about. Or you can read them just for fun. Reading good writing can help you improve your own writing without your having to lift a pen.

RESOURCES AND WRITING WITH A PURPOSE

The table below lists the 14 chapters of *Writing with a Purpose*, Ninth Edition, and the experiments in this book that correspond to them.

RESOURCES FOR FOR WRITING WITH A PURPOSE

PART ONE
EXPERIMENTS

I
PREPARING

　　　　THE DOUBLE-ENTRY JOURNAL

Even if you don't intend to keep a daily journal, you are going to need a notebook
for class notes and exercises, so you might consider using your notebook as a
writing journal. As you become comfortable with a particular notebook, writing
time, and writing style, you will probably keep more than notes in your notebook
and it will become a journal, an important part of your writing and thinking.

You will get the most out of your notebook if you keep it as a double-entry
journal. The concept is simple: you make a journal entry — a response to any of the
experiments in this book, for instance — then later reread your initial entry and
comment on it in writing.

What's the point? Commenting on your initial entries helps you make sense of
your own processes of thinking, reading, and writing. In a second entry you might
speculate on why you thought of second-grade recess when you were freewriting. Or
you might put your enthusiastic response to the essay "Book Learning" in perspective by noting that you enjoyed reading some of E. B. White's other essays in high
school. We learn to improve our writing and our thinking by becoming more
conscious of them as processes, discovering what we do well and what gives us
trouble. Double-entry journals help writers make the connections between ideas and
experiences that are essential to effective thinking and to learning.

How do you go about it? Everyone has a different method. Experiment with
some of these and choose one that seems most effective for you.

■ Draw a vertical line on each page, making the side for first entries somewhat
larger than the second-entry side.

■ Get a notebook with wide ruled margins and write your comments in the
margins.

■ Write first entries on the backs of the pages, second entries on the fronts of the
following pages.

■ Use a different color ink for your second entries.

Be sure to date each entry and to keep your notebook with you as much as
possible. Trade notebooks occasionally with classmates if you feel comfortable
about doing so. Keep quotations from your reading or from conversations, lists,

names, notes, freewriting, and writing tips in your journal — anything that could conceivably help you with your writing.

To get started, read Patricia Hampl's "To Create a National Music," Lorna Dee Cervantes's "Refugee Ship," or Baron Wormser's "I Try to Explain to My Children...." As soon as you finish your reading, write down all your reactions without worrying about trying to write correctly. Then reread the selection carefully and make a second entry in your journal, explaining or commenting on your initial entry. Think about ways in which writing is really thinking. If you want to continue working on this subject, follow this experiment with experiments 9, 17, and 33.

2   **WRITING PROCESS SELF-ANALYSIS**

One of the best ways to learn about your own writing process is to analyze how you created one particular paper. Which parts of the process were effective and which would it be better to change or eliminate? To do such an analysis, you need to reconstruct how you went about writing something. It's helpful if you have recently written an important paper, but think back to last year if necessary. Or if you have a big paper assignment coming up, do this experiment after you've finished it.

After you've focused on a particular paper, follow these steps:

■ Copy the questions below, writing them on the left side of a notebook page.

■ Answer the questions, writing your answers in the next column.

■ Look over your answers and determine whether the steps you've written down would be the same for most of the papers you write, or whether some steps are unique to that paper. Make some kind of notation (perhaps "T" for *typical* and "D" for *different*) in a third column.

■ Finally, on the right side of the page, note the steps that you'd like to change and suggest ways that you might change them. Your teacher may be able to suggest ways to make the changes you're interested in.

If you find this process useful, try repeating it regularly, or even for every paper you write, constantly looking for aspects of your writing process that you should change and parts that work well and that you should expand on. Try experiment 14, as well, to help you make the best use of the results of your self-analysis.

Question	Answer to the Question	Typical?/ Different?	Changes
Why did I write this paper?			
How did I come up with this subject?			

Question	Answer to the Question	Typical?/ Different?	Changes
Did I talk to anyone about my subject?			
How did I refine the subject?			
What did I do to "plan" the paper before the first draft? [List as many steps as you can think of; if you did it all in your head, say so.]			
What tools [e.g., pens, typewriters, dictaphones] did I use?			
How did I make the first draft into a final draft? [List the steps.]			
How did I come up with my opening paragraph?			
Did anyone read any of my drafts?			
What reaction did I get from my teacher (or other reader)?			
What part(s) of the process were particularly difficult or painful?			
What parts were easy or enjoyable?			

3   **EXPERIMENT WITH TOOLS, TIMES, AND PLACES**

Some professional writers can write anywhere, anytime. But almost all writers prefer to write in particular places, at particular times, and with particular tools. Over the next few weeks, experiment as much as you can with when, where, and how you write. Record your results. Any discovery you make about when you write your best can be extremely useful to you for all your future writing.

If you need something to write about, try responding to one of the readings, for example, Lynda Van Devanter's "Short-Timers," Ed Ward's "Reggae," or Alice Walker's "Nuclear Madness: What You Can Do." Then try writing just before bed, after you've had your morning coffee, in the five minutes between classes, or on Sunday afternoons when you have no commitments until dinnertime. Are you more meticulous in the morning, more creative in the afternoon?

Go to the library, the crowded cafeteria, your dorm room when your roommate's playing Jimi Hendrix. You may be surprised to discover the place you work best. Many people get ideas for writing while taking walks or showering. Some writers work best in crowded coffee shops. Sit under a tree and see if you get any inspiration before you get uncomfortable. See if you can find *the spot* where writing will always go well for you.

Try pencils on notecards, felt pens on yellow pads, ballpoints in your journal. Compose at the typewriter. Many writers use superstitions to help them through their fear of the blank page, so if you have a favorite pen, use it; if you like to write on the backs of envelopes, do it. Pamper yourself to get those words flowing. If you have a chance, by all means experiment with a word processor. Initially it will require a bigger investment of time than any other tool, but it will repay your effort. (See experiment 4.)

Keep notes on every writing session — just jot down quickly:

1. Where you were;
2. What time it was;
3. What you were using;
4. Whether you accomplished anything; and
5. Whether you enjoyed it or found it painful.

Every now and then go back over your notes and look for patterns. After a while you should begin to feel — or to see in those patterns — that one combination is the best for you.

---

4   USING A WORD PROCESSOR

Many writers were slow to take advantage of personal computers. They thought that computers were too mechanical and inhuman to be used in the arts and humanities and worried that writing on one would somehow drive the life from their writing. Yet I've never met a writer who bought a computer for writing and was sorry. Writing on a computer after typing all your life is like changing from a bicycle to a car. You don't want to forget how to ride the bike, but when you want to go far or fast, you take the car.

Here are a few of the many reasons to invest time (if not money) in writing on a computer.

■ Writing on a computer saves you time — lots of time. If you've ever retyped a ten-page paper because you left a crucial paragraph out on page 2, you have some idea of the potential savings. The more drafts you tend to write, the more of a perfectionist you are, the faster your investment in a computer will pay off for you.

■ Writing on a computer speeds and aids you through many planning, drafting, and revising strategies. Most typists find they type faster on a computer keyboard then they ever did on a typewriter, so freewriting on a computer can reach nearly the speed of talking into a tape recorder. Some word processors can create outlines for the writer, numbering or bulleting different sections. (Bulleting means listing items vertically and marking each item with a dash, asterisk, or dot.) All make almost every aspect of revision easier and more enjoyable, from moving whole paragraphs to correcting misspellings.

■ Writing on a computer creates a better finished product. A computer won't write your papers for you, but it allows you to improve your paper up until the last minute, and if you have the programs, it may help you with spelling and sentence problems.

■ Writing on a computer can make writing more interesting. With the drudgery of retyping virtually eliminated, writing can become more creative, less tiresome. Watching things appear and disappear at your command can give you a sense of playfulness about your writing.

■ Writing on a computer is a good skill to have. Even if you don't buy a computer yourself, you're likely to interview some day for a job for which knowledge of computers is required. It will be nice to know — and to show — that you're not computer-phobic.

You may not want to invest in your own computer (unless you foresee a continuing need for one), but you will surely write at least a dozen papers in the next few years, so learning to write on a computer will be a worthwhile investment of your time.

At many schools, people who don't have their own computers can still get access to them. Some offer students use of clusters of computers or have computers available for students in certain departments. Many computer stores offer rentals by the hour or by the month. And the person down the hall with an Apple may let you use it if you offer to buy the next box of printout paper. Since you often can't transfer a disk from one computer to another, try to locate a computer that you can get access to throughout the semester. There isn't much point in getting access to a computer for only a few hours, except that playing with it for that time can help you to decide whether you should get your own.

Once you locate a machine, you will probably be swamped with specific instructions on how to use it. Here are a few general suggestions to keep in mind as you sit down for the first time in front of keyboard and screen. If you don't understand some of the computer jargon now, you will once you've been introduced to the machine you'll be working on.

■ Be prepared to be frustrated (everybody is) and to waste time (everybody does) as you're learning. If you're getting good help, you should be able to print out your first "document" in only a few minutes, but to become comfortable with a computer will take weeks, especially if you're not a good typist.

■ Don't work on anything crucial for the first few hours. It is possible (though it's rare) to destroy an individual "file" or a whole disk and all the work it contains. If you're careful, you should never lose anything important, but while you're learning you don't want to have to worry about it. So play around instead. Write letters. Read something and then write some quick reactions to it. Try reading "Sex and Violence: Pornography Hurts" or Sissela Bok's "To Lie or Not to Lie — The Doctor's Dilemma" or *Business Week's* "Education Has Been Neglected Long Enough."

■ Being careful means always keeping backup copies of your disks. That will probably mean buying an extra disk or two, but that's a good insurance investment. If you keep backup copies you're much less likely to contribute to the growing collection of computer horror stories.

■ Save your file every few minutes. The fact that something appears on the screen may give you the impression that it is *there*, fixed and permanent. But it isn't. Until you write your file onto a disk, it can get wiped out by a power loss or a mistake on your part.

■ Don't get power-crazy. Some people become infatuated with the power and possibilities of computers and want to play all the games, to use all the programs, or to create programs of their own. Such impulses may lead to computer "hacking," and from there to a career in computers. But they probably won't help you to learn quickly how to write on a computer.

5   ## LOOKING AND LISTENING FOR SUBJECTS

Many of your paper topics may be assigned or may grow out of your reading, but chances are your teacher will want you to come up with at least a few paper topics on your own. If so, you will be faced with the question that terrifies students of writing everywhere: What will I write about? Of the many answers to that question we will explore in the following experiments, one of the most basic is "The world around me." There are endless subjects in the people and things around us. We just have to open ourselves up to them and start thinking like writers.

Take your journal or notebook with you to familiar places and look for subjects. Go to the mall, the student union at its most crowded, a rock concert on campus, the gym. Look for what Ken Macrorie, in *Telling Writing* calls "fabulous realities," small bits of information that surprise, amuse, or startle us, giving us insight into people and ways of thinking. One of my favorites is a bumper sticker that read "If it's metric, we don't want it" on a Toyota, every bolt of which was metric. Little ironies like that can turn into paper topics.

Look for connections, contradictions, ironies, surprises. What do you notice about fashions, hair styles, the number and type of people smoking cigarettes? What new insights do you have into the behavior of groups of high school students? What do store window displays tell you about our society? What kinds of people are asking for money or handing out pamphlets these days? Try not to feel "I must get a paper out of this." Just observe and think and connect. Jot things down, then go back later and ask yourself why you wrote down that particular observation.

After testing your own observational powers, read Donald Hall's "Ox Cart Man" and see how they transform observations of everyday things into poetry. Or read Patricia Hampl's "To Create a National Music" and note how composer Antonin Dvořák turned the sounds of birds, waterfalls, and trains into music. Follow this experiment with experiments 6, 7, or 38; then if you think you're onto a good idea, focus it with experiments 21 or 28, and begin drafting with number 33.

---

6   **SENSORY EXPERIMENT**

As observers, we all tend to rely too much on our sight and hearing. We don't pay enough attention to the information available to us through our other senses, and we seldom just sit and use our senses without interacting with the world. This experiment is designed to get you in touch with all five of your senses and to sharpen the observational powers that are crucial for a good writer.

Pick a spot on or near campus — a laundry room, the bowling alley, the library's newspaper room, a pizza joint. Go there with your journal or notebook and stake out a good position for observation. Then spend twenty-five minutes there — five minutes "observing" with each of your five senses. You'll have no trouble hearing, seeing, and touching things, but at first you may think there's nothing to smell or taste. But don't give up — spend your whole five minutes smelling and tasting. Move around if you want to. A laundry room does have a particular taste, as does a library. It takes some work to find ways to express what you smell or taste in an empty classroom, but doing such work will open up new areas of insight into the world around you.

After you've spent your full time "sensing," try getting together with friends or classmates who have observed in the same place. Compare your observations, looking for points of agreement and for surprises. Pick the best observation from your group for each of the five senses and compose a sentence embodying that observation. Combine the five sentences into one sentence or into a short paragraph that will give a reader the best possible idea of what your observation area was like. This process of sorting through sensory details to find the most expressive and representative one is often frustrating, but it's fundamental to the writer's art. And when you have that one detail, the sentence that really captures your place, you should feel a sense of accomplishment that lets you know why writers keep writing.

Now read Michael Herr's "Illumination Rounds," or Fred Reed's "A Veteran Writes," and observe the way they use sensory details. How do you react to sensory details that are neither seen nor heard? After this experiment, try experiments 7, 44, 59, or 70.

---

7   **FREEWRITING FOR TOPICS**

In freewriting as a way of coming up with topics, anything goes. Start writing whatever comes into your head and follow your train of thought without trying to make sense of it and without paying attention to grammar, spelling, punctuation, propriety, or anything that might slow you up. Follow tangents if that's where your pen leads you. If your brain starts feeling empty and written-out, get ready — that's often the best time for a thought from left field (or third grade) to pop into your consciousness. Many people who are used to writing only for a specific purpose — slow, painful, "correct" writing — find it very difficult to freewrite, just as some tennis players who compete constantly get fidgety rallying. But if you freewrite often enough and long enough, you'll find that it allows you to see writing, for the first time, as a relaxing, creative, and perhaps even enjoyable experience.

Start by freewriting for ten or twelve minutes, then immediately read back over what you've read while you shake the cramps out of your hand. Look for words or phrases that surprise you, connections that you don't completely understand. Compare your first idea to your last, and see if you can make a sensible statement about how they are connected. You won't always hit pay dirt when you freewrite, but if you keep trying it, and keep an open mind about the results, you'll soon find yourself saying, "Yeah, I could write about that."

Now try experiments 8, 9, 17, 18, 29, 40, or 42. If you need to produce a draft quickly, write some quick discovery drafts (experiment 34), then organize your thoughts with experiment 41.

---

8   **WHAT DO YOU WANT TO KNOW ABOUT?**

Most writing is done from a position or strength, expertise, and information. The ex-CIA agent writes spy novels, not rock record reviews. But one of the joys of writing and research is digging into a subject that has always interested you but that you've never had a chance to explore. Through the writing and research, you make yourself an expert on the subject. Then when you're done, you not only have a paper to hand in, you also have a new strength, a sense of authority about a new area. You've expanded and broadened your world, and you might possibly follow this new subject in your education or career.

So in this brainstorming experiment, list subjects that you'd like to explore and become more knowledgeable about, not subjects you already know about. Don't worry, for now, about the practicality of writing on any of these subjects. You can't easily become a true expert on, say, the theory of relativity, but you could become an authority on it relative to your friends. You might decide it would be fun to write a paper explaining the theory to people who haven't a clue about it.

Take about fifteen minutes and jot down all the subjects you can think of that you'd like to dig into. Keep this list in a special place in your notebook and periodically glance back at it and add to it. Occasionally, when you are searching for a subject for a paper, consider doing some of that digging.

Now read Susan Fraker's "Why Women Aren't Getting to the Top," Georgakas and Rubenstein's "Interview with Jane Fonda," Donald Barthelme's "Report," or

Alex Haley's "My Furthest Back Person — 'The African.' " What and how much did the authors learn in the process of researching and writing about their subjects? Write about this question in your journal or discuss it with friends or classmates. Follow this experiment with experiments 7 or 18.

9   FOCUSING WITH FRIENDS

Your experiences constitute a rich source of paper topics — they are unique to you and they contain more lessons and themes than you could ever hope to write down. Yet student writers often become frustrated in trying to write about their experiences. They have trouble stepping outside of the events and making sense of them; they can't see the point or focus that would help a reader grasp the essential meaning of the experience.

Many of the experiments in Section II will help you transform experiences into essays, and you can start the process by working with a group of friends or classmates.

As a warm-up, read Vo Thi Tam's "From Vietnam, 1979" and discuss what point the author makes and what point you would make from the same material. Consider whether there are a number of possible essays contained in the experience.

Now think of a story you often tell friends about some meaningful event in your life. Without trying to figure out the focus or importance of the story, tell it to your group as you would normally tell it, giving as many details as you can. After you have finished, ask your friends to play teacher, giving you feedback on four specific questions:

1. What should the focus, point, theme, conclusion, or moral be for an essay written about the experience? What idea related to the experience would make people think, feel, or act differently?

2. Once you've agreed on the focus from question one, discuss how the story could best be told to highlight that focus. Which details would hook the reader into the paper and which should come last to resonate in the reader's mind?

3. What parts of your story need to be expanded, clarified, or explained? What extra context could you provide to help readers make sense of the whole thing?

4. What details need to be cut? This is often the hardest part for many writers — you get really attached to the detail about all the funny nicknames people called your brother, but you have to realize that that detail really doesn't help you make your point about teenage pregnancy. Three or four friends saying, "Nah, that doesn't fit," may convince you of something about which you couldn't convince yourself. (Don't throw the detail away, however. Delete

it from the essay you are working on but note it in your journal; it could become the basis for an entirely new essay.)

Chances are your friends won't agree on their responses to your questions, but that's fine — it leaves you with many options open. You don't want other people to be dictating to you the meaning of your experience. But with some help from your friends, you're likely to be able to see your own experience as something worth writing about.

From here you might want to go to experiments 10, 19, 22, 31, 33, or 40.

___

10   ## ANALYZING A SPECIFIC AUDIENCE

You've learned about the concept of audience, and you may have discussed the characteristics of the general audience to whom you'll be writing most of your papers. Often writers find it useful to take this process one step further and analyze a specific audience, perhaps even an audience of one. Even when writing for a large audience, many people find they can focus their ideas better if they imagine that they're just writing for one particular person — a friend or parent or teacher or a "typical" member of the larger audience.

For this experiment, think of one particular person that you're likely to write for — a boss, friend, or teacher — and analyze that person by answering the questions below. When you next have to write something important outside of class, use these questions to analyze your new audience.

1. Who is my primary audience?

2. Is there a secondary audience — someone else who is likely to read what I am writing?

3. What does my audience know about me?

4. What is the relationship between me and my audience in terms of the hierarchy of school, company, or family?

5. What am I likely to represent to my audience?

6. What does my audience know about my subject?

7. How is my audience likely to perceive my knowledge about my subject?

8. How is my audience likely to feel about my approach or conclusions?

9. What is the age, sex, education, and background of my audience?

10. What in their background is likely to affect their perception of me and my subject?

11. What have I heard about how my audience reacts to writing? Does my audience insist that every paper be a certain length, or that papers be typed and presented in a specific way?

Read Michael Goldberg's "Los Lobos," Yoko Ono's "On Yoko Ono," or Steven H. Madoff's "A Way to Pay That's Not Just Academic," and describe the kind of person the author seems to be writing for. Then try experiments 11, 12, 13, or 32.

11   QUESTIONS TO ASK YOUR TEACHERS

Teachers may be the most important audiences that you write for at the moment, as well as the most confusing. Every teacher has individual preferences and pet peeves; unfortunately, many teachers assume that their preferences are universal. Your writing teacher will probably tell you what sorts of things will earn you a higher or lower grade, but your teachers in other subjects may not. This experiment is designed to help you analyze your teachers as audiences and therefore to write papers in the style and format that they approve.

This is not advice to write "just what the teacher wants to hear." By all means, stick to your own ideas, interpretations, and conclusions. But discovering the quirks of individual teachers will ensure that you are graded on the basis of your ideas and writing, not on whether you broke some unspoken rule about format or presentation. If you become good at analyzing your teachers as audiences, you're likely to carry that skill over to the work place, where you will need to analyze your boss or your clients or customers in the same way.

First, try experiment 10 to get you thinking about specific audiences. Then, when you're given an assignment, or at some other time when you're discussing writing for a particular class, ask the teacher — politely and respectfully — as many of the following questions as you feel are relevant.

1. What kind of format do you expect?
   a. Title page?
   b. Summary?
   c. Name, date, and class section or number in a particular place?
   d. Margin size?
2. Is there a page minimum or maximum?
3. Should a particular kind of analysis or particular steps be included?
4. Do you like, or object to, headings and subheadings, numbered lists, etc.?
5. Should the paper contain enough background information so that it makes sense to anyone who might pick it up, or should I write it assuming that the audience has some knowledge of my subject?
6. Should I avoid using "I"? Are contractions acceptable?
7. Do you expect particular theories or terms to appear in my paper?
8. Do you have a preferred footnote or citation form?

9. Is it OK to have other students read and critique my paper?

You might try doing this with a friend, as in experiment 27, or preparing for this particular teacher's essay exam with experiment 65.

---

12 WRITING FOR DIFFERENT AUDIENCES

This experiment should show you how much your sense of your audience can affect the way you write about a given subject.

1. Read Thomas Murray's "The Growing Danger from Gene-Spliced Hormones," Norman Ellenberger's "We Have to Make Money," or Peter Drucker's "The Basic Skill," and think about the subject that the selection discusses.

2. Select four audiences from the college community that would have an interest in that subject: students, teachers, administrators, parents, alumni, coaches, taxpayers, athletes, employers, and so on.

3. Write a paragraph to each of your four different groups, trying to explain your stance on the issue while also appealing to their specific interests. (You'll find this easier if you've already done experiment 10.) Remember how many different elements of a paragraph can — and probably should — change as you change audiences: style and tone, emphasis, choice of facts (what you mention and what you leave out), diction, and amount and arrangement of detail.

4. Compare your paragraphs with those of classmates who wrote to the same audiences. Discuss why you made the choices you did for that particular audience.

Now read Gene Santoro's "Paul Simon — Graceland." Can you describe his audience? Discuss how the review might change if it were to appear in *Time*, *Rolling Stone*, or your school newspaper. (The review originally appeared in *Downbeat*, a magazine that caters to serious music lovers, particularly jazz fans.)

To avoid becoming paralyzed by writing *for* your audience, try the next experiment or use the material you gathered here for experiments 25, 28, 41, or 47.

---

13 CREATING YOUR AUDIENCE

We often talk about audience as though each person were a fixed, unchanging entity, reacting to the same information in the same way every time, as a computer does. But in your own experience as an audience — reader or listener — you know that what may strike you as funny one day can seem stupid the next, and that the presentation of an idea may strongly affect the way you react to that idea. Generally, we react not only to what a writer says, but to the writer's stance and assumptions about us as well. If the writer is angry and assumes we're going to be unsympathetic and unfair, we'll probably respond with more anger than justice. On the other hand, if the writer approaches us assuming our good will, we're more likely to respond with thoughtfulness and good judgment.

Therefore, to some extent, we can as writers create the audience that we would like for our writing. But to do so, we have to control carefully what we write. This experiment gives you practice in taking such control.

Imagine that you have been given what you think is an unfair grade by your chemistry teacher, Mr. Zinc. You got three *Bs*, an *A*- and a *C*- on the tests that determine your grade. Yet Mr. Zinc gave you a *C*+ for the course. For a number of reasons (make up your own!) you haven't liked Mr. Zinc from the first, and you suspect that he lowered your grade because he sensed your lack of respect. You'd like to tell him off, but you'd also like to get your grade raised.

First, write a letter to Mr. Zinc — an immediate response to your grade. You're very angry, and you want to let Mr. Zinc know about all the stupid things he's been doing all semester. Let loose. When you're finished, reread the letter, or exchange letters with a friend, and imagine the response you'd get from Mr. Zinc.

Now write a second letter in which you carefully consider your audience and purpose. You want to get your grade raised, but you don't want to do it simply by lying or by flattering Mr. Zinc. Write your letter to a Mr. Zinc who's fair and caring and who will certainly change your grade once he sees the miscalculation.

Again, exchange letters and imagine how you would react. Many people would write — and send — the first letter because, they say, it makes them "feel better," even if it doesn't give them any realistic hope of accomplishing their goal of raising their grade. Writing the second letter may not give you the emotional satisfaction of the first, but it's much more likely to get you the more lasting satisfaction of an improved grade. As long as you don't misrepresent any of your feelings, you're not being false. No letter ever includes all of a person's feelings. You're simply choosing to say those things that will help you reach your goal and to ignore others that wouldn't get you anywhere.

To practice applying this concept, follow this experiment with experiments 58 or 67.

14   **SELF-ASSESSMENT**

This experiment will help you make the most of your evolving skills as a writer. Use it in conjunction with experiment 2; together they will help you to assess periodically your progress throughout the term.

The idea is to get down on one page all the most useful things you've learned about your writing and yourself as a writer, the things that you want to remember long after this course is over. Answer the following questions as specifically and completely as you can. If you don't write another paper for a year, you may be very glad that you've written down the things that helped you create a good paper.

1. What works for me?
   a. What subjects?
   b. What tools?
   c. What processes?
   d. What critics? (Which friends make good critics?)
2. What words, phrases, approaches, or constructions should I stay away from because they confuse my readers or because I overuse them? [For instance, I use "but" and "it seems" too much, and I have to be careful about not letting my sentences get too long.]
3. What parts of my writing have teachers or classmates praised throughout the semester? That is, what am I good at?
4. What have I learned about reading, writing, grammar, spelling, audience, and so on, that I want to remember for future writing tasks?

Repeat this experiment periodically throughout the term, and especially at the end of your writing course.

Use the results of experiments 3, 8, 38, 39, 45, 51, 59, 61, and 64 to make your self-assessment more detailed and accurate.

II
PLANNING

15   PROCRASTINATION

Many, perhaps most, student writers when faced with a writing assignment take the same first step: they procrastinate. Putting your work off until the last minute isn't *necessarily* a bad thing to do. Some very successful writers work that way, figuring out in their heads what they're going to say, then furiously writing it all down. But before you label yourself as a "last-minute person," honestly answer two questions about the last paper you did at the last minute:

1. Was it as good as you could have made it?
2. Did you enjoy the process?

If you answered *yes* to both questions, keep procrastinating. If you didn't, try following the method outlined below for the next paper you write.

■ Start as soon as you're given the assignment, but do only a little. Jot down ideas for fifteen minutes, and then get on to other things.

■ Continue to work in short, frequent sessions. Do some brainstorming or free-writing one day, come up with an outline or an introduction the next.

■ Reward yourself for successfully completing your short writing sessions. Get yourself an ice-cream cone or go play with a frisbee. Make a half-hour or an hour of writing a pleasant, natural part of every day.

■ Set false deadlines for yourself. Arrange with a friend to read a draft of your paper five days before it's due.

■ Don't punish yourself with writing. If you hear a party going on downstairs but tell yourself that you won't go until you get some writing done, you're punishing yourself with writing and you'll hate it. Try instead to see every page as its own reward, as something you can feel good about having accomplished for the day, as a weight taken off your shoulders.

■ Get your teacher involved. If your teacher's willing to meet with you to discuss your ideas or rough drafts, agree on a meeting time well before the paper is due so that you'll feel compelled to come up with something to show your teacher.

■ Pay close attention to what you discover about your writing process as you do the other exercises in this book. It's most important for you to determine what kind or stage of writing is the easiest and least painful for you. For me, the least painful step is sitting with a yellow pad and jotting notes, making lists, or coming up with connections. So I do as much of my writing as possible in that fashion.

■ Whatever you do, get the paper typed early enough so you have plenty of time to proofread it. The first time you go through this process, you'll probably be looking for any excuse to return to your old ways, and a low grade, resulting from a poorly proofread paper, could be just such an excuse. An hour spent proofreading may have more of an effect on your grade than an hour spent on any other stage of the process.

To conquer your procrastination, you're going to have to analyze yourself and figure out what you gain and lose from putting your work off. Chaining yourself to your desk doesn't work. Figure out the games that you play with your own mind and learn how to win those games. If you can improve your writing habits, the improvement may carry over into your other study habits, making you a better student all around.

If you want to change your habits — start now. Read Alice Guy Blaché's "Woman's Place in Photoplay Production," Lorna Dee Cervantes's "Refugee Ship," or Sissela Bok's "To Lie or Not To Lie? — The Doctor's Dilemma." As soon as you finish reading, spend fifteen or twenty minutes freewriting or brainstorming, jotting down whatever thoughts occur to you in relation to what you have just read. Then, a day or two later, go back, read what you wrote, and try to appreciate how much closer you are to having ideas for a paper than you would have been if you hadn't written anything down. A little writing today can make you feel better about the whole project tomorrow.

Keep track of changes in your habits using experiment 1 or 14, and keep your mind open for new changes as you do other experiments, particularly 16, 34, 45, 52, and 64.

---

16   **INTERVIEW A PROFESSIONAL**

This experiment is intended to help you learn more about writing processes rather than to make you into a great interviewer, although it should provide practice for the interviewing experiments later in this section. Students often have the sense that professional writers are a different kind of being who magically, effortlessly, turn out page after page of perfect prose. In order to realize that they, too, can become good writers, many students need to learn that every writer must work at it, that we all suffer from fear of the blank page, that even writers with hundreds of publications and prizes sometimes wake up in the morning and think "everything I've written is worthless."

Your teacher can probably help you find a professional writer. Most professors are professional writers (in order to keep their jobs they must publish articles and books) and your teacher probably works with scores of other writing teachers who are also poets, novelists, playwrights, and journalists. Most will be delighted to be treated as professional writers with valuable experience. Ask for a fifteen or twenty minute interview. Before the interview, read Georgakas and Rubenstein's "Interview with Jane Fonda" to see the kinds of questions two interviewers asked of Jane Fonda. Become more aware of your own approaches to writing by performing experiments 2, 14, or 15. During the interview, find out everything you can about how your subject writes, focusing on planning with questions like these:

1. Where do you get your ideas?
2. What's the first step you take once you've decided to work on a subject?
3. Do you freewrite? Brainstorm? Use maps or lists?
4. What kinds of tools do you use? Do these tools change as you advance through the process?
5. At what stage in the process do you first write complete sentences?
6. Do you try to get all your research done before you write anything, or do you cycle between writing and research?
7. Do you use stock sets of questions, like "Who? What? When? Where? Why? How?" Or do you let the questions grow out of the subject?
8. What's hardest for you?
9. What's easiest?
10. What do you most enjoy?

Follow this experiment with numbers 23, 26, or 27.

---

17   **FOCUSED FREEWRITING**

Consider the concept "practical education." Freewrite for ten minutes on what it means to you.

Now read Donald M. Murray's editorial "What Is a Practical Education?"

Did reading the editorial change your views, even slightly? If so, in what ways? What did Murray do to try to persuade you of his view? Which of his arguments seemed particularly successful to you? Can you figure out why?

Write down what you see as Murray's purpose in writing this editorial. Did he succeed?

Consider writing a paper on your own definition of "practical education." You don't necessarily have to agree or disagree with Murray. Just try to explain your own ideas as they emerged from your freewrite and in your reaction to Murray's editorial. If you're interested in this subject, read other selections from the section "What Is a Good Education?" and do experiments 18, 23, 28, or 34.

18   ## MAKING AN AUTHORITY LIST

A common complaint among young people taking writing courses is "I haven't lived that long or done that much — what can I write about?" This experiment is designed to show you that you have more experience, knowledge, opinions, and expertise than you might think.

Read E. B. White's "Book Learning," Ralph Waldo Emerson's "Education," David Weinberger's "Computer Literacy Is Not Literacy," or Meg Greenfield's "Creating a 'Learning Society'" in the section, "What Is a Good Education?" Think about what you might write on the general subject of education and literacy. You probably don't have expertise on the subject equivalent to that of the authors of the readings. Yet you are an authority on education — you've spent thousands of hours in educational institutions. So before you go any further, make yourself an authority list. List aspects of education that you know something about, your perspectives on education gained from your years in school, the opinions you hold about the educational system even if, at the moment, you can't back up those opinions. Remember, you don't need to be the world's leading expert on something to write about it. You just have to know more than your audience does or to have thought more about your subject. Relative to your current teachers, you're probably an authority on what high school is like now. And relative to people in high school, you're an authority on college.

Spend fifteen or twenty minutes thinking of both the specific and the general aspects of education that you know about. Don't overlook the expertise gained by going to different kinds of schools (for example, public and private); the role of "teacher" you may have taken on for younger siblings or kids at camp; all the extracurricular aspects of school — sports, musical groups, socializing; what was unique about your school; what you've learned about schools and education from talking to relatives and teachers. You should come out with a long list, because, in fact, you are an authority on education.

This process should teach you that you know more and have more opinions than you may think you do. And every time you start working on a new subject, consider creating an authority list to give yourself confidence and to help you decide what to focus on. Balance this experiment with number 8, or expand on it by doing experiments 17, 19, or 38.

19   ## FILL IN THE BLANKS FOR FOCUS

Usually writers will discover the best focus or theme for their subjects through the kinds of thoughtful writing and brainstorming emphasized in many of these experiments. But sometimes it helps just to fill in the blanks, to force yourself to answer simple, basic questions about your subject. As part of your planning, after you've done some freewriting or listing, try completing the following sentences and see if that process helps you clarify what you'd like to say about your subject.

1. What I'm trying to say is that _____ .
2. The main problem with this subject is _____ .
3. What really interests me about this idea is _____ .
4. The major question I'd like to answer is _____ .
5. _____ got me interested in this subject in the first place.
6. I think that _____ results from _____ .
7. If I had to put my idea into one sentence, I'd say _____

_____ .

8. When they get through reading my paper, I'd like people to be thinking about

_____ .

9. What really irritates me about this problem is _____ .

Now choose the completed sentence that best captures the idea and continue clarifying your subject with experiments 20, 21, 22, 28, 29, or 31.

20 **PROBING QUESTIONS**

The questions below include journalists' standard probes as well as others designed to help you look at your subject from a number of different perspectives. These questions are most useful for ensuring that you've covered all important aspects of your subject, so use them after you have done some initial writing or thinking about a subject. Try to answer these questions in your head as you deal with each new subject. Then read Barry Commoner's "An Inherently Dangerous Technology" or Daniel Egger's "West Germany Pours Hot Milk," and ask yourself how many of these questions the author has answered.

Who?

What?

When?

Where?

Why?

How?

What caused it?

What will it affect?

What are its parts?

What is it part of?

What does it look like?

How would I define it?

What are its functions?

What is it like?

What is it unlike?

What does it connect or relate to?

How did it start?

How will it end?

How is it relevant to our lives?

How do I feel about it?

Why am I interested in it?

Who else is interested in it?

   After answering these questions, see if you can pose a question central to your subject and use it for experiment 22.

---

21   THE PHYSICISTS' METAPHORS

In their book, *Rhetoric: Discovery and Change*, Richard E. Young, Alton L. Becker, and Kenneth L. Pike suggest thinking of your subject in terms of three metaphors from physics. Because metaphors are, by definition, a verbal connection between two things that allows us to see one of the things in a new way, using metaphors can help writers to see their subjects in a fresh light. The three metaphors are *particle* (or object), *wave* (or action), and *field* (or network).

   Read Barry Commoner's "An Inherently Dangerous Technology" and Edwin Diamond's "Twelve Days of Terror! The Three Mile Island Story" and think about writing a paper on the Three Mile Island accident. Then consider the accident in each of these ways:

■   *As a particle or object.* What is the accident in itself? How could you define it? What are its boundaries? To describe fully the accident as a particle, you'd need to give a reasonably complete and objective description of those events that you feel constitute the "accident."

■   *As a wave or action.* A wave exists in time — something precedes it and something else follows it. What led up to the TMI accident? What resulted from it?

■   *As a field or network.* Imagine the accident as part of a field of interconnected lines. (It may help to think of it as a spider web; when you touch one part of the web, everything else moves.) To what parts of our society and way of life is Three Mile Island connected? (Because so much relies on electricity, almost everything is connected to the power plant at TMI. But don't stop with that realization. Think about the possible connections with the military, space research, politics, Chernobyl, coal mining, drug testing, etc.)

This experiment should leave you with a sense of how much there is to say about almost any subject and of the interconnectedness of all things. Having thought of the accident in terms of a particle, a wave, and a field, you should have a better sense of how to narrow your topic to one aspect of the whole, to one segment of the unfolding events, to one connection or cause-and-effect link, or to one comparison to something else in the same field.

If you want to keep working on this subject, take one of the insights developed through this experiment and expand on it using experiment 22, 28, or 29.

---

22   USING AN ANALYSIS TREE

This experiment introduces you to a systematic method of analyzing a subject before writing about it. Starting with a large, perhaps overwhelming, question, you break it down into its parts until you're left with relatively small questions that can often be answered with data. This method works much better for some subjects than for others, so before you try it, be sure you can formulate the central question that you're trying to answer. If you're working on an appropriate subject and your goal can be summed up in one question, this method can create for you both a checklist of information you need and an outline of the points you're going to make.

Read the essays "The Lessons of Chernobyl" by Mary McGrory and "The Lesson of Chernobyl" by *The Wall Street Journal* editors in the section "Nuclear Threats and Accidents," and consider your own feelings about nuclear power. A central question about nuclear power is "Should the United States continue to build nuclear power plants?" Although this question is probably too large to be answered in your paper, it could provide a good beginning for an analysis of the subject.

Put your question at the left side of a piece of paper, preferably legal size. Now break it down into two or three other questions that you must answer before you can answer the central question. Place these questions in a column to the right of your original question. In this case, the second-level questions might be:

1. What are the advantages of nuclear power?

2. What are the disadvantages?

3. What are our energy needs?

(Many other sets of second-level questions are possible.)

These questions, too, should be broken down. For example, the "disadvantages" question might break into:

What are the economic disadvantages?

What are the social disadvantages?

What are the dangers?

To answer the question about economic disadvantages, you'd have to break the question down to cover the disadvantages for the companies involved, for the surrounding area, for the nation's balance of trade, and so forth. As you continue to create subcategories of questions, create new columns for them, moving to the right across your page.

If you continue to break all these questions down into smaller ones, you'll eventually come down to questions like "How does building a nuclear power plant affect a utility company's financial balance sheet?" and "How does a local nuclear plant affect an area's property values?" These still will not be easy questions to answer, but they're getting further away from opinions and closer to facts. They're now research questions. If you were lucky, you might find in the library the results of a study done on property values around a new nuclear power plant. Answering that one small question would help you answer the next larger question and so forth, as you build back towards the big question on the left of your page.

A side benefit of this approach is that after seeing how many questions you need to answer before you can argue for either side, you might decide it is necessary to limit your topic to one much narrower than you originally had in mind. You might decide just to address one of your subsidiary questions, for example, "What economic effects does the building of a nuclear power plant have on the people in the surrounding area?"

Once you have analyzed your question and chosen, if necessary, an appropriately narrow one, you can either confirm your choice by having others react to your idea, as in experiment 71, or begin turning your question into a thesis using experiments 31, 33, and 41.

---

23   "INTERVIEW" AN AUTHOR

After reading Alice Walker's "Nuclear Madness: What You Can Do," Calvin Trillin's "Investment Opportunities," or Michael Herr's "Illumination Rounds," create an imaginary interview with the author. Ask questions pertinent both to the author's article and to a topic that you might be interested in writing a paper on. Try to take the task seriously, projecting yourself into the author's shoes and answering the questions just as the author might. This experiment is similar to one novelists use — before writing a character into a novel, they often describe the character in detail, create a history for that character, and engage the character in dialogue. This experiment might in itself produce a paper, but its real aim is to help you become more familiar with the perspective of a particular writer so you can write more intelligently about that writer's works.

You might want to follow this experiment with experiments 32, 68, or 69.

━━━━━━━━━━━

24   **RESEARCH A SPECIFIC AUTHOR**

Quickly read Gloria Steinem's "The Importance of Work," W. H. Auden's "Work, Labor, Play," or Peter Drucker's "The Basic Skill," and jot down your impressions of both the author and the article. Now, using the resources of your library, try to answer the following questions as completely as possible:

1. What makes this author an expert on her or his subject? What formed the author's outlook on the subject?
2. Where, when, and why was the article originally published?
3. Who was the original audience for the article? What kinds of knowledge and attitudes did the author expect the audience to have?
4. What is the author's purpose in writing the article?
5. What facts about the author's background seem relevant to this article?

You might start by consulting *Who's Who in America* and *Current Biography*. These general sources should give you enough information about your author so that, perhaps with a librarian's help, you can find more specific reference material. When you have answered the questions as well as you can, reread the author's article. Keep track of your reactions, and note the points you now understand more fully. List the advantages of always getting to know an author before you read any of that author's works; list the possible disadvantages. Write a paragraph — or perhaps a whole paper — on how this kind of biographical information influenced your reading.

Use this kind of research in experiments 25, 32, 53, and 68.

━━━━━━━━━━━

25   **THE DONAHUE APPROACH**

Read one of the following pairs of articles:

a. Richard D. Lamm's "America Needs Fewer Immigrants"
   Wayne A. Cornelius's "When the Door Is Closed to Illegal Aliens, Who Pays?"
b. Mary McGrory's "The Lessons of Chernobyl"
   The Wall Street Journal's "The Lesson of Chernobyl"
c. Mortimer Ostow's "That Right Belongs Only to the State"
   Norman Cousins's "The Right to Die"

Now imagine you are hosting a talk show. Your guests are the authors whose articles you've just read. Write a multiple-part conversation: pose the questions, then create the answers that your authors would give. Try to come up with some questions that the authors would agree on, some about which they'd disagree, and some which would get the audience — and perhaps the authors themselves — to see the gaps or weaknesses in the various positions. Finally, ask yourself if speaking for the two or more opposing points of view has helped you form your own opinion, an opinion about which you might write a paper. If it has, begin developing your own opinions using experiments 8, 17. 18, or 29.

26   **INTERVIEW A CLASSMATE**

Interview one of your classmates. Don't be content with learning about your classmate's year, major, and hometown. Don't settle for the kind of information that would appear in a high school yearbook. Ask your classmate about important or revealing incidents in his or her life, about unusual habits, hobbies, or obsessions. Before the interview, think up unusual questions that might catch your subject by surprise and thus elicit the unique, personal responses you are looking for. For example, you might ask:

If you had your choice, where would you live? Why?

What have you done in your life that you're most proud of?

What do you do regularly that you bet no one else in the class does?

What would you like written on your tombstone?

Don't feel that you have to ask all your prepared questions. Your interviewee's response to only one question may provide the insights you are looking for.

Write a focused essay about your classmate in which you present a thesis and back it up with three central incidents or pieces of information derived from your interview. In other words, make your classmate into an essay. You might want to read William Zinsser's "Shanghai" to see how a professional writer makes a profile of two men come alive.

When you're finished, your teacher may ask you to "present" your classmate to the class. You should also keep track of the questions that really *worked*, those that provoked the fullest, most revealing responses. Trade such questions with your classmates and use them in experiments 23 or 27.

27   **INTERVIEW *WITH* A CLASSMATE**

Interview someone — either another classmate or someone outside the class — *with* another classmate. Then, separately, establish the focus that you would give an essay about the interviewee. Compare your focus to your co-interviewer's. You both heard the same information. Why are you focusing on different things? What does this tell you about yourself as a writer? What does it tell you about your classmate? What does it tell you about the person you interviewed? This experiment should help you with numbers 28 and 73.

---

28 **EXPERIMENT WITH POINT OF VIEW**

Read Sissela Bok's "To Lie or Not to Lie? — The Doctor's Dilemma" or Baron Wormser's "I Try to Explain to My Children...." Find a word or short phrase that summarizes the piece (perhaps "doctors' lying" or "death in the nuclear age"), write it down, and circle it in the middle of a sheet of paper. Then around the circle, write down the types of people — all with their own viewpoints — who are directly affected by the subject. (For example, with the Bok piece, you could start with doctors, nurses, patients, lawyers, patients' families, and so on.) You can indicate the intensity of a group's interest in your subject by how close to the center subject you place the group's name. ("Patients" would be close to the center circle; "insurance ratepayers" would be further away.)

When you feel your list is complete (you should probably have at least twenty different points of view), jot down quickly how you think each of those kinds of people would react to the reading. Was the author writing directly to any of them? Was the writer specifically ignoring any others? Consider writing a response to the reading in which you address directly the concerns of groups apparently ignored by the author. What points would you want to make — or ignore?

Experimenting this way with your own subjects can be a useful step in any writing process after you've done some initial planning. Try it before moving on to experiments 29, 33, or 34.

---

29 **EXPERIMENT WITH TITLES AND LEADS**

"Lead" is a journalist's term referring to the opening of an article, the part that *leads* you into the rest. It's a more descriptive term than *introduction* because generally in a short paper you want to lead the reader quickly into the heart of the matter rather than present the slowly unfolding background that the word "introduction" implies to many people. We will be using leads in a number of different ways in these experiments; here we're concerned with how leads and titles can help you see the many possible approaches to your subject.

Read Ed Ward's "Reggae," Samuel G. Freedman's "Live Aid and the Woodstock Nation," or William Zinsser's "Shanghai" and think about types of music that you like and might want to write about. Then start dreaming up titles for possible papers about music. Don't worry about whether you *could* in fact write the paper or about how the titles sound. Just write them down. You should be able to come up with fifteen or twenty in a ten-minute period. Now look back at your titles and notice how, even though they're about the same subject, they point in very different directions. If you were to write papers that followed logically from each of your twenty titles, you'd probably have twenty quite different papers. Think of what you would expect from an article about reggae entitled "Jamaica's Homegrown Music" versus your expectations of "The International Beat of Reggae." As you look over your titles, trying to choose one, you're not just choosing between particular combinations of words. You're choosing between different meanings and focuses.

Now do the same thing with leads. Choose the title that you like best, put that at the top of the page, and then write four, five, or ten leads for that title. Don't change just the wording from one lead to the next; try to come up with entirely different ways of starting off. Lead the reader into different papers. Often when you get beyond the obvious openings and start pushing yourself, you will come up with something different that will excite and inspire you. Try experiment 51 for more ideas on effective leads.

If you decide to write an entire paper on music, you may choose not to use any of these titles or leads, or you may find that you can combine words, phrases, or sentences from a number of different ones into one good one. But in any case you'll have a much fuller sense of the possibilities of your topic, and you can move on more easily to experiments 31, 33, 34, or 52.

---

30   PUTTING IT ALL TOGETHER

If you've been doing a lot of the experiments, by this point you may be feeling overwhelmed and wondering how you should put all these methods together to create a paper. There is no one right way, of course; one of the reasons for focusing on the processes of writing is to introduce you to many different methods, so you can pick and choose what works for you. But if your deadline is approaching and you're looking for some guidelines on what processes to use, here's a logical progression to try, assuming you've already picked a general subject:

1. Freewrite about your subject.

2. Starting with ideas gleaned from your freewriting, brainstorm a list of related ideas.

3. Group elements in your brainstorming list and see what starts to take form.

4. Sharpen your focus by answering the questions in experiment 19.

5. Do any preliminary research, reading, or interviewing that you need to.

6. Experiment with point of view, titles, and leads to give yourself an overall picture of your subject.

Now you should be ready for the next stage — drafting.

III
DRAFTING

STEP-BY-STEP THESIS DEVELOPMENT

If these tips seem to work for you, use them on every paper you write. The examples are based on Donald Barthelme's "Report."

1. Sometimes a thesis is so vague and vast that it becomes meaningless to both author and reader: "Donald Barthelme uses many effective details in 'Report.'" You must isolate the special characteristics of the details and the reasons for their effectiveness, then define them carefully in your statement of purpose. This marks one step towards limiting your topic, a process that helps you get clear in your own mind the connections between your ideas.

2. One way to limit such a topic might be to pick one of Barthelme's thematic concerns — say the engineers' uncaring attitude towards their potential victims — and to focus on how the details shape and advance this theme. "Donald Barthelme presents his readers with detailed descriptions of what the engineers' weapons will do in order to...." (Finish the sentence yourself.) You have now limited your topic; you have something to prove, and, presumably, you have a list of the details that originally led you to your conclusions. From this list of examples and evidence you can draw smaller, more precise points about the engineers and their attitude towards their victims. You must be sure, however, that every detail you select supports your thesis statement.

3. Don't be afraid to expand upon your thesis in your opening paragraph. Think about putting it into context and, at the same time, setting out a principle of organization for your entire paper. You might start with the context:

    > Donald Barthelme shows the engineers' callous attitudes towards "the enemy" through _____ , _____ , and _____ .

    And then get down to your particular thesis:

    > But the most pervasive way Barthelme demonstrates the engineers' attitude is by having the chief engineer recount with so much relish details of what the weapons do to their victims. Barthelme uses such details to

show us three important things: _____ ,
_____ , and _____ .

Once you've filled in the blanks, you have set out the major points you intend to explore and support.

4. Avoid promising more than you can deliver. Your thesis statement should *not* cover a lot of territory, though it can suggest how your limited topic fits into the story's larger themes. It's better to stick to a single topic rather than to try to show that you know everything there is to know about the story — and all in the first paragraph! Don't make generalizations you can't back up.

5. But don't box yourself into a corner with your thesis. A too limited thesis sacrifices all complexity and all possibilities for exploring new ideas. And be careful not to prove a point that needs little proof. It's obvious to any reader that there are a lot of odd bone fractures in "Report."

Use this kind of thesis development on your own papers after doing some planning experiments and before moving on to experiments 32, 33, 40, or 51.

32   ## ANALYSIS OF PROFESSIONAL WRITING: PURPOSE, AUDIENCE, THESIS

Arrange with a friend or two to read Yoko Ono's "On Yoko Ono," Alice Walker's "Nuclear Madness: What You Can Do," or Fred Reed's "A Veteran Writes." Before discussing the piece, have each person write down its primary and secondary purpose, audience, and thesis. Then compare. If you disagree, try to figure out why. Who can point to the most convincing evidence to back up their reading? Can you put your interpretation in the form of an essay arguing for your point? Try this same technique on your own essays and use it in conjunction with experiments 31, 67, 68, or 74.

33   ## DRAFTING TITLES, LEADS, AND ENDS

If you didn't do experiment 29, refer to it for a definition of *lead*. There we were experimenting with titles and leads as a way to find the best focus for a paper; here we will use them in drafting. Working on leads separately from the body of the paper helps those people for whom the first paragraph is the hardest part of the paper to write. Many people get stuck and waste hours sweating over getting those first few sentences right.

Some writers avoid that problem by writing the body of the paper first and then writing the beginning. If that works for you, great. But if you feel you need a good first paragraph before you can get into the body of the paper, try writing — quickly — a number of experimental leads rather than trying to write one perfect lead.

Few writers know exactly what they'll say before they start a piece, but many know where they will end up. So drafting a number of ends, too, can be very useful before you start on the body. If you're lucky enough to come up with a good lead and a good end at this stage, you may feel as though the rest of the paper just writes itself. Keep your mind open to the possibility that one of your "ends" may be a "lead," and vice-versa.

First, if you don't already have something to write about, read Judith Levine's "Motherhood Is Powerless" or Michael Korda's "When Business Becomes Blood Sport" and Ellen Goodman's "It's Failure, Not Success" and do some freewriting or brainstorming on them. Then experiment with titles, keeping in mind that the ideal title is short and catchy but also an accurate reflection of the content of the piece. Next work on leads. Try a few "off the top of your head" as you did in experiment 29. Also try some leads that include one of these types of standard opening: direct statements, factual information, quotations, dramatic episodes, or anecdotes. Experiment with formal leads that state first, information or opinions shared by writer and audience; second, the reason for writing the paper; and third, the main idea or conclusion you will put forth.

Now experiment with ends. I wouldn't yet look back at your leads, but if you find that some of your ends echo your leads, all the better. Most good ends bring the essay full circle, tying in with ideas brought up in the first paragraph.

Try to choose a working title, lead, and end from your collection. Then look at the other paragraphs you've written. Sometimes a rejected lead will make an excellent second or third paragraph, and you may find that you've already written a good portion of your paper.

This experiment is excellent preparation for any kind of drafting, particularly experiments 34, 37, or 52.

---

34   MULTIPLE DISCOVERY DRAFTS

Thinking of your first draft as a "discovery" draft prepares you to recognize and appreciate the new ideas and directions that you discover as you write. The more relaxed you are and the more open you are to following new paths to your subject, the more your draft should advance your thinking. Therefore, to some extent, the more drafts you write, the better. So instead of writing a discovery draft and then analyzing and perfecting it, write three discovery drafts as quickly as you can, simply putting each aside when you're done with it, without looking at it, and starting on the next. (You don't necessarily have to do them all at the same sitting.) Your thinking will become more focused and organized as you write; your third discovery draft should be much closer to "finished" than was your first. This method may actually save you time in the long run. Just as important, it may reduce your anxiety about writing drafts; you may find you can relax and perhaps even enjoy yourself.

Try it. If you don't have a topic to work on read the two sections from Studs Terkel's *Working*, Ellen Goodman's "It's Failure, Not Success," or Patricia Hampl's "To Create a National Music," and quickly write a discovery draft. If this technique seems to work for you, try it at virtually any point in your writing process and in conjunction with experiments 42, 44, and 52.

35   **USING THE DESCRIPTIVE OUTLINE**

Use the following technique on Caroline Bird's "Where College Fails Us," Bertrand Russell's "Education and Discipline," or Daniel Yankelovich's "The Work Ethic Is Underemployed."

Descriptive Outline

1. Analyze each paragraph. First summarize what each one *says* — identify its content. Then note what each *does* to advance the author's argument.
2. Put the two types of information in different lists, one list of "says," one list of "does."
3. Look for individual summaries that are closely linked to other summaries.
4. Connect these linked summaries with arrows or brackets.
5. Continue to bracket the individual summaries into larger blocks, grouping those blocks into even larger ones.

You will probably come out with three or four major blocks that make up the whole essay. Now use these blocks to create a quick formal outline of the reading. What can you learn from doing this? Does it make the complex essay seem more like your own? Experiment 54 encourages you to apply this technique to your own work.

36   **FIND THE THESIS**

Read William Zinsser's "Shanghai," Fred Reed's "A Veteran Writes," or Jeff Jones's, "The War Is Not Over." Try to find the author's most direct statement of his thesis. Keep in mind that the thesis is not necessarily a single sentence in the first paragraph; or it may be three or four sentences, and it could come in the second or third paragraph, or in the last. Discuss your choice with others who looked at the same reading. Try condensing the thesis into one sentence and putting that sentence at the beginning of the reading. What is gained? What is lost? In what types of writing would you expect the thesis to appear in the first sentence or two?

You can combine this experiment with number 32, and use the results of your search for a thesis in published pieces to help you write your own thesis statements in experiment 31. How often does a thesis statement answer one or more of the questions in experiment 20?

---

37   EXPERIMENT WITH DISTANCE

Photography gives the teaching of writing many of its best metaphors. We use the term *focus* so much to talk about writing that we may forget its original meaning — something that the eye does. The zoom lens provides another useful metaphor. Imagine the ultimate lens, out on a satellite, able to take a picture of the Earth in space or of the eye of a bee on a flower in a field in Montana. Try to become a zoom lens as you write, sometimes giving a close-up view, sometimes backing away to put things in context.

After reading Donald Barthelme's "Report," Alex Haley's "My Furthest Back Person — 'The African,'" or Maxine Hong Kingston's "The Father from China," write a few paragraphs trying to make sense of what you read.

1. First put your reading in context — get far away from it and see how it fits into a larger scheme.

2. Next, get out your magnifying glass and focus on sentences or individual words.

3. Then zoom out and in to intermediate positions.

You may find this experiment useful simply for thinking about your subject, or you may find that your short "zoomed" paragraphs fit into an essay. Look at Donald M. Murray's "What Is a Practical Education?" and Thomas Murray's "The Growing Danger from Gene-Spliced Hormones" to get a sense of how good writers vary the distance between themselves and their subject. There's no right or wrong distance, but most good essays will give the reader a variety of vantage points on the subject.

You can use this approach on any subject and at virtually any point in the writing process. To keep working on the ideas you've come up with in this experiment, try experiments 40, 54, 69, or 70.

38   TALK IT OUT

If you've done lots of planning on a subject but now fear the big step to the first draft, talk before you write. (If you're not in the middle of another project, read Terrence Rafferty's "Platoon" or Norman Cousins's "The Right to Die" and consider this experiment as oral freewriting.)

Get yourself a friendly audience — a classmate, a roommate, a friend, even a younger sister or brother (the person doesn't have to know anything about your subject) — and try to explain your subject to that person as quickly and completely as you can. The point of this experiment is not to get feedback; simply trying to make sense of a subject to someone who doesn't know about it often helps you to frame and organize that subject in useful ways. If your listener can understand your subject well enough to make suggestions, all the better.

Talk it out whenever you're stuck, and when you're done with your oral presentation think back over what you said and ask yourself if something could be developed into a thesis (experiment 31), an organizing detail (experiment 40), or a central question (experiment 22). If you find you can't remember all those clever ideas you just poured out to your friend, try the next experiment.

39   TAPE IT

Have you ever felt that you knew exactly what you wanted to say but your brain seemed to stall when you put pen to paper? Consider that you don't have to use pen and paper at all. You can talk your draft into a tape recorder, and then transcribe it. It may feel strange, but if it works, if it relaxes you and starts the words flowing, why not? In order to use this technique successfully and produce a full, organized draft, most people need to have done a lot of planning and some preliminary drafting, as outlined in experiments 17, 22, 33, and 37.

If you want to see if recording stream-of-consciousness thoughts, rather than a draft, might work for you, read Jeff Jones's "The War Is Not Over," Mary McGrory's "The Lessons of Chernobyl," or *Business Week*'s "Education Has Been Neglected Long Enough," and then tape your reactions. Listen to what you've said and jot down any ideas worth saving.

40   FIND AN ORGANIZING DETAIL

Reexamine some planning work you've already done or read Daniel Egger's "West Germany Pours Hot Milk" or Vo Thi Tam's "From Vietnam, 1979" and prepare to write about it. (A good way to prepare for this experiment is to complete experiment 52 first.) Often looking closely at your planning or at the reading itself will reveal to you an idea that will make your draft easier to organize or focus. Is there a single event or phrase that seems to encapsulate the reading? Does a minor detail symbolize or mirror more central concerns? Is there a thematic thread or pattern throughout your planning experiments? Is there an image or design that you see in your imagination when you think about the reading? Don't expect to be able to make sense of such an intuitive idea right away, but try expanding on it and see what happens.

For intance, you might choose as an important detail the system the refugees used to get water at the Malaysian camp in Vo Thi Tam's "From Vietnam, 1979." You might decide to use the small can at the end of a string as an image in a discussion about the contrast between the technology used to kill people in Southeast Asia and that used to keep people alive. You might compare the can to some of the surreal instruments of war in Donald Barthelme's "Report." Then you might want to do some research into the money spent on armaments and weapons by various countries. You could even use the "hanging by a string" idea in your title.

After this experiment, try experiments 42, 44, or 49. If you're writing a critical paper, move from this experiment to number 70.

---

41   ANSWER THE READER'S QUESTIONS

Imagine that you are the audience for your own paper. Try to read what you have written — even if you only have a title and lead — with a fresh and questioning mind. Start with a careful consideration of your working title. What's the most important question raised by the title? Write it down, then answer it. What question does this answer raise? Answer that question. Keep going until you've answered all the important questions. Then go back and see if you can turn this string of questions and answers into an outline for a paper. Phrasing questions as *questions* in a paper can get tedious, but if you use the questions-and-answers order to organize your paper, your reader may feel as though you're a mind-reader.

An alternate method is to jot down all the questions that a reader might ask about your topic, without at first considering which are important. Then go back and number the questions, creating an order that most effectively reveals the subject to your reader. When in doubt about how to organize your paper, structuring it to respond to readers' questions is usually a safe bet.

Now read some informative articles and consider their organization. Do they proceed by raising questions and then answering them? (Try Michael Goldberg's "Los Lobos" or *Science News*'s "Sex and Violence: Pornography Hurts" or Judith Levine's "Motherhood Is Powerless.") After this experiment, start fleshing out your outline with the techniques in experiments 33, 38, or 44, or analyze the primary question with experiment 22.

42   SELECT AND DEVELOP

As you read over your planning notes or discovery draft, look for places where you've packed in the information. Especially when we've worked hard to find facts, we have a tendency to want to get them all in. Often a better way to write an interesting, convincing essay is to choose one important idea and develop it. See if you can find an underdeveloped idea, especially one hidden in a jumble of information. Expand on it, even if that will mean cutting something else out. Use sensory details (experiment 6), brainstorm what you know about the subject (experiment 18), freewrite on it (experiment 17), give it detail and context (experiment 37), or show the action (experiment 44).

Then see if you can do the same thing with a professional essay. Read *Business Week*'s "Education Has Been Neglected Long Enough" or Gary S. Becker's "Why Shouldn't College Be a Smart Investment?" Look for an idea that you think deserves more attention and expand on it, even if you have to speculate about facts or invent illustrative details.

43   STOP IN THE MIDDLE

During your next drafting session, when you feel you're getting close to using up your time, energy, or ideas, stop in the middle of a sentence in the middle of a paragraph, even if you feel you could complete it. Then, when you next have time and energy, go back and finish the sentence and the paragraph. Getting going again might be easier this way than starting each time on a new page or a new paragraph.

44   SHOW AND TELL

Most student writers have a tendency to *tell* about something, to describe it in general terms, rather than to *show* the person or action to the readers so they can see it for themselves. But generalizations don't interest or convince readers. As Don Murray points out, a good prosecuting attorney often doesn't have to say "the defendant is guilty"; instead, the attorney *shows* the jury enough evidence so that the jury reaches the conclusion, the generalization, on its own.

Read Dan Georgakas and Lenny Rubenstein's "Interview with Jane Fonda," Michael Herr's "Illumination Rounds," or Michael Korda's "When Business Becomes Blood Sport." Then take fifteen minutes to expand upon one of the vague, descriptive statements below. Try to bring the person to life, to show the person in action, to create a scene that the reader can *see*, even if it means making up some details.

Jane Fonda is political.

Michael Herr's ride was dangerous.

Michael Korda plays hardball.

Now look at your planning or discovery draft. If you find similarly vague, uninformative sentences, try to rewrite them to *show* what you previously had just told about. Keep a balance in your papers by using both this technique and the one in experiment 42. Writing and revising are often matters of expanding with more details and then whittling down for directness and conciseness.

45   LEARNING FROM OTHER PROCESSES

Using some of the questions from experiment 2, analyze a creative process you're familiar with — taking pictures, painting, cooking, figure skating. Then compare your analysis to the writing process. In what ways are the two processes similar? Do people use the same vocabulary to talk about them? Can the comparison teach you anything about writing?

Study the various kinds of work described in W. H. Auden's "Work, Labor, Play," Studs Terkel's pieces from *Working*, or Donald Hall's "Ox Cart Man." What are the similarities and differences between creative processes and work?

46   DEFINITION

Define *education* after reading Ralph Waldo Emerson's "Education," Donald M. Murray's "What Is a Practical Education?" or E. B. White's "Book Learning." Start by composing a standard formal definition. (Don't use a dictionary.) Such a definition has three parts: the *term* to be defined, the *class* to which the term belongs, and the *differentia* — the elements that distinguish the term from others in the class. Writers often forget to include the second term, the *class.* "A car is used primarily to transport passengers" isn't an adequate definition because it does not include the class. "A car [the term] is a four-wheeled, motorized vehicle [the class] used primarily to transport passengers [the differentia] " is a more complete definition.

Try to capture the author's ideas about education in your definition. Then ask yourself, "Is the author's definition consistent with a dictionary definition? Is it one that most students would give?" If it isn't, how is the author adding to, changing, or expanding the more common definition? Could focusing on the author's unusual use of this term become a paper topic?

Defining your terms clearly yet unobtrusively in a paper can be difficult. Pay particular attention to definitions when you're writing arguments (experiment 47), research papers, or critical essays (experiment 68).

▬▬▬▬▬▬▬▬▬▬

47   **ARGUMENT AND COUNTER-ARGUMENT**

Read Alice Guy Blaché's "Woman's Place in Photoplay Production," Mortimer Ostow's "That Right Belongs Only to the State," or David Weinberger's "Computer Literacy Is Not Literacy." As you read, mark points that you think are particularly convincing or particularly ineffective. Look over the points that you feel are effective to see if you can find connections between them. Do most of them use the same kind of evidence or the same kind of logic? Even if you don't agree with the author's point, can you learn anything from the essay about how to write persuasively?

Now write a letter to the editor in which you argue against the author's point. One strategy for making such an argument is to begin with a point of agreement, a point that you marked as convincing. Then show how your own conclusion follows more logically from the point of agreement than does the author's conclusion. Along the way, you'll probably want to mention the points in the author's argument that you found particularly weak.

While working on this experiment, try 46, 48, and 49, and when you're done return to experiment 13 and see if you can perfect your letter to Mr. Zinc.

▬▬▬▬▬▬▬▬▬▬

48   **THE SOUND OF GOOD LOGIC**

This experiment provides practice in logical thinking, that is, in drafting a paragraph that will ring true in a persuasive paper. Although you will only write a few paragraphs, you will find it a challenge, because you must improve on the logic of published writing.

Read Richard D. Lamm's "America Needs Fewer Immigrants," Susan Fraker's "Why Women Aren't Getting to the Top," Caroline Bird's "Where College Fails Us," or Norman Ellenberger's "We Have to Make Money." Look for examples of faulty logic. Do the authors generalize from insufficient data? Do they accept as true the points that they're trying to prove? Do you see other possible causes for or effects of the events they're studying? Do they jump from point to point without providing sufficient connections?

Compare your results with those of classmates. Now take two or three of what you consider to be the worst logical faults, rethink the ideas, and write in your own words your own logically sound paragraphs. Compare your version to the original and determine the advantages of each.

Some people plan every step their argument will take before they write a sentence. Others write more intuitively. In either case, looking for faulty logic should be part of your revising process whenever you're writing something persuasive. Use what you've learned here when you're working on experiments 13, 47, and 54.

49   **ILLUSTRATING A POINT**

Read at least two of the following:

Meg Greenfield, "Creating a 'Learning Society' "

Susan Tyler Hitchcock, "Cultural Literacy"

Robert Pattison, "On the Finn Syndrome"

Michael Goldberg, "Los Lobos"

Fred Wilcox, "Agent Orange on Trial"

Wayne A. Cornelius, "When the Door Is Closed to Illegal Aliens, Who Pays?"

Look closely at the way the authors back up or illustrate important points. Do they give a generalization and then provide specific examples? Do they provide lots of raw data and then draw conclusions from it? Do they tend to back up a general point by going into detail about one specific example or by mentioning quickly many examples? Do they seem to use examples that would be familiar to most readers? Classify the ways the two essays illustrate their points, then write a paragraph about how this examination can help you illustrate your own points.

    This experiment parallels 42 and 44 and should be used in connection with 68 and 69.

50   **PARAGRAPHING**

Have a friend — a generous friend who types well — type out the first two pages of Alex Haley's "My Furthest Back Person — 'The African,' " Steven H. Madoff's "A Way to Pay That's Not Just Academic," or Judith Levine's "Motherhood Is Powerless" without making any paragraph breaks. Copy these pages, give them to classmates, and independently decide where to make the paragraph breaks. Compare your results with your classmates' and defend your approach. Then compare your efforts with the author's. Is there a logic to the author's breaks that escaped you? Do the different ways of breaking up the text lead to different emphases, different readings? Can you learn anything about paragraphing your own essays?

    This experiment might help you understand why you have difficulty summarizing paragraphs in experiments 35 and 54 and should help you move towards greater variety and flexibility with paragraphs in all your writing.

51   WHAT HOOKS YOU?

Read just the opening paragraphs of ten or twelve essays that you haven't yet read. Think about the effect each had on you and then rate it according to how much each one draws you in, how much each makes you want to read the rest of the article. Then list the common factors in the three or four leads that attract you the most. Compare your list with those of some of your classmates. Were they drawn in by the same factors? What improvements can you make in your own leads based on the techniques the professional writers used to make you want to read an article?

This experiment is useful whenever you're focusing on leads — as in experiments 29, 31, 33, and 67.

52   PUTTING IT ALL TOGETHER — FAST

Read Lynda Van Devanter's "Short-Timers," Vo Thi Tam's "From Vietnam, 1979," or Maxine Hong Kingston's "The Father from China." Freewrite for three minutes about it. Read over your freewrite, pick a key word or idea, and brainstorm with that idea for three minutes. Bracket and connect words in your brainstorming list. Arrange your grouped ideas into a scratch outline. Then turn each heading of the outline into a complete sentence, as quickly as you can. Now from this sentence outline, write a draft — in only ten minutes.

You no doubt felt rushed, but look at what you achieved. Take a few minutes to annotate your draft, marking effective images, sentences, or passages or ideas that seem especially interesting. Some people, when introduced to new ways to approach the writing process, complain that all these steps take too long. But the more you use steps like brainstorming and freewriting, the better you will get at turning out something worthwhile very quickly. Use this approach whenever you're trying to get your ideas down on paper quickly, whether it's to prepare for one of the experiments, to write a paper at the last minute, or to write a good essay exam answer.

IV
REVISING

53   **REVISION AGENDA FOR A PROFESSIONAL**

Read Judith Levine's "Motherhood Is Powerless" or Fred A. Wilcox's "Agent Orange on Trial." The former was published in *The Village Voice*, a newspaper whose urban, politically and socially aware audience would generally know something about the Baby M case and be sympathetic with Levine's point of view. Wilcox's piece appeared in *The Amicus Journal*, put out by the Natural Resources Defense Council, an environmental group. Now imagine that the two authors wanted to write about their respective subjects for very different audiences — readers who are unsympathetic to feminism or who think that Vietnam veterans are just bellyaching.

Develop a revision agenda to modify the piece to appeal to the new audience. To create the agenda, ask yourself what changes the author would need to make in purpose, content, organization, style, and tone. What revising tasks should the author tackle first?

This experiment should help you with others that require persuasive, audience-directed writing: 12, 13, 41, 47, and 61.

54   **USING THE DESCRIPTIVE OUTLINE AS A REVISING TOOL**

You may have used a descriptive outline to analyze a professional essay in experiment 35. Now try using it for revision — on your own work. Choose a fairly long draft that you're not yet satisfied with, particularly one with organizational problems. Summarize each paragraph in terms of what it "says" — its contents — and what it "does" — how it fits into the overall movement of your piece.

Put these summaries in lists on a single page. Can you bracket some of the summaries to make logical blocks, as you did in experiment 35? Do your summaries suggest more logical or forceful connections could be made by reordering your paragraphs? Chances are you can strengthen the organization of your paper by moving some of your paragraphs around, and it's much easier to conceptualize such movement when you're playing with summaries than when you are looking at full paragraphs. If you tend to have trouble with organization in your papers, consider making this experiment a standard part of your revision strategy. Try using it in conjunction with experiment 41.

55   STUDYING EMPHASIS

Read one of the following: Bertrand Russell's "Education and Discipline," Gloria Steinem's "The Importance of Work," or Thomas Murray's "The Growing Danger from Gene-Spliced Hormones." Read the essay closely, marking the points that seem to receive particular emphasis throughout the essay. Now go back and try to determine how the authors establish that emphasis. Do they devote more space to important points? Do they put key points in particular places in sentences, in paragraphs, or in the essay as a whole? Do they use particular diction or more adjectives and adverbs? Do they become more personal and direct when they're making a more important point?

Now look at sections that seem particularly unemphasized, downplayed, or even dismissed. Do they fit into any patterns?

Professional writers achieve emphasis as much by instinct as by design. But if you seem to have trouble getting your point across, if readers take some of your minor points to be major points, then you can probably learn something from the pros about how to make sure the right ideas are highlighted. Once you've reached some conclusions about the professional essay you studied, try to apply them to one of your own papers. Keep this experiment in mind when you're working on 31, 47, and 49.

56   HUNTING FOR *BE*S

Choose one of your drafts that you've already begun revising. Go through the first two or three pages, circling every form of the verb *to be* (*is, was, are, were, am, be, being, been*). *Be* verb forms, the weakest of verbs, say simply that something exists; in combination with past participles of other verbs they form passive constructions, which are often dull and wordy. Spend twenty or thirty minutes looking carefully at the verbs you've circled, and especially at the passive constructions; in each case consider whether you should revise it, and if so how.

When you're tired of fighting your own *be*s, try the same thing with a professional essay. Circle all the *be* verb forms in the pieces by E. B. White, Calvin Trillin, or W. H. Auden, three famous stylists. How many do you find? What changes would make the sentences more active, direct, and interesting?

If you have a word processor, you may have one of the new grammar-checking programs that will highlight *be* verbs. That's a great step towards completing this experiment, though the hard part, of course, is revising the sentence. One key: look for strong verbs hidden in noun forms within the sentence. For example, look for a hidden verb in this sentence: "To ensure profit, diversification of your portfolio is crucial." Within the mouthful *diversification* is the verb *diversify*. Try to make that into the primary verb of the sentence: "To ensure profit, diversify your portfolio."

57   COLLOQUIAL BEAUTY

Read the Studs Terkel selections from *Working*, Dudley Randall's "Booker T. and W. E. B.," or the poem by Lorna Dee Cervantes. Circle colloquialisms and uses of non-standard English. Find more standard synonyms and phrasings and rewrite the passages to conform with standard English. What are the differences between the two versions in terms of reading ease, amount of information conveyed, sound and color of language, and personal voice of the author? Which version do you like better?

Try rewriting some of the passages with the most colorful, descriptive language you know, even if it's slang. Discuss the reasons why you might choose one version over the others. Are your various versions perfectly synonymous in meaning or does the meaning of each version vary somewhat with the changes in diction?

Can you write with a colloquial vocabulary? If you grew up using a non-standard version of English, do you see any advantages in that linguistic background? One obvious one: most non-standard users can slip into standard English if they want to, but few people who speak "by the book" can convincingly take on other dialects.

58   WHAT DO OUR WORDS REVEAL?

Read Donald Hall's "Ox Cart Man," Michael Korda's "When Business Becomes Blood Sport," or Yoko Ono's "On Yoko Ono." Freewrite for ten or fifteen minutes about what sort of person you think the author is. Can you tell anything about the author's politics, outlook on the world, ethnic background, or social or economic class? Would you like to meet the author?

Now go back to the author's piece and see if you can figure out what gave you the impressions you just wrote down. Did they come from the subject matter, sentence structure, diction, or tone?

Try reading one of your own papers looking for what it reveals about you. What sort of person do your readers imagine when they think about the author of your papers? Is that the sort of person you want to project? Can you change the person you project? The next time you hear a speaker you've never heard before, even in a brief interview on the evening news, do a similar analysis.

We make assumptions and draw conclusions about people almost any time we communicate. If you're more aware of the clues you're picking up, you'll have more control over how you react to people — and how people react to you.

In conjunction with experiments 57, 59, 60, and 61, this process should make you more sensitive to all the messages that your words may carry.

59   CONCRETE AND ABSTRACT

Reread a selection that you remember reading with particular enjoyment. Pay attention to the abstract or general statements (like "She was a good coach") and to the more specific or concrete statements or details related to them (like "She never lost a game and all her players still sent her Christmas cards"). Is there a consistent ratio of abstract to concrete? That is, is each abstract statement eventually phrased in more concrete terms?

Now do the same analysis on a selection that you didn't enjoy reading, particularly one that you found boring. Is the second reading significantly more or less abstract? Would you say that your sensibility is "abstract," "concrete," or "balanced"? What ratio of concrete to abstract do you find in your writing? Go back to experiments 42, 44, and 49 and see if using the terms *abstract* and *concrete* helps you understand what you were doing in those experiments.

60   OBJECTIVITY

Read Daniel Egger's "West Germany Pours Hot Milk" or Dan Georgakas and Lenny Rubenstein's "Interview with Jane Fonda." The first piece is a news analysis, the second an interview. These are generally thought to be fairly objective forms of writing, certainly more objective than an argument or editorial. Note any places where the author's opinions show through. Is it acceptable for an interviewer's or journalist's opinions or biases to affect an interview or news article? If you have found evidence of subjectivity in the piece, do you think it would be possible to revise the piece for complete objectivity? What would the piece gain and what would it lose through such a revision?

Make a quick list of the ways authors can express their own opinions in a piece of writing, short of saying directly "I think...." Look at the subjects the interviewers ask about, the way they phrase their questions, the comments that they pursue further and the ones that they let stand. Notice, too, the facts and details included and the connections made between facts and ask yourself if different details or different connections might lead to different conclusions. Then use the techniques in your list to express your own opinions or when working on experiments like 41 or 47.

61   INFORMATIVE AND AFFECTIVE

Most pieces of writing try either to influence or to inform readers — they are either *affective* or *informative* or some combination of the two. To distinguish between the two types of writing, ask yourself whether the author draws conclusions and presents opinions, or whether he or she is content to give readers the facts and to let them draw their own conclusions. Read Ellen Goodman's "It's Failure, Not Success," Ed Ward's "Reggae" or Samuel Freedman's "Live Aid and the Woodstock Nation" and Gene Santoro's "Paul Simon — Graceland." Create a scale with *affective* on one end and *informative* on the other, like this:

Affective   Informative

Now place the two pieces you read on this scale. From this sample, which kind of writing appeals to you more? Do you find the "affective" writing to be at all informative, and vice-versa? Can you remember reading a selection that was both affective and informative? Freewrite on whether you, as a writer, want more to inform people or to affect them. This choice constitutes a major part of your purpose for writing. Making a decision about it early in the writing process can help you clarify your thinking more quickly. Once you've mentally established your affective and informative purposes for a piece of writing, keep returning to them as you do experiments like 33, 68, and 73.

62   DISTANCE ANALYSIS

Read Gary S. Becker's "Why Shouldn't College Be a Smart Investment?" or Ed Ward's "Reggae." Analyze the essay in terms of distance from the subject. Does the author often bring us close to the subject, letting us see specific, individual details of human lives, or do we more often see general humanity as we deal with larger concepts and issues? Does the author adopt one stance at the beginning and stick to it, or does the distance from the subject vary from paragraph to paragraph?

Find a place in the essay where you think either stepping back from the subject and putting it in context, or moving closer and giving details, would make the essay more convincing or more interesting. Write a paragraph in which you supply the "missing" section.

Use this same technique when you're "developing," "showing," or "illuminating" material in experiments 42, 44, 49, or 68.

63   FRIENDLY CRITIQUING

All writers, even the best professional writers, need editors, friends, colleagues, or spouses to read their writing and comment on it. Professional writers covet such readers, and many famous authors would never have made it into print without the help of not-so-famous readers. After working on a piece of writing for a while, we're simply too close to it to be able to spot the shrill expression, the vague phrase, or the key idea buried in the middle of a paragraph. Almost anyone who can read can help you improve your writing. If your ten-year-old brother says, "I don't understand this part," you should give it another look.

Finding the right person to read our drafts is often difficult. It depends on luck and cooperation. The guidelines below will help you to identify the qualities that make a good writer-reader relationship. Proceed by trial and error with anyone willing to help you. Remember that you will be able to offer similar help in return. Remember, too, that no one person may be the right reader for all the different types of writing you do.

To Be a Good Reader for Someone Else

- Ask the writer how you can help. What should you look for? If the writer is thinking about completely changing the subject or organization, your comments about sentence structure will be irrelevant and perhaps irritating. You'll get along much better if you let the writer be the first to say, "Do you think this end works? I don't."

- Be positive. Most of us are trained to see the flaws rather than the near-perfection. Try to start off by mentioning a number of things in the piece that you thought worked well.

- Consider the writer's ego. You may think of the writer as the most confident person you know, but chances are the writer is very nervous about what you're going to say. Never be flippant with your criticism; never say things like "This part stinks" or "I was really bored here."

- Be honest. You're not helping the writer if you avoid mentioning a problem. The trick is to balance criticism with praise and to make your criticism productive, as outlined below.

- Be specific. Telling a writer that a page is "vague" or a sentence is "awkward" probably won't help, and will just make the writer anxious. On the other hand, the writer will probably see the problem if you say, "I don't understand exactly what you mean by 'productivity' on this page," or "Let's see if we can change the phrase, 'to not unfeelingly fire the foreman.'" Such criticism will often make the writer feel encouraged about the possibility of making the writing better.

■ Be constructive. If you can suggest a way to revise a sentence, great. But if you don't have the time to revise someone's work, or feel you don't have the expertise, you can still make your criticism sound like praise: "A couple of examples in this section would make your idea crystal clear"; "If you could get your fourth paragraph next to the first, no one could argue with your conclusion."

■ Deal with big questions first. Talk about the overall meaning of the piece and its organization before you get into questions of spelling and punctuation. If problems with organization lead to a major revision, the writer may throw out all those misspelled words anyway.

When Your Writing Is Being Critiqued

■ Try not to get defensive. A writer's natural reaction is often that the reader is being purposefully thick-headed, obtuse, and picky. But if you lash out at your reader even once, the chances of a constructive dialogue will be diminished.

■ Indicate where you need help. This may enable you to see the piece in a new light, and it will almost certainly make the reader's job easier.

■ Take notes while you're discussing your writing. You may feel foolish, but your reader will feel flattered, and you'll be glad you did when you start revising the draft.

■ Don't always knuckle under. On a question of style or emphasis, your first instinct may be better than your critic's. Get another opinion. Often two readers will give contradictory advice about a particular point. It's your piece, after all, and you have to answer for it when it reaches its ultimate audience. So don't change something unless you honestly agree that it needs changing.

Try to make a friendly exchange of papers part of your writing process for every important piece you produce.

64 LOOKING BACK

If you can, locate a paper you wrote in high school or at least before you started taking this class. Read it over, quickly marking things that you would change if you were going to revise it now. What types of things would you pay particular attention to now? Write down the specific ways that you've changed as a writer and what you've learned about writing since you wrote the old paper. Try to remember these points when you write and revise new papers.

V
SPECIAL ASSIGNMENTS

65   PREPARING FOR AN ESSAY EXAM

Put yourself in your professor's shoes. List the major concepts covered in the course, especially the points that the professor emphasized. Form a number of questions about those concepts and answer your questions by constructing a brief outline or in a simple list. Review your course texts, separating key points from background details and then generating more questions. Answer these questions, too, briefly. Compare your two lists or outlines, looking for blocks and patterns of information.

A good essay question will force you to do more than simply regurgitate facts; it will lead you to tie ideas or information together in new ways or it may ask you to apply what you've learned to completely new situations or contexts. So when you're studying, try to think in terms of the large picture. Make associations, relate the course to events in "real life," and memorize only those facts that you will need to make such arguments or connections. Consider the professor's biases; how does he or she think? What kinds of things does he or she want (or not want) to hear? These points will help you to anticipate questions. Use what you've learned from previous experiments, particularly 10 through 13, 18, and 41. Know your audience!

66   READING THE QUESTION

The answers you prepared in experiment 65 are probably good answers to possible exam questions, so one of the hardest things you may have to do during the exam itself will be to abandon your answer. Do not make the mistake that many people make of not carefully reading the question. Many people, if they have prepared an answer about a particular subject and then see a question about that subject, start rattling off their prepared essay without noticing that the question requires a very different approach from the one they'd prepared.

When you first get the question, circle the key verb in the directions (*define*, *explain*, *compare*) and underline the major nouns. This will help you to focus on what the question is really asking. Then, while writing your answer, stop yourself every now and then and re-read the question, asking yourself "Am I really answering the question?" It's better to realize that you're off-track when you're in the middle of the essay than to find it out when you get your grade. The work that you did for experiments 55, 58, and 61 may help you to figure out exactly what kind of response an essay question requires.

----

67   STARTING RIGHT

The first sentence in an essay exam response is crucial. If you're running out of time, getting down a good thesis statement will probably earn you more credit than producing a couple of paragraphs of evidence without a thesis. A good thesis gives your essay a frame that will hold your argument together, even if some of your supporting material goes astray.

The simplest and most logical way to write such a thesis statement is probably the best (unless you have some other great idea): turn the question into a statement. If the question is "What were the causes of the Civil War?" your answer should probably start with some variation of "The causes of the Civil War were...."

Read Samuel G. Freedman's "Live Aid and the Woodstock Nation." Then turn the following questions into statements and use one of them to write a brief answer; take ten minutes to complete your answer.

1. What does Freedman learn from the comparison between the two concerts?

2. Which event does Freedman seem to prefer?

3. According to Freedman, what social and political changes have taken place since the 1960s? What brought those changes about?

4. Are Freedman's ideas convincing? If not, choose one to argue against.

You may find that this method of turning a question into the beginning of an answer will help you write thesis statements (experiment 31) or to come up with better leads (experiment 33).

----

68   THE CRITICAL ESSAY: ILLUMINATING THE TEXT

One of the major purposes of almost any critical essay is to illuminate the subject being discussed, to allow other readers, listeners, or viewers of the subject to understand and appreciate it in ways they might not on their own. Good critical essays provide new details, new contexts, new backgrounds, or new perspectives on their subjects. Reading a good critical essay, you should, at some point, think "Now I understand." or "I never thought about it that way before."

Seeing how professional writers provide such illumination may help you to come up with ideas for your own critical essays. Read any of the review essays, for example, Terrence Rafferty's "Platoon," Robin Wood's "Beauty Bests the Beast," Susan Tyler Hitchcock's "Cultural Literacy," Fred Wilcox's "Agent Orange on Trial," Robert Pattison's "On the Finn Syndrome," or any of the essays about music. Try to pick an essay that covers a subject you already know something about. As you read, note the ways in which the authors help you to understand and appreciate the works being discussed. Do they give you personal feelings, the author's gut reactions, to the works? Do they provide facts about the work itself, details about its creation, background on the artist, comparisons to similar works, opinions, other critical reactions?

Use the work you did in experiments 46, 49, 51, 55, and 57 through 62 to help you answer these questions. As you write your own critical essays, try to illuminate the works you're discussing in similar ways.

---

69   EXAMINE YOUR GUT REACTION

Many inexperienced writers of critical essays seem to think that the point of a critical essay is to be esoteric, to dig up allusions or focus on symbols that no one else has noticed or to point out how the work in question is similar to something else. But most effective critical essays grow out of the critic's deeply felt emotional reaction, not out of a purely analytical search for "hidden inner meaning." Most start in the heart (or the gut) even if they seem to end up in the head. If the critic doesn't care about the subject, the essay is likely to sound hollow and false. So one of the first steps towards writing a good critical essay is to latch onto a strong feeling about the piece you're critiquing.

Read Lynda Van Devanter's "Short-Timers," Alice Guy Blaché's "Woman's Place in Photoplay Production," or Richard Lamm's "America Needs Fewer Immigrants." Before talking with anyone about it or even consciously thinking about it yourself, freewrite about it for eight to ten minutes. Let your thoughts wander wherever they will. Then go back over what you've written and see if you can finish the sentence "My gut reaction is...." (Or "What I feel strongly about here is....") Now analyze that reaction. Why did you react that way? What details can you point to that contributed to that reaction? How much does your reaction say about you and how much about the reading? Can you come up with some rational, logical reasons for what is essentially a non-rational, intuitive reaction? Can you find indications that the author wanted you to feel the way you do? See if you can turn your gut reaction and analysis into a paper, using techniques like those in experiments 17, 19 through 25, and 31 through 42.

▬▬▬▬▬▬▬▬

70   DETAIL EXPERIMENT

Choose a detail from Robin Wood's "Beauty Bests the Beast," Thomas Murray's "The Growing Danger from Gene-Spliced Hormones," or Susan Fraker's "Why Women Aren't Getting to the Top." Consider why that detail struck you, why it seems meaningful. How does that detail fit into and contribute to the complete piece? Write a short essay about why that detail stuck in your mind and how it relates to the meaning of the piece. The more you think — and write — about the detail, the more you may find that it symbolizes or encapsulates the entire essay for you. You may, in fact, find that by closely examining this detail and relating it to other points within the essay, you can explain a major part of what the essay is all about. If so, you've got a good start on writing a critical paper. (See experiment 40 for more about focusing on details.)

▬▬▬▬▬▬▬▬

71   RESEARCH QUESTIONS

Before you begin writing your research paper, jot down answers to these questions:

1. What is my subject?

2. Why am I interested in this subject?

3. What got me started thinking about it?

4. What do I already know about the subject?

5. What kinds of sources do I expect to consult?

6. What conclusions do I think I might reach about it?

7. What questions would I like to answer about it?

Answering these questions for yourself should give you a good sense of where you stand in relation to your research subject. Formulating questions that you want your paper to answer should give you a sense of the present direction and focus of your thinking.

You'll probably want to stick to some of your initial goals as you develop your paper, but finding out how an audience reacts to your subject may lead you to change others as you expand and re-focus your thinking. To get such audience input, pass your list of questions and answers around to your classmates. Have each of them read what you wrote, add a question to the bottom of the list, and put a check mark next to any other questions on the sheet that seem important or interesting. If you get the whole class to respond to your research ideas, you should end up with a list of questions that can guide your library research and the organization of your paper itself. (See experiments 22 and 41.)

72   ANALYZING SOURCES

Read closely Edwin Diamond's "Twelve Days of Terror! The Three Mile Island Story," the *Science News* article, "Sex and Violence: Pornography Hurts," or Daniel Yankelovich's "The Work Ethic Is Underemployed." Consider the different sources the author must have used to write the piece. You may want to research the author's background (experiment 24) to get a better idea of the kinds of materials the author might have used.

Which kind of information from which kind of source affects you most? That is, are you most convinced by individual, personal anecdotes of the kind that President Reagan uses in his speeches, or do you look more for facts, statistics, and survey results? Does the piece you read rely on one type or a combination of types of documentation? Would the piece be less effective if the types of documentation were less diverse? Would the piece be better if it drew on still more sources? How does the author's explicit reference to sources affect the way you read the article? Compare your list with a classmate's. Could either of the articles you and your classmate analyzed have been written solely with information available in the library?

As you plan and begin to research your own paper, keep in mind what you've learned about how professionals use sources.

73   KEEP THAT IDEA YOUR OWN

When they begin to read source material for a research paper, some writers have difficulty keeping track of their own ideas, insights, interests, and feelings — the things that convinced them to write about the subject in the first place. When such writers find sources that seem to articulate their ideas, they're liable to forget that they ever had ideas of their own on the subject. Losing sight of their own ideas leads such writers to produce the kind of research paper you may have written in high school — a collection of quotations from various sources patched together with a few lines of your own.

Most college professors won't want to see a collection of other people's ideas in a research paper — they'll want to see your ideas and your synthesis of other people's ideas. They'll want you to pick and choose from among your sources, rather than to be controlled by those sources. So keeping your own interests and goals in sight as you do research should be a major goal — and can be a major struggle.

One way to win that struggle is to keep returning to your own ideas and writing them down, using some of the most basic planning strategies. Before you even go to the library, jot down as many ideas as possible about where you plan to go with the paper, what you would like to focus on, and what your own feelings and opinions are. Then, after you read each important source, brainstorm or freewrite briefly on how you can use that source, how it connects to your main ideas and to your other sources, and how it helps you to change or expand your original ideas. By writing a little after reading each book or article, you'll be more in control of your material and less likely to wonder, "Do I really have anything of my own to say here?" When it comes time to write your first draft, you'll probably find that the results of these periodic efforts at brainstorming and freewriting will provide you a good base to build upon.

74   RESEARCHING TO UNDERSTAND

Read Dudley Randall's "Booker T. and W. E. B." Unless you've studied W. E. B. DuBois or Booker T. Washington before, you'll have trouble understanding and appreciating the poem. Go to the library and see how much information you can find on the two men in an hour. Try to locate information that relates to the ideas in the poem. Write a two or three page essay about what you understand to be the essential differences in the philosophies of the two men. If this interests you, consider making a full-fledged research paper out of the subject.

Now go back and reread the poem. Does it seem consistent with what you've discovered about the two men? Do you find that it now seems to say in a very condensed fashion things you were trying to say in your short paper? A good poem will do that — it will seem deceptively simple at first, but the more you get into it the more you realize that it's saying, in only a few words, what an essayist might try to say in many more. Consider writing a research paper on the poem, its subjects, and how it deals with its subjects in such short space.

PART TWO
READINGS

I
MUSIC-
BRIDGING
CULTURES

The selections in this section focus on music that crosses national and cultural boundaries. You will read about Jamaican reggae bringing African and Caribbean rhythms to America via Britain; about Chinese musicians' introduction to improvisational American jazz; about the journey of American blues up the Mississippi and across the Atlantic; about Chicano musicians who tap the roots of many different cultures; about a Czech composer's vision of a uniquely American music. The two reviews of contemporary music and the two articles on reggae provide contrasts in styles and audience directedness. "Live Aid and the Woodstock Nation" makes a familiar comparison between concerts of today and those of twenty years ago, but reaches some unusual conclusions.

And this section introduces many of the themes followed throughout the readings. What constitutes American culture and what does that culture owe to sources outside the United States? What defines literacy? (If you know every note of Dvořák's music but none of Bob Marley's, are you culturally literate?) How have we been changing as a people and a culture during your lifetime? How do the arts reflect and change our attitudes and beliefs?

To start exploring some of these connections, you might read William Zinsser's "Shanghai" and then something from section IV, A Nation of Immigrants. Or read Ed Ward's "Reggae" and Susan Tyler Hitchcock's "Cultural Literacy" from Section X and discuss how American culture absorbs the ideas and vocabularies of other cultures.

SHANGHAI

William Zinsser

1 Jazz came to China for the first time on the afternoon of June 2, 1981, when the American bassist and French-horn player Willie Ruff introduced himself and his partner, the pianist Dwike Mitchell, to several hundred students and professors who were crowded into a large room at the Shanghai Conservatory of Music. The students and the professors were all expectant, without knowing quite what to expect. They only knew that they were about to hear the first American jazz concert ever presented to the Chinese. Probably they were not surprised to find that the two musicians were black, though black Americans are a rarity in the People's Republic. What they undoubtedly didn't expect was that Ruff would talk to them in Chinese, and when he began they murmured with delight.

2 Ruff is a lithe, dapper man in his early fifties who takes visible pleasure in sharing his enthusiasms, and it was obvious that there was no place he would rather have been than in China's oldest conservatory, bringing the music of his people to

---

From William Zinsser, *Willie and Dwike: An American Profile*, Harper & Row, 1984.

still another country deprived of that commodity. In 1959 he and Mitchell — who have played together as the Mitchell-Ruff Duo for almost thrity years — introduced jazz to the Soviet Union, and for that occasion Ruff taught himself Russian, his seventh language. In 1979 he hit on the idea of making a similar trip to China, and he began taking intensive courses in Chinese at Yale, where he is a professor of music and of Afro-American studies. By the winter of 1981 he felt that he was fluent enough in Mandarin to make the trip.

3   Now Ruff stood at the front of the room surveying the Chinese faces. He looked somewhat like an Oriental sage himself — or at least like the traditional carving of one; he is the color of old ivory, with a bald head and the beginnings of a Mandarin beard. He was holding several sheets of paper on which he had written, in Chinese characters, what he wanted to tell his listeners about the origins of jazz.

4   "In the last three hundred and fifty years," he began, "black people in America have created a music that is a rich contribution to Western culture. Of course three hundred and fifty years, compared to the long and distinguished history of Chinese music, seems like only a moment. But please remember that the music of American black people is an amalgam whose roots are deep in African history and also that it has taken many characteristics from the music of Europe."

5   Ruff has an amiable voice, and as he declaimed the first sentences, relishing the swoops and cadences of his latest adopted language, he had already established contact with the men and women in the room. They were attentive but relaxed — not an audience straining to decipher a foreigner's accent.

6   "In Africa the drum is the most important musical instrument." Ruff went on. "But to me the intriguing thing is that the people also use their drums to talk. Please imagine that the drum method of speech is so exquisite that Africans can, without recourse to words, recite proverbs, record history and send long messages. The drum is to West African society what the book is to literate society."

7   I wondered what the audience would make of that. Not only was China the oldest of literate societies, we were in the one Asian city that was encrusted with Western thought as transmitted in books, in journals and in musical notation — a city whose symphony orchestra, when it was founded in 1922, consisted entirely of Europeans. Even the architecture of Shanghai was a patchwork of Western shapes — a residue of the days when the city had a huge foreign population and was divided into districts that were controlled by different European countries. At the conservatory we were in the former French concession, and its main building was in a red brick French provincial style, with a sloping red tile roof and a porte cochere. Another French-style building housed the conservatory's library of one hundred thousand books about music — definitely not the oral tradition. Newer buildings served as classrooms and practice rooms, and the music that eddied out of their windows was the dreary fare of Western academic rigor: vocal scales endlessly rising, piano arpeggios repeated until they were mastered, chamber groups starting and stopping and starting again. We could have been in Vienna of the nineties or Paris of the twenties. In any case, we were a long way from Africa. And we were farther still from music created spontaneously.

8   "In the seventeenth century," Ruff continued, "when West Africans were captured and brought to America as slaves, they brought their drums with them. But the slave owners were afraid of the drum because it was so potent; it could be used to incite the slaves to revolt. So they outlawed the drum. This very shrewd law had tremendous effect on the development of black people's music. Our ancestors had to develop a variety of drum substitutes. One of them, for example, was tap dancing — I'm sure you've all heard of that. Now I'd like to show you a drum substitute that you probably don't know about, one that uses the hands and the body to make rhythm. It's called hambone."

9   There was no translating "hambone" into Mandarin — the odd word hung in the air. But Ruff quickly had an intricate rhythm going, slapping himself with the palms of his hands and smacking his open mouth to create a series of resonating pops. Applause greeted this proof that the body could be its own drum.

10   "By the time jazz started to develop," Ruff went on, "all African instruments in America had disappeared. So jazz borrowed the instruments of Western music, like the ones we're playing here today." He went over to his own instrument, the bass, and showed how he used it as a percussion instrument by picking the strings with his fingers instead of playing them with a bow. "Only this morning," he said, "I gave a lesson to your distinguished professor of bass, and he is already *very good.*"

11   Moving from rhythm to terrain that was more familiar to his listeners, he pointed out that jazz took its structural elements from European harmony. "Mr. Mitchell will now give you an example of the music that American slaves found in the Christian churches — Protestant hymns that had been brought from Europe. Slaves were encouraged to embrace Christianity and to use its music. Please listen."

12   Mitchell played an old Protestant hymn. "The slaves adopted these harmonies and transformed them into their own very emotional spirituals," Ruff said. "Mr. Mitchell and I will sing you a famous Negro spiritual from the days of slavery. It's called 'My Lord, What a Morning.' " With Mitchell playing a joyful accompaniment, the two men sang five or six choruses of the lovely old song, Mitchell carrying the melody in his deep voice, Ruff taking the higher second part. The moment, musically beautiful, had an edge of faraway sadness. I couldn't help thinking of another alien culture onto which the Protestant hymns of Europe had once been strenuously grafted. It was just beyond the conservatory gates.

13   "Mr. Mitchell will now show you how the piano can be used as a substitute for the instruments of the orchestra," Ruff said. "Please notice that he uses his left hand to play the bass and also to make his rhythm section. Later he will use his right hand to play the main melody and to fill in the harmony. This style is called ragtime." Mitchell struck up a jaunty rag. The students perked up at the playful pattern of the notes. Ruff looked out at his class and beamed. The teacher in him was beginning to slip away, the musician in him was tugging at his sleeve and telling him to start the concert.

14   . . . When Mitchell finished his ragtime tune the audience clapped — apparently glad to hear some of the converging elements that Ruff had talked about earlier. "Now,"

Ruff said, "we're going to give you an example of blues." It was another word that didn't lend itself to Mandarin, and it sounded unusually strung out: *blooooooze*. "One of the fundamental principles of jazz is form." Ruff continued, "and blues are a perfect illustration. Blues almost always have a twelve-bar form. This twelve-bar form never changes. It wouldn't change even if we stayed here and played it all night." He paused to let this sink in. "But you don't have to worry — we aren't going to play it that long." It was his first joke in Chinese, and it went over well. Mitchell then played an easygoing blues — a classic example of what came up the river from New Orleans, with a strong left hand ornamented by graceful runs in the right hand. Ruff joined in on his bass, and they played several twelve-bar choruses.

15   After that Ruff brought up the matter of improvisation, which he called "the lifeblood of jazz." He said that when he was young he worried because his people hadn't developed from their experience in America a written tradition of opera, like Chinese opera, that chronicled great or romantic events. "But later I stopped worrying because I saw that the master performers of our musical story — Louis Armstrong, Ella Fitzgerald and so many others — have enriched our culture with the beauty of what they created spontaneously. Now please listen one more time to the blues form, and count the measures along with me." He wanted his listeners to count, he said, because the rules of jazz require the improviser, however wild his melodic journeys, to repeat the harmonic changes that went into the first statement of the theme. "After you count with me a few times through, Mr. Mitchell will begin one of his famous improvisations."

16   Mitchell played a simple blues theme, emphasizing the chord changes, and Ruff counted the twelve bars aloud in English. Mitchell then restated the theme, embroidering it slightly, and this time Ruff counted in Chinese: "*Yi, er, san, si, wu, liu, qi, ba . . .*" This so delighted the students that they forgot to join him. "I can't hear you," Ruff said, teacher fashion, but they kept quiet and enjoyed his climb up the numerical ladder. Mitchell then embarked on a series of improvisations, some constructed of Tatum-like runs, some built on strong chord progressions (he can move immense chord clusters up and down the keyboard with incredible speed). Next, Ruff took a chorus on the bass; then they alternated their improvised flights, moving in twelve-bar segments to an ending that seemed as inevitable as if they had played it a hundred times before.

17   Changing the mood, Ruff announced that Mitchell would play a song called "Yesterday." Jerome Kern's plaintive melody is hardly the stuff of traditional jazz, nor was Mitchell's rendition of it — a treatment of classical intricacy, closer to Rachmaninoff (one of his heroes) than to any jazz pianist. The students applauded with fervor. Staying in a relatively classical vein, Ruff switched to the French horn and the two men played Billy Strayhorn's "Lush Life" in a mood which was slow and lyrical, almost like a German *lied*, and which perhaps surprised the students with its lack of an obvious rhythm.

18   The next number was one that I didn't recognize. It moved at a bright tempo and had several engaging themes that were brought back by the piano or the French horn — the usual jazzmen's game of statement and response. Twice, Mitchell briefly introduced a contrapuntal motif that was a deliberate imitation of Bach, and each

time it drew a ripple of amusement from the professors and the students. It was the first time they had heard a kind of music that they knew from their own studies.

19   "That number," Ruff said, "is called 'Shanghai Blues.' We just made it up." The audience buzzed with amazement and pleasure.

20   I had been watching the professors and the students closely during the concert. Their faces had the look of people watching the slow approach of some great natural force — a tornado or a tidal wave. They had been listening to music that their experience had not prepared them to understand. Two black men were playing long stretches of music without resorting to any printed notes. Yet they obviously hadn't memorized what they were playing; their music took unexpected turns, seemingly at the whim of the musicians, straying all over the keyboard and all over the landscape of Western tonality. Nevertheless there was order. Themes that had been abandoned came back in different clothes. If the key changed, as it frequently did, the two men were always in the same key. Often there was a playfulness between the two instruments, and always there was rapport. But if the two players were exchanging any signals, the message was too quick for the untrained eye.

21   From the quality of the listeners' attention I could tell that the music was holding them in a strong grip. Their minds seemed to be fully engaged. Their bodies, however, were not. Only three pairs of feet in the whole room were tapping — Mitchell's, Ruff's and mine. Perhaps this was a Chinese characteristic, this stillness of listening. But beyond that, the music wasn't easy. It never again approached the overt syncopation of the ragtime that Mitchell had played early in the program; that was where the essential gaiety of jazz had been most accessible. Nor did it have the flat-out gusto that an earlier generation of black musicians might have brought to China — the thumping rhythms and simpler harmonies of a James P. Johnson or a Fats Waller.

22   It wasn't that Mitchell and Ruff were playing jazz that was pedantic or sedate; on the contrary, I have seldom heard Mitchell play with more exuberant shifts of energy. But the music was full of subtleties — even a Westerner accustomed to jazz would have been charmed by its subtlety and wit. I had to remind myself that the Chinese had heard no Western music of any kind from 1966 to 1976. A twenty-one-year-old student in the audience, for instance, would only have begun to listen to composers like Mozart and Brahms within the past five years. The jazz that he was hearing now was not so different as to be a whole new branch of music. Mitchell was clearly grounded in Bach and Chopin; Ruff's French horn had echoes of all the classical works — Debussy's "Reverie," Ravel's "Pavane" — in which that instrument has such uncanny power to move us.

23   After "Shanghai Blues" Ruff invoked the ancient device of teachers who know they have been presenting too much material too fast. He asked for questions. The serious faces relaxed.

24   "Where do people go to study jazz in America?" a student wanted to know. "What kind of courses do they take?"

25   Ruff explained that jazz courses, where they existed at all, would be part of a broad college curriculum that included, say, languages and history and physics.

"But, really, jazz isn't learned in universities or conservatories," he said. "It's music that is passed on by older musicians to those of us who are younger."

26   It was not a helpful answer. What kind of subject doesn't have its own academy? A shyness settled over the room, though the students seemed full of curiosity. Professor Tan got up and stood next to Ruff. "I urge you to ask questions," he said. "I can assure you that jazz has many principles that apply to your studies here. In fact, I have many questions myself."

27   An old professor stood up. "When you created 'Shanghai Blues' just now," he said, "did you have a form for it, or a logical plan?"

28   "I just started tapping my foot," Ruff replied, tapping his foot to reconstruct the moment. "And then I started to play the first thought that came into my mind with the horn. And Mitchell heard it. And he answered. And after that we heard and answered, heard and answered, heard and answered."

29   "But how can you ever play it again?" the old professor said.

30   "We never can," Ruff replied.

31   "That is beyond our imagination," the professor said. "Our students here play a piece a hundred times, or two hundred times, to get it exactly right. You play something once — something very beautiful — and then you just throw it away."

32   Now the questions tumbled out. What was most on the students' minds quickly became clear: it was the mystery of improvisation. (The Chinese don't even have a word for improvisation of this kind; Ruff translated it as "something created during the process of delivery.") All the questions poked at this central riddle — "Could a Chinese person improvise?" and "Could two strangers improvise together?" and "How can you compose at such speed?" — and it was at this point that Ruff took one question and turned it into a moment that stood us all on our ear.

33   Was it really possible, a student wanted to know, to improvise on any tune at all — even one that the musicians had never heard before?

34   Ruff's reply was casual. "I would like to invite one of the pianists here to play a short traditional Chinese melody that I'm sure we would not know," he said, "and we will make a new piece based on that."

35   The room erupted in oohs and cheers. I caught a look on Mitchell's face that said, "This time you've gone too far." The students began to call the name of the young man they wanted to have play. When they found him in the crowd he was so diffident that he got down on the floor to keep from being dragged out. But his friends dragged him out anyway, and, regaining his aplomb, he walked to the piano and sat down with the formality of a concert artist. He was about twenty-two. Mitchell stood at one side, looking grave.

36   The young man played his melody beautifully and with great feeling. It seemed to be his own composition, unknown to the other people. It began with four chords of distinctively Chinese structure, moved down the scale in a stately progression, paused, turned itself around with a transitional figure of lighter weight, and then started back up, never repeating itself and finally resolving the theme with a suspended chord that was satisfying because it was so unexpected. It was a perfect small piece, about fourteen bars long. The student walked back to his seat and Mitchell went back to the piano. The room got very quiet.

37 Mitchell's huge hands hovered briefly over the keys, and then the young man's melody came back to him. It was in the same key; it had the same chords, slightly embellished near the end, and, best of all, it had the same mood. Having stated the theme, Mitchell broadened it the second time, giving it a certain majesty, coloring the student's chords with dissonances that were entirely apt; he gave the "Chinese" chords a jazz texture but still preserved their mood. Then Ruff joined him on his bass, and they took the melody through a number of variations, Mitchell giving it a whole series of new lives but never losing its integrity. I listened to his feat with growing excitement. For me it was the climax of years of marveling at his ear and at his sensitivity to the material at hand. The students were equally elated and astonished. For them it was the ultimate proof — because it touched their own heritage — that for a jazz improviser no point of departure is alien.

38 After that a few more questions were asked, and Mitchell and Ruff concluded with a Gershwin medley from *Porgy and Bess* and a genial rendition of "My Old Flame." Professor Tan thanked the two men and formally ended the concert. Then he went over to Mitchell and took his hands in his own. "You are an artist," he said.

39 Later I told Mitchell that I thought Ruff had given him an unduly nervous moment when he invited one of the students to supply a melody.

40 "Well, naturally I was nervous," he said, "because I didn't have any idea what to expect. But, you know, that boy phrased his piece *perfectly*. The minute he started to play I got his emotions. I understood exactly what he was feeling, and the rest was easy. The notes and the chords just fell into place."

LIVE AID AND THE WOODSTOCK NATION

Samuel G. Freedman

1 It was the word on everybody's lips at the Live Aid concert last Saturday in Philadelphia. "Woodstock II," said the rock star Neil Young. "It's your Woodstock," the singer Joan Baez told the crowd in John F. Kennedy Stadium. Seventeen-year-old Tom Teter of Vineland, N.J., agreed: "It's our Woodstock and it's just as good."

2 There was abundant reason for the comparison. The organizers of Live Aid consciously harkened to the 1969 festival, a counterculture conclave that led Abbie Hoffman to coin the term "Woodstock Nation" for America's young. And certainly Live Aid as an event, a spectacle, addressed the desire of many fans — people in their teens or 20s who know Woodstock as an icon of the decade they worship — to enact their vision of the 1960s.

3 But if Woodstock was the obvious point of reference for the mammoth Live Aid shows in Philadelphia and London — seen by 162,000 fans in Kennedy and

Samuel G. Freedman, "Live Aid and the Woodstock Nation," *The New York Times*, July 18, 1985.

Wembley Stadiums and an estimated 1.5 billion on a worldwide television broadcast — it was not necessarily the right one. If anything, the distance from a rain-soaked dairy farm in Bethel, N.Y., to a state-of-the-art stage in Philadelphia is measured in much more than 16 years and a few hundred miles.

4   Between then and now, rock-and-roll has moved from the turbulent, youthful fringe into the vast middle ground of American culture and commerce. Its audience — and in many cases, performers — has turned from social rebels to solid citizens. Woodstock was on the surface an apolitical event, promising merely "three days of music and peace," which took on enormous resonance more by what it represented than by what it said outright. Live Aid was a political event — in that it was created solely to raise money for African famine relief — that largely appealed to fans as a megaconcert.

5   "You've got to face the reality of the event," said Bill Graham, the promoter of the Live Aid concert. "People are concerned about the plight in Africa, but if there was no famine, we'd have sold as many tickets." Whatever the motive, the harvest was handsome indeed. In a single day, Live Aid raised an estimated $70 million, far outstripping the figure from such renowned rock charity events as George Harrison's 1971 Concert for Bangladesh.

6   The differences between Woodstock and Live Aid, which is to say between America in 1969 and America in 1985, show up in many specific ways, too. Woodstock was a chaotic, anarchic happening that sprawled over three days; Live Aid's 14-hour Philadelphia concert ran only three minutes overtime. Where hippie entrepreneurs sold hallucinogens at Woodstock — there were two drug-related deaths and hundreds of "bad trips" from LSD — the drug of choice at Live Aid was beer. The lasting images of Woodstock include skinny-dippers in a wallow called "Passion Puddle"; the crowd at Live Aid had short hair and waved the Stars and Stripes. One fan arrived in a limousine, from which his chauffeur watched the show on a built-in television.

APPEAL FOR 40-YEAR-OLDS

7 Live Aid was the kind of rock concert even a parent could like, especially since the typical parent of teenage children today grew up on the Beatles, Bob Dylan, and Elvis Presley. And that was part of the point in the packaging of Live Aid.

8   "This show was designed to be most appreciated by a 40-year-old," said Michael C. Mitchell, president of Worldwide Sports and Entertainment, the company that produced the Live Aid telecast. "It's their music — Joan Baez, Mick Jagger, Bob Dylan. We took a lot of performers from 1960 to 1980 and very few since. If the show aimed only at the kids — the 16-, 17-, 18-year-olds — we'd have a problem. They don't give money."

9   Besides individual performers with roots in the 1960s in general and Woodstock in particular, Live Aid offered the reunions of period bands such as the Who, Led Zeppelin, and Crosby, Stills, Nash, and Young. These performances added to the sense of a once-in-a-lifetime event, but they also threw the passage of time into clear relief. David Crosby, Stephen Stills, Graham Nash, and Neil Young played

together in public for the first time ever at Woodstock. By the time they re-assembled for Live Aid, Mr. Nash was graying at the temples, Mr. Stills had a double chin, Mr. Crosby has been convicted on drug- and gun-possession charges and Mr. Young has endorsed Ronald Reagan for president

"LONGING FOR THE 60s"

10 Such 1960s stars, though, continue to carry a mythological importance for the teen-aged audience that filled Kennedy Stadium. "It might be that the children of the 80s are longing for a Woodstock, longing for the 60s," Miss Baez said. "The similarity I felt between Woodstock and Live Aid was that desire for some un-written solidarity, for a chance for their community to come together." Another part of the nostalgia for the 60s is the desire for a sense of commitment, and the African famine, like the campaign for American institutions to divest themselves of their holdings in South Africa, provided such a rallying point.

11   At the same time, Miss Baez said, she doubted how much Saturday's audience really shared with the 500,000 at Woodstock. "I wondered what kind of problems they have," she said of the Live Aid spectators. "At Woodstock, you had the war, rebellion against parents, bad acid — a rainbow of things. These kids in Philadelphia had cooled out to 'feel good about themselves.' It's not easy to ruffle them."

12   Other observers attacked what they saw as the concert's calculated show of conscience. "I think it's great if the money raised does save lives," said Greil Marcus, author of *Mystery Train* and rock music columnist for *Art Forum* magazine. "But it was an enormous orgy of self-satisfaction, self-congratulation."

13   "It's good people wanted to do something about the famine and I'll be gladder when the money gets to Africa," said Marshall Berman, a professor of political science at the City University of New York and the author of *All That Is Solid Melts Into Air: The Experience of Modernity.* "But a little humility and wariness wouldn't hurt."

A GLOBAL LANGUAGE

14 What seems indisputable, however, is that Live Aid deeply changed the rules of what a rock concert is. While Woodstock ushered in the era of the gargantuan out-door festival — Altamont, Powder Ridge, and Watkins Glen followed — Live Aid was a case of what Neil Young called "high tech meeting the 60s." If the concert itself was modeled on Woodstock, the broadcast borrowed more from the 1984 Olympics and the Jerry Lewis telethon.

15   In place of Woodstock's community on a soggy hillside, Live Aid's worldwide audience overwhelmingly experienced the event through television. The broadcast intercut footage from concerts in Philadelphia, London, and several foreign coun-tries with fund-raising appeals by prominent politicians, artists, and sports stars. Even in Kennedy Stadium itself, the crowd did not watch the performers as much as it watched their images on several huge video monitors. It was the Marshall McLuhan "global village" prophecy come to pass.

16   The fact that rock-and-roll was the Esperanto of the "global village" was itself significant. In 1969, Woodstock's promoters had to scramble to find anybody willing to provide land for a festival. In 1985, Philadelphia officials grabbed the Live Aid concert as a way of rehabilitating the city's image in the aftermath of the Move tragedy. The concert in turn was carried by network television, FM rock stations and a 24-hour rock cable station — manifestations of a rock-based economy that was only in its infancy during Woodstock.

17   "Finally, the music industry was looked at on such a high level," said Mr. Graham, who began promoting rock concerts 20 years ago and has organized a number of charity shows. "And finally, the world at large realizes there are people in our industry who do things about their beliefs. For the world I work in, this was our finest hour. By far."

LOS LOBOS

Michael Goldberg

1 Elvis Costello played one of their songs on a recent tour. Mick Jagger was spotted trying to slip into one of their sold-out club dates. John Fogerty contributed hand claps to their latest video. Last year, a track from their EP, "*. . . and a time to dance*," won a Grammy award, and their latest record, an LP called *How Will the Wolf Survive?*, has been showing up on several critics' Top Ten lists for 1984.

2   The group is Los Lobos, and after eleven years of playing in rank bars and tacky Mexican restaurants, at weddings and bar mitzvahs, neighborhood barbecues and Hollywood punk clubs, they have become one of the most talked-about groups in rock & roll. "I think we're really fortunate to be in this situation. It's hard to keep from wondering, 'Do we really deserve it?'" says singer and guitarist Cesar Rosas as he sits in a funky Japanese restaurant in East Los Angeles, eating from a four-dollar plate of sushi and teriyaki chicken. He smiles and fingers his bushy goatee. "The only thing that's missing is the money."

3   Though Los Lobos' finances may be shaky, there's no question about their talent. Eschewing synthesizers, drum machines and other newfangled equipment in favor of old-fashioned Fender guitars, sax and button accordion, Los Lobos plays everything from classic rock & roll to blues, zydeco, soul, C&W and Tex-Mex. They can rip into "Don't Worry Baby," a raw blues, with the sweaty fury of the late Howlin' Wolf, then waltz through "Corrida #1," a Norteña polka, sounding as sweet as Buddy Holly.

4   "People have to remember that rock & roll came from a cross-pollination of a lot of different cultures," says drummer and songwriter Louis Perez. "The black, the hillbilly, all that rural culture: that's what rock & roll is all about. I don't find what we're doing any different from what Elvis was doing."

Michael Goldberg, "Los Lobos," *Rolling Stone*, April 11, 1985.

5   The four original members of Los Lobos — Rosas, 29, Perez, 30, singer, guitarist and songwriter David Hidalgo, 29, and bassist Conrad Lozano, 32 — grew up
together in East Los Angeles, a working-class Chicano community that they still
call home. All four are happily married. All four have children. And all four are
about as low-key and unpretentious as you can get. "We're just normal people,"
explains Rosas. "You can't expect to have a kid and then be playing loud shit all
day, having all the boys come over and whipping out the drugs and drinking beer.
We look forward to coming home to a peaceful house. That's the only thing that
holds you together."

6   Los Lobos are also adamantly attached to their roots: their parents, their
neighborhood, their families, their Latino culture. "You can't make rooted music,
music as solidly based as the music Los Lobos play, without having that fundamental foundation," says Steve Berlin, the twenty-eight-year-old sax player who
joined the group last year after quitting another of L.A.'s roots-oriented bands, the
Blasters. "It *does* show in the music."

7   Like so many other groups, Los Lobos got their start playing in Top Forty
cover bands. Getting drunk every night and having little in the way of responsibility seemed fun at first, but after a while the band members began to get bored.
"Once you realize, like, hey, I've been playing at this club for a year, it kind of
shocks you," says Rosas. "You think, I want to go somewhere else. And it turns
out you can't. You just go to another club, and it's the same."

8   So Rosas and his friends decided to try something different. They began
spending afternoons learning to play old Mexican folk songs on acoustic guitars.
Soon they were calling themselves Los Lobos — Spanish for "the Wolves" — and
embarking on six years of intensive study of Mexican folk music. The quartet
sought out and learned how to play obscure Mexican stringed instruments: the
requinto jarocho, the jarana, the guitarrón, the bajo sexto.

9   "A lot of people in East L.A. used to think we were crazy," says Hidalgo. But
after a couple of years Los Lobos became known as a "cultural unit," four young
men helping make other Mexican-Americans aware of their musical heritage. In
1978, they raised some money and recorded an acoustic album, *Just Another Band
from East L. A.* By the end of the Seventies, however, Los Lobos were bored again.
"We were turning into a jukebox," says Perez.

10   What turned things around was a Los Angeles concert that they opened for
former Sex Pistol John Lydon's band, Public Image Ltd. The audience was an
obnoxious pack of L. A. punks who weren't in the mood for long-haired Chicanos
strumming acoustic guitars. "It was like an ocean of fingers, flipping us off," says
Rosas. "Then they started getting nasty, saying, 'You bunch of spics, go back to
Mexico.' "

11   Steve Berlin was in the audience that night, hearing Los Lobos for the first
time. "I had never seen more effluvia thrown at anybody," he recalls. "I was
thinking, these must be the bravest men in the world!"

12   Despite that debacle, the energy and freshness of the punk scene appealed to
the band, so they hauled the old Fender amps and electric guitars out of the closets.
"This time we had brand-new ears," says Perez. "We had already explored all this

cultural music, regional music of Mexico, and we came back to rock & roll with a whole different mentality. It was like a new chapter.''

13   They began making regular commutes to Hollywood, opening for groups like the Blasters, X and the Circle Jerks at such punk clubs as the Club 88 and Cathay de Grande. This time they found audiences who loved their music. The money was bad, but rave reviews in the L. A. press brought interest from filmmakers (Los Lobos' songs were included on soundtracks for *Eating Raoul* and *Chan Is Missing*) and major labels like Motown and CBS and A&M. Eventually, they made a deal with Slash Records.

14   Their new album, *How Will the Wolf Survive?*, has already become the biggest seller in Slash's six-year history, and Warner Bros. Records, which distributes the smaller label's product, has undertaken a major promotional campaign on behalf of the record. But none of the band members seems to have unreal expectations about the future. "I don't really expect Tex-Mex songs sung in Spanish to reach the top of the pop charts," says Perez. "The industry pretty much relies on the latest trends to make money real quick. But there has to be a place for people who play music that's a lot more durable than that."

15   No matter what happens, it seems unlikely that Los Lobos will lose sight of where they've come from. "What would I do with lots of money?" Perez says. "Paint my car. I don't know, man. I like it where I live. I wouldn't move away from here, that's for sure. Where else would I go? I wouldn't know anyone. Here I know the ice-cream vendor who comes by the house tinkling his bell. I know the folks at the corner store. The Ease Side is my home."

PAUL SIMON – *GRACELAND*

Gene Santoro

1 Toward the end of Simon and Garfunkel's long career, Paul Simon began dabbling in different sounds to color that rather monochromatic duo's music: *El Condor Pasa* drew on Andean panpiping, while *Bridge Over Troubled Waters* elaborated on gospel changes and a key religious image. On his own over the years, Simon extended his attempts to refract his ideas through a prism of styles: jubilee spirituals (*Loves Me Like A Rock*), salsa (*Me And Julio Down By The Schoolyard*), second-line soul (*Take Me To The Mardi Gras*).

2   But none of these previous dips into generic crosscurrents matches the total immersion on *Graceland*, a release that's as catchy and danceable as its implications are provocative. Deftly juggling a variety of South African styles, American r&b and c&w, zydeco (courtesy of Rockin' Dopsie on *That Was Your Mother*), Tex-Mex-flavored rock & roll (via Los Lobos on *All Around The World Or The Myth Of Fingerprints*), and Tin Pan Alley tunesmithing, Simon hasn't so much fused his

Gene Santoro, "Paul Simon – *Graceland*," *Downbeat*, December 1986.

elements as he has created a musical space they all inhabit as neighbors. And they interact, just like in the real world, where latin polyrhythms collide with American r&b to produce zydeco, or with eastern European polkas to spawn Texas two-steps, where congas and talking drums nestle next to c&w in Sunny Ade's juju, where funk gives birth to Afrobeat. It's a process as old as the hills.

3 The various ironic tensions Simon sets up, however, are very much of our time. "These are the days of miracle and wonder/This is the long-distance call," he sings over the loping lead bass of *The Boy In The Bubble*, but the miracles include lasers in the jungle, babies with baboon hearts, and modern terrorism ("The bomb in the baby carriage/was wired to the radio"). For the title track, the Nashville-via-Nigeria pedal steel of Sunny Ade's Demola Adepoju entwines with the Everly Brothers' harmonies to float behind lyrics that first metaphorically relate the bottleneck Delta blues and the Civil War — the opening struggle against American apartheid — and then seek to transcend the glitz reality of Elvis' residence under the pressure of loss: "Losing love is like a window in your heart/Everybody sees you're blown apart/Everybody sees the wind blow."

4 That dialog — or lack of it — between the historical and the introspective powers the lyrics over a collection of dance grooves that chatter with guitar cross-talk while the lead vocal spouts inconclusive cocktail party exchanges (*I Know What I Know*), stride to a skaish Zulu walking beat tickled by accordion (*Gumboots*, which are the shoes worn by South African miners), or sway to a gentle guitar lick stung on the chorus by the stuttering Tower of Power horns (*Diamonds On The Soles Of Her Shoes*), as New York City street scenes commingle with reminders of one of South Africa's prime money-making industries.

5 And so on. Without ever making any direct political statements, without ever abandoning the infectious musicality that first drew him into this project, Simon demonstrates that apartheid — apartness — is not only racist and stupid but ultimately untenable in a shrinking world whose confluent cultures create crosscurrents as rich as these. And by returning home for the last two cuts with Dopsie and Los Lobos, he brings us face to face with the implications of the music — and ourselves.

REGGAE

Ed Ward

1 "Reggae" is the collective term for a number of successive forms of Jamaican popular music, isolated examples of which have washed onto the shores of the U.S. Top 40 since the early Sixties. Characterized by a loping beat, a strong dose of R&B and recording techniques as original as they are primitive, reggae has had an

From Ed Ward, "Reggae," *The Rolling Stone Illustrated History of Rock 'n' Roll*, Random House, 1980.

impact on rock in the Seventies that is vastly disproportionate to its apparent commercial success.

2   In a way, this isn't really surprising. When someone used to sluggish rock is confronted with a sensory blitzkreig like Big Youth's "Screaming Target," for instance, with its heavily-accented chanting and echoplexed screaming over a track that seems to come and go at will, an immediate reassessment of pop aesthetics seems in order. What in the world is this guy raving about? Isn't there another song buried down there in the mix? What's this conversation at the start about guns and the "outasite movie Dirty 'arry," which segues into a rap about education? Searching out the answers to such questions can lead the quester down the alleyways of an alien world, where familiar assumptions about language, music and religion are all turned upside down. More importantly, it can lead one to a world where pop music is made like it used to be, where a song takes as long to cut as it does to play, where the resulting spontaneity leaps off a record with a long-forgotten immediacy.

3   Reggae's origins are found in diverse places. African-derived children's games, the ecstatic Christian Pocomania cult, the Garveyite Rastafarians, and the style of rhythm and blues played in New Orleans and beamed, in the late Fifties, over clear-channel stations: all these elements have had a role in the development of reggae. These influences did not converge, however, until the introduction of the transistor radio awakened a Jamaican interest in recorded pop music. The island's local stations featured sober programming in the BBC style, but on a clear day one could easily pick up commercial stations in the U.S. and Cuba, broadcasting the hits. From hearing the hits to wanting to make your own is a logical step, and it wasn't long before enterprising Jamaicans started doing just that.

4   Radios created a demand for music that stations on neither the island nor the mainland could easily respond to, and thus was born the "sound system man." These were electronically inclined entrepreneurs who assembled a "sound system" featuring huge speakers and a generator-powered hi-fi rig that could be mounted on the back of a flatbed truck and hauled out to the country for dances. Fronted by an operator who usually had a classy handle like Prince Buster or Duke Reid, these systems soon created their own followings. Operators competed for the best records, making weekly flights to Miami or New Orleans to pick up test pressings, making sure to have an "exclusive" by scratching the label information off, so no competitor could know where to get another copy.

5   It wasn't too big a jump for most of the operators from the system to a primitive sort of recording studio, and by 1960, there were several on the island. The first recordings were bad copies of New Orleans music — Fats Domino, in particular, was revered in Jamaica. For some reason, Jamaican musicians couldn't get the New Orleans rhythm "right." And, since the only other form of popular music on the island was a jazz-style instrumental music called "mento," there was no alternative but to keep at it, trying to duplicate the subtle swing of the Crescent City jump bands.

6   Suddenly this task became more urgent, because the early Sixties saw the talent in New Orleans dry up. When imported output dropped, the sound system men were forced to make their own records. Somehow, the "wrong" rhythm tri-

umphed, and ska, Jamaica's first internationally popular music, was born. With its strict, mechanical emphasis on the offbeat (mm-*cha!* mm-*cha!* mm-*cha!* mm-*cha!*), ska took Jamaica by storm.

7   The first ska groups included the Skatalites, who recorded for the island's first important studio, Coxone Dodd's Studio One. Among the group's members were Ernest Ranglin, the guitarist whose playing helped define the Jamaican style; Tommy McCook, a keyboard artist who has probably been on more sessions in Jamaica than any other musician; and Don Drummond, a moody trombone player who gave the Rastafarian sect its first popular hero (though mental problems landed him in an institution, where he died in the early Seventies).

8   Ska took off modestly in the U.S. with Millie Small's (British-produced) hit "My Boy Lollipop" selling respectably, paving the way for her white Jamaican-born producer, Chris Blackwell, to found Island Records in 1964. Producer Byron Lee took a ska band to the New York World's Fair, and fronted it with a teenaged vocalist named Jimmy Cliff, who'd had some Jamaican hits with producer Leslie Kong. And there was a U.S. *Do the Ska* album by Lee, complete with numbered footprints on the cover.

9   By 1965, in the inexorable Jamaican way, ska was "finish." It was replaced by the slower, even more rhythmic "rock steady," which was better for "rubbin' up a daughter" on the dance floor. Around this time, the sound system men escalated their competition by introducing disc jockeys. A DJ would "toast" or talk over the instrumental B-side of a record, improvising rhymes about his own prowess as a lover and the greatness of the sound system operator. The first successful toaster was Prince Buster, who scored a freak talk-over rock steady hit in the U.S. with "Ten Commandments," a sexist classic; but he is better-known in Jamaica and Britain for his series of "Judge Dread" records, in which a stern jurist sentences "rude boys" — the Jamaican juvenile delinquents who sang and danced to much of this music — to harsh terms in jail. Rock steady DJs not only did their toasting live, but recorded the best for posterity. Sir Collins and King Stitt were among the first, but the biggest star was U Roy, who brought deejaying to the top of the island's charts with "Wear You to the Ball." The practice was also known as "dubbing" not only because the DJs were dubbing in voices, but because some of the dub was "rude," (i.e., dirty), and in Jamaican slang "dub" is exactly equivalent to "fuck." In fact, during the rock steady era, the rude record came into its own, epitomized by Max Romeo's under-the-counter million-seller "Wet Dream," which Romeo claimed was about sleeping under a hole in his roof.

10   A slight variation in rock steady's beat (or "rydim," a Jamaican term that encompasses most of the backing track) produced poppa-top, reggae's direct precursor. Sounding just like its name, it was bubblier, and loosened up the rydim to the point where greater rhythmic division was possible. Poppa-top's great exponent was Desmond Dekker, a former rock steady star whose 1969 hit "Israelites" reached Number 12 in the U.S.

11   In 1968, the Maytals, a vocal trio that had been around for some time, led by the charismatic Frederick "Toots" Hibbert, released a record called "Do the Reggay," although neither Toots nor anyone else seemed to know where the word

came from. The music had been expanding the role of the bass for some time, and reggae brought the bass into the forefront, emphasizing a complex interrelationship between it, the trap drums, and the percussion instruments. The rydim was shot through with silences, and to this day few non-Jamaicans can play it. The pulse is divided as finely as 64 times, and cross-rhythms abound. The bass seems to be the lead instrument, and the guitar is reduced to playing "changa," mere scratching at a chord. Keyboards and occasional "country" (i.e., out-of-tune) horn sections thicken the texture.

12   Reggae might have remained an isolated phenomenon, picked up by a few cognoscenti in the U.S. if it hadn't been for a white Jamaican filmmaker, Perry Henzell, who, starting in 1968, began researching and filming the story of a rude boy who comes to Kingston, records a smash hit, is cheated by an all-too-typical record businessman, commits a murder, goes on the lam, and is sought by both the Jamaican army and the producer, who wants another hit. Henzell's film, *The Harder They Come*, was a classic case of the right movie being made in the right place at the right time. Its star, Jimmy Cliff, was at his peak as a singer, reggae was at perhaps its highest level of artistic development and Henzell was the perfect filmmaker, a man who clearly loved his subject. The film was fraught with danger, problems and delay, an actor died midway through, and money was constantly tight, but when it was finally released in the U.S. in 1973, it became an immediate cult hit.

13   The world *The Harder They Come* showed was, unfortunately, all too close to the real world of reggae. Producers tended to tie in with sound systems, and few if any of their performers ever saw royalties or sales figures from their records. If they complained, the producer wouldn't work with them any more, their records wouldn't get played at the sound system dances, and they would fade from the minds of one of the most fickle audiences anywhere. Live music was rare because most of the records used the same basic pool of studio talent, and because most Jamaicans couldn't afford night clubs or stage show performances even if they could get to Kingston to see them. The music world was truly what the vernacular had it to be, a "Mafia," and those who worked outside the system had very little hope for success.

14   Still, there were those who tried. The most famous was a rebellious songwriter, Bob Marley. His vocal trio with Peter Tosh and Bunny Livingstone, the Wailers, had worked with just about every producer in Kingston before they were signed, in 1970, to Chris Blackwell's Island Records, a label with a reputation for integrity and distribution in England and America as well as in Jamaica. Blackwell gave Marley the kind of money and artistic freedom he'd never experienced before. He had always been an intensely political writer, but now his topics became even more focused. He wrote new lyrics protesting conditions in Kingston's Trench Town ghetto ("Concrete Jungle"), decrying random searches by army troops ("Rebel Music [3 O'Clock Road Block]"), and glorifying the Rastafarian life ("Natty Dread"), all in songs that were gloriously melodic, well recorded, and both rootsy enough to satisfy the Jamaican audience and rock-oriented enough for the U.S. market. Both music and lyrics struck a responsive chord with American fans, and

Marley's records continue to be the only reggae records to sell in appreciable numbers here, although many feel that the true fire of the group disappeared shortly after Tosh and Livingstone left in 1974. A key factor to Marley's success has been his incessant touring, not only in the U.S., but also in Europe and Africa; he is held in high esteem in places like Nigeria and Ghana as well as in Jamaica.

15 . . . "W'at you t'ink, mon," I was asked in Jamaica in 1975, "reggae gon' go international?" "Maybe," was my response, and it looks like I was right. Reggae has given a new rhythmic concept to rock, as performers as far apart as Eric Clapton, the Grateful Dead, the Clash and Jimmy Buffett have proven. But the "roots reggae" has stayed down Yard, because its artists have chosen to serve the cultural and informational needs of the people who gave it birth, instead of trying for the big time in Hollywood and New York. Although the current output seems relatively stagnant, it is loved in Jamaica by Jamaicans, and continues to support the world's most successful self-contained Third World record business — which, in the long run, may be its finest achievement.

TO CREATE A NATIONAL MUSIC

Patricia Hampl

THEN

1 On Monday, June 5, 1893, Antonín Dvořák stepped off the noon branch line train coming from the Iowa river town of MacGregor, onto the station platform of the village of Calmar in the northeastern part of the state. He was accompanied by his wife Anna and her widowed sister Mme. Terezie Koutecká, along with the six Dvořák children, a housemaid, and Dvořák's secretary Josef Kovařík. . . .

2 Dvořák was spending two years as director of the National Conservatory of Music in New York and had been persuaded by his secretary to spend the long summer vacation in his hometown in Iowa. Spillville, the younger Kovařík said, would provide the Master (as he faithfully called Dvořák) with the peace and quiet he needed for composition. Besides, it was a Czech settlement where he would hear his own language spoken on the street. He would be at home.

THE BELOVED

3 . . . Passing through this spring farmland, the love of place creates a desire to pause for description. I wish to describe the lilacs. A lyric wish. As far as I can tell, I want to describe them for no reason — because they're there, as climbers are supposed to say of mountains.

Patricia Hampl, *Spillville*, Milkweed Editions, 1987.

4   Was that how it was for Dvořák? "I know that my new Symphony and also the string quartet and quintet (composed here in Spillville) would never have been written in the manner in which I have written them, had I not seen America." He bird-dogged the scarlet tanager all over the woods and meadows of Spillville, trying to get its song transcribed accurately. And it's there, chirruping through the *scherzo* of the Opus 96 string quartet. The joy of description.

5   Yet, Dvořák sensed the isolation here too, the *strangeness*, as he called it: "Few people, a great deal of empty space." New York may have been crowded and noisy, but Iowa was stunned with quiet as if God, at first acting like a good Czech, had made the right landscape, but then faltered, sketching in the peasants haphazardly, too faintly.

6   Dvořák's rhapsodic voice is not a gush of feeling. That's the common mistake, to think of Romantics as "emotional." In fact, the Romantic consciousness is bred not of feeling, but of faith. Sometimes too much faith for the contemporary sophisticated audience which prefers an edgier sound to Dvořák's swells and murmurs. Birds, wind, moving water — these form his compact with life.

7   No wonder Dvořák never had much luck with opera, the human drama. His only great operatic triumph is *Rusalka*, the story of a mermaid who falls in love with a human. The most beautiful aria is Rusalka's song to the moon, the pantheistic swoon of a solitary. People are walk-ons, their frantic dilemmas overwhelmed by the greater punishments and assurances of creation itself. Landscape alone is real. Landscape and its true love, the poetic consciousness, the lyric intelligence which contemplates and reiterates the created world. The Romantic.

8   Once Dvořák had his singing bird, his wind zinging through a wheatfield, his rushing waterfall, he was companioned — not as human beings seeking relation with other human beings are companioned, but as the soul seeking God is companioned. The scarlet tanager didn't make him *feel* good, certainly it didn't inspire love; he called it his "damn bird." But its song, fleet and difficult to capture, formed an article of his faith.

9   The faith, put plainly, was that God was in the song; God was even in the difficulty. And what do you do with God but serve Him? Get out the notebook and transcribe.

10   The chilly spaces left between people must always have remained for him, as he said, *strange*. As a Central European travelling with his family entourage, he could observe that strangeness, even be dismayed by it, without being harmed. But that loneliness was part of human feeling. Whereas, the relationship to bird, wind, rushing water was part of divine faith. Landscape and faith formed the foundation and arc that enclosed human endeavor in all its frantic loneliness. Faith didn't provide a warm, comfortable sensation (Dvořák was one of the scowling Romantics), but it gave the sense of vocation, of productive servitude, without which an artist is left to rely on the inflation of personal qualities, on "originality," on "being unique."

11   But what is it, now, to wish to get out the notebook and transcribe, to describe the lilacs? Where's the divinity in description?

12   The desire to describe the lilacs, the lyric impulse, is easily disparaged. You want a description of the lilacs? Consult the Romantic poets, go to the nineteenth century. They took care of all that. A little sentimental, but pretty.

13   And for God's sake, we keep warning each other these days, don't be sentimental.

THE KINGDOM

14 "The Americans expect great things of me. And the main thing is, so they say, to show them to the promised land and kingdom of a new and independent art. In short, to create a national music. Now, if the small Czech nation can have such musicians, they say, why could not they, too, when their country and people are so immense?"

15   He believed the answer lay in the music of the slaves, Negro spirituals, and in American Indian music, especially its insistent, patient rhythms. And, as always, as everywhere, the birds, wind, moving water. This was how he'd done it in Bohemia: go to nature, go to the people. He was a peasant, had apprenticed first as a butcher, following his father, until his talent for music somehow commanded him. He was taken to study at the choir school in the cart his father used for market.

16   Maybe he could not perceive the American hesitation. In the old country "the peasants" were himself, his family. His people. In America there was a boundary. Black and white, red and white. We call it racism. He stepped over the line easily, perhaps thinking Indian drum beats were as accessible to white American composers as Czech folk music was to him. He didn't hear the heavier hit of the drum on the ear, the black wail it is impossible to borrow.

LAUGHING WATER

17 [Dvořák] wanted to write an opera based on Longfellow's *The Song of Hiawatha*. He had read the poem in translation. Naturally, its admiration for the indigenous culture appealed to Dvořák. So did Longfellow's lyrical, if rather didactic, restatement of landscape and the beauties of nature. Dvořák never found a good libretto, and the project fizzled. He stood by the falls, asked Kovařík for a pencil (nobody had any paper), and wrote something on his cuffs. It was the theme for the Sonatina, Opus 100, a piece he wrote later, after he left Spillville.

18   Dvořák loved the gash in the landscape, the great outpouring a waterfall is, and on the way back to New York the family stopped at Niagara where, of course, he was even more impressed than by the decorous Minnehaha, Laughing Water.

19   He wanted those big, bellowy sounds, too, not just the small voices of birds, the spirit whoosh of wind. He used to stand outside the train station in Prague and is said to have known the time of each train and, what is more unusual, the number of every locomotive. To his ear, each engine had a distinct tone. Engines, the sound of them, their big, pounding hearts. Get it down on the cuffs . . . .

MOVING WATER

20 . . . "And so it is very wild here," Dvořák wrote home shortly before he left Spill-ville. "And sometimes very sad. Sad to despair. But habit is everything."

21   We get used to the way we live, the way we must live — I suppose that's what he meant. But despair — do people get used to that?

22   He could afford to see the "few people and a great deal of empty space" as foreign, to wonder at the alien, lonely sensation. To shiver and depart. But for us? This strangeness *is* home. Heartland, it's called, as if the chief occupation were love.

23   "The Americans expect great things of me . . . to show them to the promised land."

24   And then he went back to Vysoká where the Bohemian Forest edged in closer than the Spillville woods, where people lived knit together, not spread out, not sad to despair. Dvořák lived within the family circle, his wife, his six children. Even his nation was more family than country: a language and a people without an inde-pendent government, a culture, not a country. America had best figure out its art forms for itself. Let it study as he had: with the birds, flowers, trees, with God, and with its own strange self . . . .

25   And it is beautiful, the gravity of moving water, the stars just starting up in the navy sky. Studying with them. And the silence of these small river towns at night when the traffic on the highway, which crashes like a falls, is well behind us some-where, people going wherever they must go.

II
WOMEN
AND FILM

Women's role in the film industry has been at the center of recent controversies about pornography, violence against women, exploitation of women's bodies, and the making of political statements through films. This section examines some of these issues, but also explores the role of women behind the camera. Alice Guy Blaché's article, written in 1914, corrects the notion that women have only recently taken a hand in creating films. The interview with Jane Fonda captures the actress a few years into the more political phase of her career, long before "doing Jane" became synonymous with an aerobics workout. Two of the articles grapple with the questions of violence in film, and Yoko Ono's — well, you'll just have to read that one yourself.

Ideas in this section echo those in other sections. Not everyone approved of Jane Fonda's political activism, as you will see in Fred Reed's "A Veteran Writes." (Fonda was widely criticized for visiting North Vietnam during the Vietnam war.) The theme of neglect and indifference toward women's contributions comes up again in Lynda Van Devanter's "Short-Timers" about nurses in Vietnam. Articles in section VI, Medicine, Ethics, and the Law, further examine the mix of ethical, legal, and cultural issues that debates about pornography stir up. And like section I, Women and Film examines the role of art in our society as a whole.

WOMAN'S PLACE IN PHOTOPLAY PRODUCTION

Alice Guy Blaché

1 It has long been a source of wonder to me that many women have not seized upon the wonderful opportunities offered to them by the motion-picture art to make their way to fame and fortune as producers of photodramas. Of all the arts there is probably none in which they can make such splendid use of talents so much more natural to a woman than to a man and so necessary to its perfection.

2   There is no doubt in my mind that a woman's success in many lines of endeavor is still made very difficult by a strong prejudice against one of her sex doing work that has been done only by men for hundreds of years. Of course this prejudice is fast disappearing, and there are many vocations in which it has not been present for a long time. In the arts of acting, music, painting, and literature, woman has long held her place among the most successful workers, and when it is considered how vitally all of these arts enter into the production of motion pictures, one wonders why the names of scores of women are not found among the successful creators of photodrama offerings.

Alice Guy Blaché, "Woman's Place in Photoplay Production," *Moving Picture World*, July 11, 1914.

3   Not only is a woman as well fitted to stage a photodrama as a man, but in many ways she has a distinct advantage over him because of her very nature and because much of the knowledge called for in the telling of the story and the creation of the stage setting is absolutely within her province as a member of the gentler sex. She is an authority on the emotions. For centuries she has given them full play while man has carefully trained himself to control them. She has developed her finer feelings for generations, while being protected from the world by her male companions, and she is naturally religious. In matters of the heart her superiority is acknowledged and her deep insight and sensitiveness in the affairs of Cupid give her a wonderful advantage in developing the thread of love that plays such an all-important part in almost every story that is prepared for the screen. All of the distinctive qualities that she possesses come into direct play during the guiding of the actors in making their character drawings and interpreting the different emotions called for by the story. For to think and to feel the situation demanded by the play is the secret of successful acting, and sensitiveness to those thoughts and feelings is absolutely essential to the success of a stage director.

4   The qualities of patience and gentleness possessed to such a high degree by womankind are also of inestimable value in the staging of a photodrama. Artistic temperament is a thing to be reckoned with while directing an actor, in spite of the treatment of the subject in the comic papers, and a gentle, soft-voiced director is much more conducive to good work on the part of the performer than the over-stern, noisy tyrant of the studio.

5   Not a small part of the motion-picture director's work, in addition to the preparation of the story for picture-telling and the casting and directing of the actors, is the choice of suitable locations for the staging of the exterior scenes and the supervising of the studio settings, props, costumes, etc. In these matters it seems to me that a woman is especially well qualified to obtain the very best results, for she is dealing with subjects that are almost a second nature to her. She takes the measure of every person, every costume, every house, and every piece of furniture that her eye comes into contact with, and the beauty of a stretch of landscape or a single flower impresses her immediately. All of these things are of the greatest value to the creator of a photodrama, and the knowledge of them must be extensive and exact. A woman's magic touch is immediately recognized in a real home. Is it not just as recognizable in the home of the characters of a photoplay?

6   That women make the theatre possible from the box-office standpoint is an acknowledged fact. Theatre managers know that their appeal must be to the woman if they would succeed, and all of their efforts are naturally in that direction. This being the case, what a rare opportunity is offered to women to use that inborn knowledge of just what does appeal to them to produce photodramas that will contain that inexplicable something which is necessary to the success of every stage or screen production.

7   There is nothing connected with the staging of a motion picture that a woman cannot do as easily as a man, and there is no reason why she cannot completely master every technicality of the art. The technique of the drama has been mastered by so many women that it is considered as much her field as a man's and its adapta-

tion to picture work in no way removes it from her sphere. The technique of motion-picture photography, like the technique of the drama, is fitted to a woman's activities.

8   It is hard for me to imagine how I could have obtained my knowledge of photography, for instance, without the months of study spent in the laboratory of the Gaumont Company in Paris at a time when motion-picture photography was in the experimental stage, and carefully continued since [in] my own laboratory in the Solax Studios in this country. It is also necessary to study stage direction by actual participation in the work, in addition to burning the midnight oil in your library, but both are as suitable, as fascinating, and as remunerative to a woman as to a man.

SEX AND VIOLENCE: PORNOGRAPHY HURTS

1 Sexual attacks against women — our newspapers, magazines, novels, movies and television shows are full of such incidents. Considering the long history and continued prevalence of this kind of violence, it might seem that little can be done to curb it. But the situation may not be so bleak. Social scientists are beginning to pinpoint the many factors associated with violence, and the National Institute of Mental Health recently has concluded that an understanding of the conditions that lead to sexual attacks against women should be a major goal of research. Some of that research was presented last week in Montreal at the annual meeting of the American Psychological Association.

2   Pornography and its possible role as a causative factor in eliciting violent behavior against women is one of the many areas currently being investigated. And the findings contradict much previous research. Ten years ago, the Presidential Commission on Obscenity and Pornography concluded that there was no relationship between exposure to erotic presentations and subsequent aggression, particularly sexual crimes. This conclusion was attacked by some researchers at the time and has been attacked by many (especially feminists) since. Now researchers are reevaluating the data, reexamining the question and finding solid evidence that at least one kind of pornography is responsible for attitudinal and behavioral changes that result in increased aggression by men against women. The type of pornography in question is called aggressive-erotic. It contains explicit sexual violence against women, and in recent years it has been produced and shown with increasing frequency. Two research projects, each taking a different approach to the study of sexually violent material, were among those described at the APA meeting.

3   Edward Donnerstein of the University of Wisconsin in Madison conducted one of the experiments. In order to examine the effects of aggressive-erotic material on male aggression toward females, 120 male college students were either angered

---

"Sex and Violence: Pornography Hurts," *Science News*, September 13, 1980.

or treated neutrally by either a male or female confederate of the experimenter. The subjects then were shown either a neutral, erotic or aggressive-erotic film. Several minutes later they were given an opportunity to deliver electric shocks to the fingertips of the original male or female confederate — as part of what they were told was a study of the effects of stress on learning. The subjects were unaware of the true purpose of the research, and they did not realize that the films they had seen were part of the same experiment. Debriefings following the experiment, says Donnerstein, indicate that the subjects really had been tricked by the rather complex research design.

4   The results showed that exposure to an aggressive-erotic film increased aggressive behavior (giving shocks) to a level higher than for the erotic film. These findings were even more pronounced in subjects who had previously been angered by the confederates. When angered subjects were paired with a male, the aggressive-erotic film produced no more aggression than did the erotic film. When paired with a female, however, the subjects displayed an increase in aggression only after viewing the aggressive-erotic film.

5   Donnerstein's study and others like it find consistent results, but they are open to criticism on several counts — the artificiality of the laboratory setting, and the aggression is seen only immediately after exposure to violent pornography. "There clearly exists a need to assess the effects of mass media stimuli that fuse sexuality and violence outside the laboratory context," say Neil M. Malamuth and James V. Check of the University of Manitoba in Winnipeg. And that's what they have done.

6   Hundreds of students were sent to the movies as part of an experiment to test the effects of exposure to films that portray sexual violence as having positive consequences. The movies they saw were not pornography, just everyday sex and violence. They included *Swept Away* (a violent male sexual aggressor and a woman who learns to crave sexual sadism find love on a deserted island) and *The Getaway* (a woman falls in love with the man who raped her in front of her husband, then both taunt the husband until he commits suicide). The control films used, *A Man and a Woman* and *Hooper*, show tender romance and nonexplicit sex.

7   Within a week of viewing the movies, an attitude survey was administered to all students in the introductory psychology sections from which the subjects had been signed up for the experiment. The students did not know that the survey had anything to do with the films they had seen, but embedded within the survey were questions relating to acceptance of interpersonal violence, acceptance of the rape myth (that women enjoy being raped) and adversarial sexual beliefs. Subjects rated from "strongly agree" to "strongly disagree" statements such as "A man is never justified in hitting his wife" and "Many women have an unconscious wish to be raped and may then unconsciously set up a situation in which they are likely to be attacked."

8   The results of the survey indicated that exposure to the films portraying violent sexuality increased male subjects' acceptance of interpersonal violence against women. A similar (though nonsignificant) trend was found for acceptance of rape myths. For females the trend was in the opposite direction. Women exposed to violent-sexual films tended to be slightly less accepting of interpersonal violence

and of rape myths than were control subjects. "The present findings," say the researchers, "constitute the first demonstration in a nonlaboratory setting . . . of relatively long-term effects of movies that fuse sexuality and violence."

9   Why do these findings differ from those of several years ago? Check says that "what's in the pornography is the important factor." Recent findings still suggest nonviolent pornography has no immediate negative effects (though long-term effects have not been studied), but the new pornography is much more violent. Donnerstein agrees: "We're looking at different material now . . . . Ten-year-old pornography is very bland in comparison." Also, he adds, the women's movement affected us. "Women raised the question, and now social scientists have the responsibility of proving or disproving." And what we have found comes as no surprise, he adds. Many studies, such as those with children and televised violence, have shown similar effects. Now it has been found with violence in pornography. "Everyone finds the same results, no matter what measures they use . . . . There are no discrepant data here at all."

BEAUTY BESTS THE BEAST

Robin Wood

1 Confronted over the past few years with the proliferation of escalatingly violent and gruesome low-budget horror movies centered on psychopathic killers, one may take away the impression of one undifferentiated stream of massacre, mutilation, and terrorization, a single interminable chronicle of bloodletting called something like *When a Stranger Calls After Night School on Halloween or Friday the Thirteenth, Don't Answer the Phone and Don't Go Into the House Because He Knows You're Alone and Is Dressed to Kill.* In fact, the films are distinguishable both in function and in quality, and however one may shrink from systematic exposure to them, however one may deplore the social phenomena and ideological mutations they reflect, their popularity (especially – indeed, almost exclusively – with youth audiences) suggests that even if they were uniformly execrable they shouldn't be ignored; an attempt both to understand the phenomena and discriminate among the films seems valid and timely.

2   The films can be seen to fall into two partially distinguishable categories, answering to two partially distinguishable cultural "needs": the "violence-against-women" movie (of which Brian De Palma's *Dressed to Kill* is the most controversial – as well as the most ambitiously "classy" – example) and what has been succinctly dubbed the "teenie-kill pic" (of which the purest – if that is the word – examples are the three *Friday the 13th* movies). The distinction is never clear-cut. The two cycles have common sources in Tobe Hooper's *The Texas Chainsaw Massacre* and John Carpenter's *Halloween* (which in turn have a common source in

From Robin Wood, "Beauty Bests the Beast," *American Film*, September 1983.

Psycho); the survivor in the teenie-kill movies — endurer of the ultimate ordeals, terrors, and agonies — is invariably female; the victims in the violence-against-women films are predominantly young. But the motivation for the slaughter, on both the dramatic and ideological levels, is somewhat different: In general, the teenagers are punished for promiscuity, and the women are punished for being women.

3   Both cycles represent a sinister and disturbing inversion of the significance of the traditional horror film: There the monster was in general a "creature from the id," not merely a product of repression but a protest against it, whereas in the current cycles the monster, while still "produced by" repression, has become essentially a superego figure, avenging itself on liberated female sexuality or the sexual freedom of the young. What *hasn't* changed (making the social implications even more sinister) is the genre's basic commercial premise: that the customers continue to pay, as they always did, to enjoy the eruptions and depredations of the monster. But where the traditional horror film invited — however ambiguously — an identification with the "returnof the repressed," the contemporary horror film invites an identification (either sadistic or masochistic or both simultaneoulsy) with punishment.

4   On the whole, the teenie-kill pic seems the more consistently popular of the two recent cycles, and one can interpret this as a logical consequence of a "permissive" (as opposed to liberated) society. The chief, indeed almost the *only*, characteristic of the films' teenagers (who are obviously meant to be attractive to the youth audience as identification figures) is a mindless hedonism made explicit by a character in Steve Miner's *Friday the 13th Part 3*, who remarks (without contradiction) that the only things worth living for are screwing and smoking dope. The films both endorse this and relentlessly punish it; they never suggest that other options might be available. (After all, what might it not lead to if young people began to *think*?) What is most stressed, but nowhere *explicitly* condemned, is promiscuity — the behavior that consumer capitalism in its present phase simultaneously "permits" and morally disapproves of.

5   The satisfaction that youth audiences get from these films is presumably two-fold: They identify with the promiscuity as well as the grisly and excessive punishment for it. The original *Friday the 13th*, directed by Sean S. Cunningham, dramatizes this very clearly: Most of the murders are closely associated with the young people having sex (a principle that reaches ludicrous systematization in the sequels, where one can safely predict that any character who shows sexual interest in another will be dead within minutes); the psychopathic killer turns out to be a woman whose son (Jason) drowned because the camp counselors who should have been supervising him were engaged in intercourse. In the sequels, Jason himself returns as a vaguely defined mutant monster, virtually indistinguishable from Michael of the *Halloween* films, introducing another indispensable component of the cycle, the monster's unkillability: The sexual guilt which the characters are by definition incapable of analyzing, confronting, or understanding can never be exorcised.

The violence-against-women movies have generally been explained as a hysterical response to sixties and seventies feminism: The male spectator enjoys a sadistic revenge on women who refuse to slot neatly and obligingly into his patriarchally predetermined view of "the way things should naturally be." This interpretation is convincing so long as one sees it as accounting for the intensity, repetitiveness, and ritualistic insistence of these films, and not for the basic phenomenon itself: From *Caligari* to *Psycho* and beyond, women have always been the main focus of threat and assault in the horror film.

6   There are a number of variously plausible explanations for this. As women are regarded as weak and helpless, it is simply more frightening if the monster attacks *them*; the male spectator can presumably identify with the hero who finally kills the monster, the film thereby indulging his vanity as protector of the helpless female. That he may also, on another level, identify with the monster in no way contradicts this idea; it merely suggests its inadequacy as a *total* explanation. Second, as men in patriarchal society have set women up on (compensatory) pedestals, and thereby constructed them as oppressive and restrictive figures, they have developed a strong desire to knock them down again.

7   As in every genre, the archetypal male-constructed opposition of wife-whore is operative. In the traditional horror film, the women who got killed were usually whore-figures, punished for "bringing out the beast" in men; the heroine who was terrorized and perhaps abducted (but eventually rescued) was the present or future wife.

8   The ideological tensions involved here are still central to our culture. The films obliquely express what Hitchcock's films, for example, consistently dramatized: the anxiety of the heterosexual male confronted by the possibilty of an autonomous female sexuality he can't control and organize. But the key point is that in the traditional horror film, the threatened heroine was invariably associated with the values of monogamous marriage and the nuclear family (actual or potential): The eruption of the Frankenstein monster during the preparations for his creator's wedding in the 1931 James Whale movie was the locus classicus. What the monster really threatened was the repressive, ideologically constructed bourgeois "normality." Today, on the other hand, the women who are terrorized and slaughtered tend to be those who *resist* definition within the virgin-wife-mother framework. As with the teenie-kill movies, the implications of the violence-against-women films are extremely disturbing.

9   The dominant project of these overlapping, interlocking cycles is, then, depressingly reactionary, to say the least. However, as both can be shown to have their sources in contemporary ideological tension, confusion, and contradiction, both also carry within them the potential for subverting that project . . . .

10   Feminists (of both sexes) have been quite vociferous on the subject of violence against women, and this can be credited with provoking various degrees of disturbance in recent specimens of the genre, ranging from vague uneasiness to an intelligent rethinking of the conventions.

ON YOKO ONO

Yoko Ono

October 1968

on *Film No. 4, 1967* (in taking the bottoms of 365 saints of our time)

1 I wonder why men can get serious at all. They have this delicate long thing hanging outside their bodies, which goes up and down by its own will. First of all having it outside your body is terribly dangerous. If I were a man, I would have a fantastic castration complex to the point that I wouldn't be able to do a thing. Second, the inconsistency of it, like carrying a chance time alarm or something. If I were a man, I would always be laughing at myself. Humor is probably something the male of the species discovered through their own anatomy. But men are so serious. Why? Why violence? Why hatred? Why war? If people want to make war, they should make a color war, and paint each other's city up during the night in pinks and greens. Men have an unusual talent for making a bore out of everything they touch. Art, painting, sculpture, like who wants a cast-iron woman, for instance.

2   The film world is becoming terribly aristocratic, too. It's professionalism all the way down the line. In any other field: painting, music, etc., people are starting to become iconoclastic. But in the film world — that's where nobody touches it except the director. The director carries the old mystery of the artist. He is creating a universe, a mood, he is unique, etc., etc. This film proves that anybody can be a director. A filmmaker in San Francisco wrote to me and asked if he could make the San Francisco version of *No. 4*. That's OK with me. Somebody else wrote from New York, she wants to make a slow-motion version with her own behind. That's OK, too. I'm hoping that after seeing this film people will start to make their own home movies like crazy.

3   In fifty years or so, which is like ten centuries from now, people will look at the film of the 1960s. They will probably comment on Ingmar Bergman as a meaningfully meaningful filmmaker, Jean-Luc Godard as the meaningfully meaningless, Antonioni as meaninglessly meaningful, etc., etc. Then they would come to the *No. 4* film and see a sudden swarm of exposed bottoms, that these bottoms, in fact, belonged to people who represented the London scene. And I hope that they would see that the 1960s was not only the age of achievements, but of laughter. This film, in fact, is like an aimless petititon signed by people with their anuses. Next time we wish to make an appeal, we should send this film as the signature list.

4   My ultimate goal in filmmaking is to make a film that includes a smiling face snap of every single human being in the world. Of course, I cannot go around the whole world and take the shots myself. I need cooperation from something like the post offices of the world. If everybody would drop a snapshot of themselves and their families to the post office of their town, or allow themselves to be photographed by the nearest photographic studio, this would be soon accomplished. Of

Yoko Ono, "On Yoko Ono," *Film Culture*, Winter/Spring 1970.

course, this film would need constant adding of footage. Probably nobody would like to see the whole film at once, so you can keep it in a library or something, and when you want to see some particular town's people's smiling faces you can go and check that section of film. We can also arrange it with a television network so that whenever you want to see faces of a particular location in the world, all you have to do is to press a button and there it is. This way, if Johnson wants to see what sort of people he killed in Vietnam that day, he only has to turn the channel.

INTERVIEW WITH JANE FONDA

Dan Georgakas and Lenny Rubenstein

1 *Q:* What kind of problems has becoming a political activist created for you as a performer?

2   *A:* One of the first things was to resolve certain contradictions that were posed in my life, if I should continue acting or not, and if I continued, in what way? Should I continue in Hollywood films or should I join a group like Newsreel? I almost decided that it would be better to totally disappear into the faceless crowd of organizers (I thought then there were crowds) in the GI coffeehouses. The people who dissuaded me were John Watson and Ken Cockrel. That must have been 1970 or 1971. They sat me down and said: "We've seen too many people with very important middle-class skills — doctors, lawyers, and others — who have rejected their class, and with it their talents. There's a need for doctors and lawyers, and there's a need for people who can reach mass audiences. You must continue." That was a very important statement for me to consider.

3   *Q:* What about the kind of roles you decided to play?

4   *A:* Well, I had always been the kind of actress who waited for people to come to me with scripts and ideas. The performers in Hollywood who are active producers are almost all men. Producing was an area that had been mystified. I found myself not working very much because I didn't like the roles coming my way. I think the problem with Hollywood is that the directors, and the writers even more so, don't view things historically and don't view things socially. Stories are unraveled in the context of an individual's particular personality and psyche and in the events of one life, never against a social background. You never see things dialectically, which means they are lying to people. They lead people down blind alleys.

5   I started to realize that if I was going to work, and if there were going to be movies made that I thought were important, and if I wanted to remain in the context of the mass media, I was going to have to produce them msyelf.

Dan Georgakas and Lenny Rubenstein, "Interview with Jane Fonda," *from* "I Prefer Films that Strengthen People," *Cinéaste* 4, no. 4, 1975.

6   *Q:* Is it feasible to expect roles with ideas in them that are in any way compatible with your political views if you are not producing?

7   *A:* It's not impossible. I'm doing a film . . . based on a story by Lillian Hellman called "Julia." It's a true short story from a book of hers called *Pentimento* [1973]. It's the story of Lillian Hellman and a woman she knew who became a socialist. Well, you don't know for sure. All you know is that the woman becomes a committed activist who joins the French antifascist underground and gets killed by the Nazis. It's a very beautiful story about two women. It's about why people change and about the relationship of women with strong social commitments. I think it could be a very exciting film.

8   *Q:* There have been suggestions that you should play famous revolutionaries like Rosa Luxemburg and Emma Goldman.

9   *A:* I'm very wary of playing any role which makes me look like I view myself as La Pasionaria. I would rather play a fascist, if that exposed something about racism and power, than to play a famous revolutionary. Someone wanted me to play one of the Weather-women killed in the town house explosion. A rumor has me playing Patty Hearst. Those kinds of roles are the last thing I would think of doing. There is one revolutionary woman I would like to play though, but only when I'm old and shriveled. That's Mother Jones. That would be a great joy to do.

10   Actually, the kind of parts that I think are the most exciting to play and the most viable in terms of communication are characters that are complex; that is, characters that are full of contradictions that can be shown, that are in motion, that are trying to deal with problems that are real to people. I prefer films or any kind of cultural expression that strengthens rather than weakens people. That's why I would rather not play a villain's role or, if I did, I would want her to be at least moving in an upward direction. I think all of us are trying to figure out — what is a progressive movie, what is a revolutionary movie? Is it really possible to make a movie that is a weapon for political change? I don't know. I honest-to-God don't know. I do have the feeling that, at this stage, in this country anyway, it wouldn't necessarily be a film that offers a solution. I have a feeling that there is a kind of frustration that may be progressive at this point. Perhaps the best we can do now is create in the audience a sense of hopeful frustration. Perhaps they should leave the theatre with a sense of wanting to move and a feeling that there is good reason to move.

11   *Q:* Most of the films made by Americans who consider themselves leftists are documentaries. Why are there so few fiction films that are radical and that appeal to masses of people?

12   *A:* There's *Billy Jack* [1972]. Maybe you don't share my view of it. I think it was an extremely progressive film. You're not going to make a mass movie that is revolutionary. You're not going to make a *Battle of Algiers* [1967] that is a mass movie. I think it's important to do a picture that is going to be seen by a lot of people. *Billy Jack* takes the American superman as its main image, and that has to be improved on, but here you have a Vietnam veteran who comes to the aid of a minority people and you have a real debate about pacificism versus armed resistance . . . .

13   *Q:* You've expressed interest in doing a movie based on Harriet Arnow's *The Dollmaker.* Would such a film be more like *Grapes of Wrath* [1940] in terms of themes and characters? Is it likely we'll see such films if the recession should deepen into a major depression?

14   *A:* I think so, but we must always remember that it's not 1929 and nothing repeats itself. I wouldn't want *The Dollmaker* to be a downer the way a lot of the Depression films were. I think it can be hopeful. I met with Harriet Arnow and we both share the sense that it can be a positive movie. I disagree with the thinking in Hollywood on the part of producers that people don't want to think, that they only want to be entertained. People want to be led out of the morass or at least to have a little help in clearing away the confusion. The problem is what we said earlier. People who have a social vision haven't found a way to express it in a mass language. There's so much rhetoric and so much sectarianism. It gets manifested in the cultural field and I think that's why culture gets left in the hands of the entertainers.

15   *Q:* How would you rate your own film, *They Shoot Horses, Don't They?* [1969].

16   *A:* I think that was a movie a lot of people related to on a political level. The author of the book was definitely drawing an analogy with American society: the tragedy of all those people killing each other for a prize that doesn't exist at the behest of one man who they could replace if they were conscious of what was being done to them. I realize the shortcomings of the movie. The woman who does realize what is going on commits suicide. No, really something worse: she has a man kill her. I think for what is possible, however, it was a good movie. It would be wonderful if someone could go around with the movie and, after it was over, have a discussion with the audience about what it means. It's too bad that movies are sort of thrown out and left that way.

17   *Q:* You improvised the scene in the analyst's office in *Klute* [1971]. What does that mean exactly? Did you have any script to begin with, or what?

18   *A:* That was the last scene we shot, and by that time I knew the character very well. You find areas in yourself that relate to the character and then learn how those things are expressed differently than you would express them. By that time, I knew Bree well enough to improvise the scene. I think it worked real well. I didn't have to think about it too much, but I set myself certain tasks. Bree was the kind of woman who at a crucial point in her analysis would find an excuse, like it was costing too much or that it wasn't doing her any good, to keep from revealing another layer of herself. She would create barriers and conflicts. It was wonderful fun to do that scene. We did it real quick. We didn't do anything twice.

19   *Q:* That seems an example where the performer gets rid of the director and writer at least in one scene and sort of takes charge.

20   *A:* Not really. We all worked closely. The director and I had a lot of discussion beforehand about how the scene was going to be used and what we wanted to convey. It was his idea that the analyst be a woman and that was an important decision. Bree would not have talked the same way if it had been a male analyst. Someone else decided where the camera should be and that was important. What's

so wonderful about movies and so frustrating if you're working in Hollywood is that filmmaking really is a collective effort even though the director has the final control. That's what seems exciting about filmmaking in a socialist country. Filmmaking is a socialized process. When it is working right, everyone is participating. The cameraman is doing the lighting and setting the angles in conjunction with what is being attempted in the overall effort. Everyone has thoroughly discussed and understood what is being undertaken.

21   I was very interested to talk to the film people in Vietnam. They described how everyone worked together. The performers, the directors, the technicians would discuss a story and carefully work out what was to be conveyed and how to tell a story. It would all be done very collectively. The writers would then write and there would be more discussion. They all said this, laughing about the fact that everything takes so long.

22   *Q:* Sometimes in discussing the films you made before you became politically involved you seem defensive, especially about the subjects of nudity and sex. Nowadays the left is generally puritanical about sex, but this wasn't always so. At the turn of the century, leftists were attacked as often for their sexual beliefs as for their political beliefs.

23   *A:* I don't object to the movies I made because of the nudity in them. I don't think that nudity is the problem. It's how it's used. The problem is that movies that are made with sex and nudity, including some of the films I participated in, were exploitive of sex. *Barbarella* [1968] is a film that's always brought up, but as a matter of fact, I was hardly ever nude. Most of the pictures where I was dressed to the teeth and played a cute little ingenue were more exploitive than the ones with nudity because they portrayed women as silly, as mindless, as motivated purely by sex in relation to men. The simplest way to explain why women do that in this country is because there are limited avenues open to women to gain some power. One of the avenues is to marry a powerful man; another is to become a sex symbol. Things are changing slowly, but it used to be if a woman got offered one of those avenues, she didn't generally turn it down.

24   I don't think I'm particularly sexy. I don't know why I should be made a symbol of anything. At that time, it didn't occur to me to say, wait a minute, this isn't what I am. I never felt like Barbarella. I never felt like the American Brigitte Bardot. I always felt slightly out of focus. There was Jane and there was this public figure. It was extremely alienating. I never liked it. I never felt comfortable with it. I'm not defensive about it anymore. I think it's important to try to understand why women do that and how it is possible to change. It's hard to tell what a revolutionary future might bring. Some people think marriage should be abolished. Who knows? I believe that you can't build a mass movement around the questions of sex and marriage. I've been in a revolutionary society where marriage is very much an institution. It did not appear to be particularly oppressive for women because the power distribution within the institution is different than here. We would call Vietnam extremely puritanical. I think the importance that is placed on sex is a cultural thing. I don't think that in a healthy society there would be all the importance put on sex that we do. I don't think that in a healthy society you would have to show anybody naked on the screen. I don't think it would be an issue.

25 *Q:*   You were in France in May of 1968. How did those events affect you?

26   *A:* ... It didn't happen as dramatically for me as perhaps for Godard who looked out the window and there were his people in the streets. I looked at television and saw my people, where I came from, and I suddenly felt I was in the wrong place. I was extremely pregnant at the time. I lived in the country and my husband wouldn't let me go into Paris because I was about to give birth. I wanted to do something, yet I knew that wasn't my place. I subscribed to *Ramparts* and *The Village Voice* at the time and I read everything I could get my hands on. I identified with Joan Baez. It was new. It was like rumblings going on inside all the time . . . .

27   What was important about being in France was that for the first time I realized that it really could all come down. There were days there when we thought it was going to stop. Who would have thought that students and maybe workers were going to bring France to a halt. No gas. No food. No nothing. We were beginning to stockpile basic provisions. People were leaving Paris to come stay with us because we had a vegetable garden. Many of the people I knew were "at the barricades." It so happened that at that time my husband, Vadim, had just been made head of the union of cinema workers. So he was having to drive to Paris all the time for these mass meetings of all the movie people, including technicians and other workers, to decide if the studios were going to close down, or what. I just felt — let's get this baby out, I want to pack it up and go home, I want to get involved. And that's what I did.

III
VIETNAM—
IT'S NOT
OVER YET

The end of the war in Vietnam did not mean an end to controversy. The selections in this section show some of the ways in which people affected by the war have sought to understand the experience.

Donald Barthelme's short story, the only piece written during the war, explores the psychology of people involved in preparing for war. In a selection from *Dispatches*, one of the first and most widely acclaimed retrospective books about the war, reporter Michael Herr describes his introduction to what Vietnam was really like. Linda Van Devanter, in a selection from her book *Home Before Morning*, lets us see the nurses' side of the war, and Fred Reed's "A Veteran Writes" shows the anger some Vietnam veterans feel at the conclusions drawn about the war by people who were not there. Vo Thi Tam's narrative lets us glimpse the aftermath of the war from a Vietnamese perspective and provides a moving preview of section IV, A Nation of Immigrants. Terrence Rafferty reviews the most popular movie about the war, the critically acclaimed *Platoon*, tracing in the process some of the ways in which a complex and traumatic event moves into the popular consciousness. Articles by Fred A. Wilcox and Jeff Jones focus on one of the war's bitter legacies, the lasting damage done by the chemical defoliant Agent Orange.

Reading these selections may begin to give you a sense of what the war was like, of the place it occupies in American culture and consciousness, and of the nature of the force it continues to exert as its veterans find ways of dealing with their experience and its effects.

ILLUMINATION ROUNDS

Michael Herr

1 We were all strapped into the seats of the Chinook, fifty of us, and something, someone was hitting it from the outside with an enormous hammer. How do they do that? I thought, we're a thousand feet in the air! But it had to be that, over and over, shaking the helicopter, making it dip and turn in a horrible out-of-control motion that took me in the stomach. I had to laugh, it was so exciting, it was the thing I had wanted, almost what I had wanted except for that wrenching, resonant metal-echo; I could hear it even above the noise of the rotor blades. And they were going to fix that, I knew they would make it stop. They had to, it was going to make me sick.

2   They were all replacements going in to mop up for the big battle on Hills 875 and 876, the battles that had already taken on the name of one great battle, the battle of Dak To. And I was new, brand new, three days in-country, embarrassed about my boots because they were so new. And across from me, ten feet away, a

Michael Herr, "Illumination Rounds," *Dispatches*, Knopf, 1978.

boy tried to jump out of the straps and then jerked forward and hung there, his rifle barrel caught in the red plastic webbing of the seat back. As the chopper rose again and turned, his weight went back hard against the webbing and a dark spot the size of a baby's hand showed in the center of his fatigue jacket. And it grew — I knew what it was, but not really — it got up to his armpits and then started down his sleeves and up over his shoulders at the same time. It went all across his waist and down his legs, covering the canvas on his boots until they were dark like everything else he wore, and it was running in slow, heavy drops off of his fingertips. I thought I could hear the drops hitting the metal strip on the chopper floor. Hey! . . . Oh, but this isn't anything at all, it's not real, it's just some *thing* they're going through that isn't real. One of the door gunners was heaped up on the floor like a cloth dummy. His hand had the bloody raw look of a pound of liver fresh from the butcher paper. We touched down on the same lz we had just left a few minutes before, but I didn't know it until one of the guys shook my shoulder, and then I couldn't stand up. All I could feel of my legs was their shaking, and the guy thought I'd been hit and helped me up. The chopper had taken eight hits, there was shattered plastic all over the floor, a dying pilot up front, and the boy was hanging forward in the straps again, he was dead, but not (I knew) really dead.

3   It took me a month to lose that feeling of being a spectator to something that was part game, part show. That first afternoon, before I'd boarded the Chinook, a black sergeant had tried to keep me from going. He told me I was too new to go near the kind of shit they were throwing around up in those hills. ("You a reporter?" he'd asked, and I'd said, "No, a writer," dumbass and pompous, and he'd laughed and said, "Careful. You can't use no eraser up where you wanna go.") He'd pointed to the bodies of all the dead Americans lined in two long rows near the chopper pad, so many that they could not even cover all of them decently. But they were not real then, and taught me nothing. The Chinook had come in, blowing my helmet off, and I grabbed it up and joined the replacements waiting to board. "Okay, man," the sergeant said. "You gotta go, you gotta go. All's I can say is, I hope you get a clean wound."

SHORT-TIMERS

Lynda Van Devanter

1 At least five companies were tangling with the NVA at different locations throughout Pleiku Province and all of them were getting trounced. We couldn't empty the dust-off choppers quickly enough. I had taken the last litter out of a Huey and was heading back to the ER when another, billowing smoke, came in low and fast, cutting in front of three choppers that were already stacked up waiting to use the landing pad. As soon as it touched down, everybody who wasn't already occupied

---

Lynda Van Devanter, "Short-Timers," *Home Before Morning*, Beaufort, 1983.

scrambled. Hospital personnel and the crew chief off-loaded the wounded while the pilot shut the engines down and carried his copilot to safety. The copilot had been shot in the stomach and through both legs. The pilot also had a couple of wounds, but both of his were in his left shoulder. Everyone bolted away from the chopper as quickly as possible, trying to get a safe distance before it blew. The other choppers headed over to the Air Force compound to unload their patients safely.

2   Flames shot out from the engine. They were working their way back along the fuel lines to the gas tank. It was only a matter of time. Coretta had what she thought was the last man. She swiftly wheeled him toward the ER, until she heard a loud plaintive moan come from the fiery bird. Everyone else, except the helicopter crew chief, was at least a hundred meters away and sprinting farther by the second.

3   "That's Jackson," Coretta's casualty said. "He's still in the chopper."

4   "We've got one more," Coretta yelled to the few free people who were maintaining a safe distance. No one made a move toward the Huey. Even the crew chief was fleeing the burning wreck without any thought for Jackson. He was practically a blur as he passed Coretta.

5   "Wait," she shouted. "You forgot one."

6   The crew chief, feeling safe at this distance, stopped. "He's gonna die anyway," he said.

7   "The hell he is!" Frustrated, Coretta yelled for someone to take her other casualty to the emergency room. Then she headed back to the chopper.

8   The crew chief stopped her. "Are you nuts, Lieutenant? It's gonna go up any second. You'll get killed!"

9   Ignoring him, Coretta returned to the burning helicopter, climbed inside, and dragged Jackson to the door.

10   "Crazy broad," the crew chief shouted. "You're gonna die."

11   She tried to lift Jackson from the litter so she could throw him over her shoulders. He was too heavy. She couldn't do it alone.

12   "Coretta, get away from there," someone cried out.

13   "Forget about him," the crew chief screamed.

14   The fire was inches from the fuel tank. It was now only a matter of seconds. The flames rose higher. Black smoke engulfed the helicopter. Coretta wasn't about to give up.

15   "Stupid!" the crew chief yelled. Yet as he said it he was sprinting toward the chopper. He grabbed Jackson's hands and ordered Coretta to help him throw the guy over his shoulder.

16   Coretta and the crew chief heaved at the same time. In a split second, they were running back toward the emergency room, accompanied by the cheers of those who watched from a distance.

17   Then it happened — the chopper blasted into pieces with such force that the concussion shook the walls of the surgical-T.

18   Neither the crew chief nor Coretta was seriously hurt. And Jackson was on the operating table within ten minutes. They said the odds weren't good, but a thoracic surgeon spent six hours rebuilding the young soldier's chest.

19   Jackson lived.

20   The head nurse in the ER put Coretta in for a Bronze Star with "V" device for valor. When it came a month later, it was missing the "V" device. The head nurse was furious and demanded to know what had happened. She was told by the C.O. that they didn't award things like that to nurses. Livid, the head nurse threatened to file a complaint.

21   "Don't bother; it's not worth it," Coretta told her. "It don't mean nothin'."

A VETERAN WRITES

Fred Reed

1 I begin to weary of the stories about veterans that are now in vogue with the newspapers, the stories that dissect the veteran's psyche as if prying apart a laboratory frog — patronizing stories written by style-section reporters who know all there is to know about chocolate mousse, ladies' fashions, and the wonderful desserts that can be made with simple jello. I weary of seeing veterans analyzed and diagnosed and explained by people who share nothing with veterans, by people who, one feels intuitively, would regard it as a harrowing experience to be alone in a backyard.

2   Week after week the mousse authorities tell us what is wrong with the veteran. The veteran is badly in need of adjustment, they say — lacks balance, needs fine tuning to whatever it is in society that one should be attuned to. What we have here, all agree, with omniscience and veiled condescension, is a victim: The press loves a victim. The veteran has bad dreams, say the jello writers, is alienated, maybe hostile, doesn't socialize well — isn't, to be frank, quite right in the head.

3   But perhaps it is the veteran's head to be right or wrong in, and maybe it makes a difference what memories are in the head. For the jello writers the war was a moral fable on Channel Four, a struggle hinging on Nixon and Joan Baez and the inequities of this or that. I can't be sure. The veterans seem to have missed the war by having been away in Vietnam at the time and do not understand the combat as it raged in the internecine cocktail parties of Georgetown.

4   Still, to me Vietnam was not what it was to the jello writers, not a ventilation of pious simplisms, not the latest literary interpretation of the domino theory. It left me memories the fashion writers can't imagine. It was the slums of Truong Minh Ky, where dogs' heads floated in pools of green water and three-inch roaches droned in sweltering back-alley rooms and I was happy. Washington knows nothing of hot, whorerich, beery Truong Minh Ky. I remember riding to bomb boats up the Mekong to Phnom Penh, with the devilish brown river closing in like a vise and rockets shrieking from the dim jungle to burst against the sandbagged wheelhouse, and crouching below the waterline between the diesel tanks. The mousse authorities do not remember this. I remember the villa on Monivong in Phnom Penh, with Sedlacek, the balding Australian hippie, and Naoki, the crazy freelance combat

Fred Reed, "A Veteran Writes," *Harper's Magazine*, December 1980.

photographer, and Zoco, the Frenchman, when the night jumped and flickered with the boom of artillery and we listened to Mancini on shortwave and watched Nara dance. Washington's elite did not know Nara. They know much of politicians and of furniture.

5   If I try to explain what Vietnam meant to me — I haven't for years, and never will again — they grow uneasy at my intensity. *My God*, their eyes say, *he sounds as though he liked it over there. Something in the experience clearly snapped an anchoring ligament in his mind and left him with odd cravings, a perverse view of life — nothing dangerous, of course, but . . . . The war did that to them,* they say. *War is hell.*

6   Well, yes, they may have something there. When you have seen a peasant mother screaming over three pounds of bright red mush that, thanks to God and a Chicom 107 [a Chinese communist rocket] , is no longer precisely her child, you see that Sherman may have been on to something. When you have eaten fish with Khmer troops in charred Cambodian battlefields, where the heat beats down like a soft rubber truncheon and a wretched stink comes from shallow graves, no particular leap of imagination is necessary to notice that war is no paradise. I cannot say that the jello writers are wrong in their understanding of war. But some-how I don't like hearing pieties about the war from these sleek, wise people who never saw it. It offends propriety.

7   There were, of course, veterans and veterans. Some hated the war, some didn't. Some went around the bend down in IV Corps, where leeches dropped softly down collars like green sausages and death erupted unexpected from the ungodly foliage. To the men in the elite groups — the Seals, Special Forces, Recondos, and Lurps who spent years in the Khmer bush, low to the ground where the ants bit hard — the war was a game with stakes high enough to engage their attention. They liked to play.

8   To many of us there, the war was the best time of our lives, almost the only time. We loved it because in those days we were alive, life was intense, the pungent hours passed fast over the central event of the age and the howling jets appeased the terrible boredom of existence. Psychologists, high priests of the mean, say that boredom is a symptom of maladjustment; maybe, but boredom has been around longer than psychologists have.

9   The jello writers would say we are mad to remember fondly anything about Nixon's war that Kennedy started. They do not remember the shuddering flight of a helicopter high over glowing green jungle that spread beneath us like a frozen sea. They never made the low runs a foot above treetops along paths that led like rivers through branches that clawed at the skids, never peered down into murky clearings and bubbling swamps of sucking snake-ridden muck. They do not remember mon-soon mornings in the highlands where dragons of mist twisted in the valleys, coiling lazily on themselves, puffing up and swallowing whole villages in their dank breath. The mousse men do not remember driving before dawn to Red Beach, when the headlights in the blackness caught ghostly shapes, maybe VC, thin yellow men mushroom-headed in the night, bicycling along the alien roads. As nearly as I can tell, jello writers do not remember anything.

10   Then it was over. The veterans came home. Suddenly the world seemed to stop dead in the water. Suddenly the slant-eyed hookers were gone, as were the gunships and the wild drunken nights in places that the jello writers can't picture. Suddenly the veterans were among soft, proper people who knew nothing of what they had done and what they had seen, and who, truth to be told, didn't much like them.

11   Nor did some of us much like the people at home — though it was not at first a conscious distaste. Men came home with wounds and terrible memories and dead friends to be greeted by that squalling she-ass of Tom Hayden's,* to find a country that viewed them as criminals. Slowly, to more men than will admit to it, the thought came: *These are the people I fought for?* And so we lost a country.

12   We looked around us with new eyes and saw that, in a sense the mousse people could never understand, we had lost even our dignity. I remember a marine corporal at Bethesda Naval Hospital who, while his wounds healed, had to run errands for the nurses, last year's co-eds. "A hell of a bust," he said with the military's sardonic economy of language. "Machine gunner to messenger boy."

13   It wasn't exactly that we didn't fit. Rather, we saw what there was to fit with — and recoiled. We sought jobs, but found offices where countless bureaucrats shuffled papers at long rows of desks, like battery hens awaiting the laying urge, their bellies billowing over their belts. Some of us joined them but some, in different ways, fled. A gunship pilot of my acquaintance took to the law, and to drink, and spent five years discovering that he really wanted to be in Rhodesia. Others went back into the death-in-the-bushes outfits, where the hard old rules still held. I drifted across Asia, Mexico, Wyoming, hitchhiking and sleeping in ditches a lot until I learned that aberrant behavior, when written about, is literature.

14   The jello writers were quickly upon us. We were morose, they said, sullen. We acted strangely at parties, sat silently in corners and watched with noncommittal stares. Mentally, said the fashion experts, we hadn't made the trip home.

15   It didn't occur to them that we just had nothing to say about jello. Desserts mean little to men who have lain in dark rifle pits over Happy Valley in rainy season, watching mortar flares tremble in low-lying clouds that flickered like the face of God, while in the nervous evening safeties clicked off along the wire and amtracs rumbled into alert idles, coughing and waiting.

16   Once, after the GIs had left Saigon, I came out of a bar on Cach Mang and saw a veteran with a sign on his jacket: VIET NAM: IF YOU HAVEN'T BEEN THERE, SHUT THE FUCK UP. Maybe, just maybe, he had something.

---

*A reference to Jane Fonda who is married to politician Tom Hayden.

FROM VIETNAM, 1979

Vo Thi Tam

1 *In the summer of 1979, the world's press and television screens were filled with heartrending photographs of the Indochinese "boat people" who fled their Communist homelands in flimsy boats. An estimated 40 percent of them died before finding temporary shelter in a refugee camp.*

2   *Vo Thi Tam was one of the lucky ones who eventually made it to the United States. A few days after her arrival here, she told her story in the living room of a small house near Seattle where she was staying with her sister's family. Tears streamed down her cheeks as she spoke.*

3 My husband was a former officer in the South Vietnamese air force. After the fall of that government in 1975, he and all the other officers were sent to a concentration camp for reeducation. When they let him out of the camp, they forced all of us to go to one of the "new economic zones," that are really just jungle. There was no organization, there was no housing, no utilities, no doctor, nothing. They gave us tools and a little food, and that was it. We just had to dig up the land and cultivate it. And the land was very bad.

4   It was impossible for us to live there, so we got together with some other families and bought a big fishing boat, about thirty-five feet long.

5   Altogether, there were thirty-seven of us that were to leave — seven men, eight women, and the rest children. I was five months pregnant.

6   After we bought the boat we had to hide it, and this is how: We just anchored it in a harbor in the Mekong Delta. It's very crowded there and very many people make their living aboard the boats by going fishing, you know. So we had to make ourselves like them. We took turns living and sleeping on the boat. We would maneuver the boat around the harbor, as if we were fishing or selling stuff, you know, so the Communist authorities could not suspect anything.

7   Besides the big boat, we had to buy a smaller boat in order to carry supplies to it. We had to buy gasoline and other stuff on the black market — everywhere there is a black market — and carry these supplies, little by little, on the little boat to the big boat. To do this we sold jewelry and radios and other things that we had left from the old days.

8   On the day we left we took the big boat out very early in the morning — all the women and children were in that boat and some of the men. My husband and the one other man remained in the small boat, and they were to rendezvous with us outside the harbor. Because if the harbor officials see too many people aboard, they might think there was something suspicious. I think they were suspicious anyway. As we went out, they stopped us and made us pay them ten taels of gold — that's a Vietnamese unit, a little heavier than an ounce. That was nearly all we had.

9   Anyway, the big boat passed through the harbor and went ahead to the rendezvous point where we were to meet my husband and the other man in the small

Vo Thi Tam, "From Vietnam, 1979," from *American Mosaic*, Joan Morrison and Charlotte Fox Zabusky, Elsevier-Dutton, 1980.

boat. But there was no one there. We waited for two hours, but we did not see any sign of them. After a while we could see a Vietnamese navy boat approaching and there was a discussion on board our boat and the end of it was the people on our boat decided to leave without my husband and the other man. [*Long pause.*]

10   When we reached the high seas, we discovered, unfortunately, that the water container was leaking and only a little bit of the water was left. So we had to ration the water from then on. We had brought some rice and other food that we could cook, but it was so wavy that we could not cook anything at all. So all we had was raw rice and a few lemons and very little water. After seven days we ran out of water, so all we had to drink was the sea water, plus lemon juice.

11   Everyone was very sick and, at one point, my mother and my little boy, four years old, were in agony, about to die. And the other people on the boat said that if they were agonizing like that, it would be better to throw them overboard so as to save them pain.

12   During this time we had seen several boats on the sea and had waved to them to help us, but they never stopped. But that morning, while we were discussing throwing my mother and son overboard, we could see another ship coming and we were very happy, thinking maybe it was people coming to save us. When the two boats were close together, the people came on board from there – it happened to be a Thai boat – and they said all of us had to go on the bigger boat. They made us all go there and then they began to search us – cutting off our blouses, our bras, looking everywhere. One woman, she had some rings she hid in her bra, and they undressed her and took out everything. My mother had a statue of our Lady, a very precious one, you know, that she had had all her life – she begged them just to leave the statue to her. But they didn't want to. They slapped her and grabbed the statue away.

13   Finally they pried up the planks of our boat, trying to see if there was any gold or jewelry hidden there. And when they had taken everything, they put us back on our boat and pushed us away.

14   They had taken all our maps and compasses, so we didn't even know which way to go. And because they had pried up the planks of our boat to look for jewelry, the water started getting in. We were very weak by then. But we had no pump, so we had to use empty cans to bail the water out, over and over again.

15   That same day we were boarded again by two other boats, and these, too, were pirates. They came aboard with hammers and knives and everything. But we could only beg them for mercy and try to explain by sign language that we'd been robbed before and we had nothing left. So those boats let us go and pointed the way to Malaysia for us.

16   That night at about 9:00 P.M. we arrived on the shore, and we were so happy finally to land somewhere that we knelt down on the beach and prayed, you know, to thank God.

17   While we were kneeling there, some people came out of the woods and began to throw rocks at us. They took a doctor who was with us and they beat him up and broke his glasses, so that from that time on he couldn't see anything at all. And they tied him up, his hands behind him like this [*demonstrates*], and they beat up

the rest of the men, too. They searched us for anything precious that they could find, but there was nothing left except our few clothes and our documents. They took these and scattered them all over the beach.

18   Then five of the Malaysian men grabbed the doctor's wife, a young woman with three little children, and they took her back into the woods and raped her — all five of them. Later, they sent her back, completely naked, to the beach.

19   After this, the Malaysians forced us back into the boat and tried to push us out to sea. But the tide was out and the boat was so heavy with all of us on board that it just sank in the sand. So they left us for the night . . . .

20   In the morning, the Malaysian military police came to look over the area, and they dispersed the crowd and protected us from them. They let us pick up our clothes and our papers from the beach and took us in a big truck to some kind of a warehouse in a small town not far away. They gave us some water, some bread, and some fish, and then they carried us out to Bidong Island . . . .

21   Perhaps in the beginning it was all right there, maybe for ten thousand people or so, but when we arrived there were already fifteen to seventeen thousand crowded onto thirty acres. There was no housing, no facilities, nothing. It was already full near the beach, so we had to go up the mountain and chop down trees to make room for ourselves and make some sort of a temporary shelter. There was an old well, but the water was very shallow. It was so scarce that all the refugees had to wait in a long line, day and night, to get our turn of the water. We would have a little can, like a small Coke can at the end of a long string, and fill that up. To fill about a gallon, it would take an hour, so we each had to just wait, taking our turn to get our Coke can of water. Sometimes one, two, or three in the morning we would get our water. I was pregnant, and my boys were only four and six, and my old mother with me was not well, but we all had to wait in line to get our water. That was just for cooking and drinking of course. We had to do our washing in the sea.

22   The Malaysian authorities did what they could, but they left most of the administration of the camp to the refugees themselves, and most of us were sick. There were, of course, no sanitary installations, and many people had diarrhea. It was very hard to stop sickness under those conditions. My little boys were sick and my mother could hardly walk. And since there was no man in our family, we had no one to chop the wood for our cooking, and it was very hard for us just to survive. When the monsoons came, the floor of our shelter was all mud. We had one blanket and a board to lie on, and that was all. The water would come down the mountain through our shelter, so we all got wet.

23   After four months in the camp it was time for my baby to be born. Fortunately, we had many doctors among us, because many of them had tried to escape from Vietnam, so we had medical care but no equipment. There was no bed there, no hospital, no nothing, just a wooden plank to lie down on and let the baby be born, that was all. Each mother had to supply a portion of boiling water for the doctor to use and bring it with her to the medical hut when it was time. It was a very difficult delivery. The baby came legs first. But, fortunately, there were no complications. After the delivery I had to get up and go back to my shelter to make room for the next woman.

24   When we left Vietnam we were hoping to come to the United States, because my sister and her husband were here already. They came in 1975 when the United States evacuated so many people. We had to wait in the camp a month and a half to be interviewed, and then very much longer for the papers to be processed. Altogether we were in the camp seven months.

25   All this time I didn't know what had happened to my husband, although I hoped that he had been able to escape some other way and was, perhaps, in another camp, and that when I came to the United States I would find him.

26   We flew out here by way of Tokyo and arrived the first week in July. It was like waking up after a bad nightmare. Like coming out of hell into paradise if only – . [*Breaks down, rushes from room.*]

27 *Shortly after she arrived in this country, Vo Thi Tam learned that her husband had been captured on the day of their escape and was back in a "reeducation" camp in Vietnam.*

━━━━━━━━━━

REPORT

Donald Barthelme

1 Our group is against the war. But the war goes on. I was sent to Cleveland to talk to the engineers. The engineers were meeting in Cleveland. I was supposed to persuade them not to do what they are going to do. I took United's 4:45 from LaGuardia arriving in Cleveland at 6:13. Cleveland is dark blue at that hour. I went directly to the motel, where the engineers were meeting. Hundreds of engineers attended the Cleveland meeting. I noticed many fractures among the engineers, bandages, traction. I noticed what appeared to be fracture of the carpal scaphoid in six examples. I noticed numerous fractures of the humeral shaft, of the os calcis, of the pelvic girdle. I noticed a high incidence of clay-shoveller's fracture. I could not account for these fractures. The engineers were making calculations, taking measurements, sketching on the blackboard, drinking beer, throwing bread, buttonholing employers, hurling glasses into the fireplace. They were friendly.

2   They were friendly. They were full of love and information. The chief engineer wore shades. Patella in Monk's traction, clamshell fracture by the look of it. He was standing in a slum of beer bottles and microphone cable. "Have some of this chicken à la Isambard Kingdom Brunel the Great Ingineer," he said. "And declare who you are and what we can do for you. What is your line, distinguished guest?"

3   "Software," I said. "In every sense. I am here representing a small group of interested parties. We are interested in your thing, which seems to be functioning. In the midst of so much dysfunction, function is interesting. Other people's things don't seem to be working. The State Department's thing doesn't seem to be work-

Donald Barthelme, "Report," *Unspeakable Practices, Unnatural Acts*, Farrar, Straus, Giroux, 1968.

ing. The U.N.'s thing doesn't seem to be working. The democratic left's thing doesn't seem to be working. Buddha's thing —"

4   "Ask us anything about our thing, which seems to be working," the chief engineer said. "We will open our hearts and heads to you, Software Man, because we want to be understood and loved by the great lay public, and have our marvels appreciated by that public, for which we daily unsung produce tons of new marvels each more life-enhancing than the last. Ask us anything. Do you want to know about evaporated thin-film metallurgy? Monolithic and hybrid integrated-circuit processes? The algebra of inequalities? Optimization theory? Complex high-speed micro-miniature closed and open loop systems? Fixed variable mathematical cost searches? Epitaxial deposition of semi-conductor materials? Gross interfaced space gropes? We also have specialists in the cuckooflower, the doctorfish, and the dumdum bullet as these relate to aspects of today's expanding technology, and they do in the damnedest ways."

5   I spoke to him then about the war. I said the same things people always say when they speak against the war. I said that the war was wrong. I said that large countries should not burn down small countries. I said that the government had made a series of errors. I said that these errors once small and forgivable were now immense and unforgivable. I said that the government was attempting to conceal its original errors under layers of new errors. I said that the government was sick with error, giddy with it. I said that ten thousand of our soldiers had already been killed in pursuit of the government's errors. I said that tens of thousands of the enemy's soldiers and civilians had been killed because of various errors, ours and theirs. I said that we are responsible for errors made in our name. I said that the government should not be allowed to make additional errors.

6   "Yes, yes," the chief engineer said, "there is doubtless much truth in what you say, but we can't possibly *lose* the war, can we? And stopping is losing, isn't it? The war regarded as a process, stopping regarded as an abort? We don't know *how* to lose a war. That skill is not among our skills. Our array smashes their array, that is what we know. That is the process. That is what is.

7   "But let's not have any more of this dispiriting downbeat counterproductive talk. I have a few new marvels here I'd like to discuss with you just briefly. A few new marvels that are just about ready to be gaped at by the admiring layman. Consider for instance the area of realtime online computer-controlled wish evaporation. Wish evaporation is going to be crucial in meeting the rising expectations of the world's peoples, which are as you know rising entirely too fast."

8   I noticed then distributed about the room a great many transverse fractures of the ulna. "The development of the pseudo-ruminant stomach for underdeveloped peoples," he went on, "is one of our interesting things you should be interested in. With the pseudo-ruminant stomach they can chew cuds, that is to say, eat grass. Blue is the most popular color worldwide and for that reason we are working with certain strains of your native Kentucky *Poa pratensis*, or bluegrass, as the staple input for the p/r stomach cycle, which would also give a shot in the arm to our balance-of-payments thing don't you know . . . . " I noticed about me then a great number of metatarsal fractures in banjo splints. "The kangaroo initiative . . . eight

hundred thousand harvested last year . . . highest percentage of edible protein of any herbivore yet studied . . . "

9   "Have new kangaroos been planted?"

10   The engineer looked at me.

11   "I intuit your hatred and jealousy of our thing," he said. "The ineffectual always hate our thing and speak of it as anti-human, which is not at all a meaningful way to speak of our thing. Nothing mechanical is alien to me," he said (amber spots making bursts of light in his shades), "because I am human, in a sense, and if I think it up, then 'it' is human too, whatever 'it' may be. Let me tell you, Software Man, we have been damned forbearing in the matter of this little war you declare yourself to be interested in. Function is the cry, and our thing is functioning like crazy. There are things we could do that we have not done. Steps we could take that we have not taken. These steps are, regarded in a certain light, the light of our enlightened self-interest, quite justifiable steps. We could, of course, get irritated. We could, of course, *lose patience.*

12   "We could, of course, release thousands upon thousands of self-powered crawling-along-the-ground lengths of titanium wire eighteen inches long with a diameter of .0005 centimetres (that is to say, invisible) which, scenting an enemy, climb up his trouser leg and wrap themselves around his neck. We have developed those. They are within our capabilities. We could, of course, release in the arena of the upper air our new improved pufferfish toxin which precipitates an identity crisis. No special technical problems there. That is almost laughably easy. We could, of course, place up to two million maggots in their rice within twenty-four hours. The maggots are ready, massed in secret staging areas in Alabama. We have hypodermic darts capable of piebalding the enemy's pigmentation. We have rots, blights, and rusts capable of attacking his alphabet. Those are dandies. We have a hut-shrinking chemical which penetrates the fibres of the bamboo, causing it, the hut, to strangle its occupants. This operates only after 10 P.M., when people are sleeping. Their mathematics are at the mercy of a suppurating surd we have invented. We have a family of fishes trained to attack their fishes. We have the deadly testicle-destroying telegram. The cable companies are coöperating. We have a green substance that, well, I'd rather not talk about. We have a secret word that, if pronounced, produces multiple fractures in all living things in an area the size of four football fields."

13   "That's why — "

14   "Yes. Some damned fool couldn't keep his mouth shut. The point is that the whole structure of enemy life is within our power to *rend*, *vitiate*, *devour*, and *crush*. But that's not the interesting thing."

15   "You recount these possibilities with uncommon relish."

16   "Yes I realize that there is too much relish here. But *you* must realize that these capabilities represent in and of themselves highly technical and complex and interesting problems and hurdles on which our boys have expended many thousands of hours of hard work and brilliance. And that the effects are often grossly exaggerated by irresponsible victims. And that the whole thing represents a fantastic series of triumphs for the multi-disciplined problem-solving team concept."

17   "I appreciate that."

18   "We *could* unleash all this technology at once. You can imagine what would happen then. But that's not the interesting thing."

19   "What is the interesting thing?"

20   "The interesting thing is that we have *a moral sense.* It is on punched cards, perhaps the most advanced and sensitive moral sense the world has ever known."

21   "Because it is on punched cards?"

22   "It considers all considerations in endless and subtle detail," he said. "It even quibbles. With this great new moral tool, how can we go wrong? I confidently predict that, although we *could* employ all this splendid new weaponry I've been telling you about, *we're not going to do it.*"

23   "We're not going to do it?"

24   I took United's 5:44 from Cleveland arriving at Newark at 7:19. New Jersey is bright pink at that hour. Living things move about the surface of New Jersey at that hour molesting each other only in traditional ways. I made my report to the group. I stressed the friendliness of the engineers. I said, It's all right. I said, We have a moral sense. I said, *We're not going to do it.* They didn't believe me.

PLATOON

Terrence Rafferty

1 Oliver Stone's *Platoon*, about a group of American infantrymen in Vietnam between 1967 and 1968, is the first Hollywood film about this country's Southeast Asian adventure that's just a war movie — and, weirdly, its straightforward genre-picture intensity makes all the other film treatments of the subject look evasive and superficial. Even leaving aside the recently popular P.O.W.-rescue movies with Sylvester Stallone and Chuck Norris, which are simply macho pulp in exotic settings, Milton Caniff on steroids, American movies haven't done very well by the horrors of Vietnam and Cambodia. All the serious films about Southeast Asia of the past ten years have been so intent on "coming to terms" with the experience that they've barely bothered to *represent* it. For all the virtues of *Apocalypse Now*, no one could possibly have learned anything about Vietnam from it. Coppola staged the war as a psychedelic opera — jungles bursting into flames with the Doors' sinister "The End" on the soundtrack, copters swooping out of the sky to the music of "Ride of the Valkyries" — and the grandiose style robbed the subject of its specificity. Coppola was so caught up in creating his huge metaphoric vision of chaos (derived, in just about equal parts, from *Heart of Darkness* and Michael Herr's *Dispatches*) that he seemed not to notice the inanity of the movie's subtext: that the war could have been won if our military leaders weren't so inept and our soldiers so stoned, if only we Americans weren't so stupid and spiritually empty.

Terrence Rafferty, "*Platoon*," *The Nation*, January 17, 1987.

2   Michael Cimino's Oscar-winner, *The Deer Hunter*, also featured a hallucinated Vietnam: the war was a bad dream that his heroes, a bunch of regular-guy Pennsylvania factory workers, couldn't wake up from. Cimino meant to contrast the supposed purity of traditional American values with the war's hellish suspension of moral categories, and he wasn't fussy about how he defined his terms — not only idealizing the "clean" sportsmanship of the heroes' deer-hunting expeditions, but also inventing a Russian-roulette torture by the group's Vietnamese captors. *The Deer Hunter* was as overblown as *Apocalypse Now*, but in a different register, like an opera scored by Springsteen. It had a heavy, plodding spirit, a populist ethos verging (probably without meaning to) on the demagogic, and a defeated air that somehow managed to congratulate us on our wounded innocence, our stunned simplicity. Neither of those big-deal movies was about Vietnam at all — they were about the shape the war took in our imaginations (which is, perhaps, why they were both so muddled and unresolved). But the war was, of course, more than a bad trip, as Coppola would have it, or a child's nightmare, as in Cimino. *Platoon* gives Vietnam back some of its reality.

3   In *Platoon*, the war is so real that it actually sobers up Oliver Stone, who, as a screenwriter (*Midnight Express, Scarface, Eight Million Ways to Die, Year of the Dragon*), has developed his own brand of hysterical machismo. The contemporary action pictures he's written may have started out as explorations of aspects of the underworld and the drug culture, but they all wound up as lurid, wired celebrations of chaos and obscenity: uneasy mixtures of tabloid moralizing and gonzo relish, stuffed into conventional genre structures that served to emphasize the filmmakers' bad faith. *Salvador*, released early last year (and now available on videocassette), was written and directed by Stone, and made a little more sense. Its hero, a Hunter Thompson-like freelance journalist played by James Woods (with even more than his usual ferrety intensity), was clearly a kind of war junkie, traveling to Central America in search of a revolution to get high on: the character seemed an acknowledgment of Stone's own guilty pleasure in out-of-control violence and reckless, "existential" tests of manhood. Although *Salvador*'s politics got a bit confused and both the action and the performances were sometimes pointlessly frenetic, the movie managed, in its self-conscious way, to convey the desperate atmosphere of crisis — and without turning its background of Third World turmoil into spectacle (as Roland Joffe's *The Killing Fields* often did with its powerful and beautiful images of the Khmer Rouge takeover of Cambodia). *Salvador* was a wild, unstable movie that, intermittently, was also a vivid essay on varieties of instability, personal and political.

4   Stone's Vietnam movie is, surprisingly, the cleanest, simplest work he has ever done. He's not exactly an austere director, even here, but he keeps the movie focused on the day-to-day experience of his platoon through a sequence of five military actions along the Cambodian border, and he has the sense to realize that the young soldiers' fear is all the subject he needs. Stone treats the war and its participants with a strange kind of reverence, as if here, at the source of his obsession with violence and madness, he doesn't need to add anything, to jack up the voltage. In some way, the failure of earlier Vietnam movies has probably helped him.

We've *had* the war as metaphor for moral chaos, and the war as rock-and-roll hallucination. Stone, who served in Vietnam in the late 1960s, must have looked at those films and asked himself if the war he'd fought was horrible because our leaders were dithering incompetents or because our soldiers were too far gone on pot or acid or Hendrix to know what was happening to them. In Stone's version, it's the soldiers who know exactly what they're doing, who kill most efficiently, like his appalling Sergeant Barnes (played by Tom Berenger, whose facial makeup transcends all previous definitions of "battle-scarred"), that are the most dangerous; and it's only the "heads" — the guys who smoke pot and listen to rock — who retain some vestige of decency and rationality. He seems to have decided that the war was awful because it was wrong to begin with, and because people were dying all around him.

5   This blunt attitude gives Stone's writing and direction a kind of ferocious concentraton they've never had before. The fact that he's drawing on his own experience obviously helps, too. He's not scattering wild notions and off-the-wall verbal exchanges all over the landscape, as he usually does: in *Platoon*, he's too busy filling in remembered details. He adopts the classic perspective of a young soldier (Charlie Sheen) seeing action for the first time, and everything is seen here with the heightened alertness of terror: the agony of night watches; the lightning-fast mayhem of a fire fight; even the smaller, peripheral dangers — snakes, insects — that help turn simple fear into panic. It's *The Red Badge of Courage*, without the courage. "Ain't no such thing as a coward out here," one weary veteran tells the young soldier before the climactic engagement: there are isolated acts of genuine heroism, but the only real prize this war has to offer is the sight of the helicopter that lifts you away from it for good. *Platoon* is even more narrowly focused than World War II movies were — there is (blessedly) little talk among the grunts about the girls they left behind or the candy store they're going to open up when they get back home or how the Yankees are doing — and the limitation is appropriate and powerful. The platoon Stone has created (or re-created) is a world of its own, where the business of survival drives everything else — even notions of home — from consciousness.

6   Stone's directorial style, which is fast, kinetic and rather literal, serves him well in the action scenes: there are few battle sequences on film as tense and frightening as these. In the intervals between skirmishes, his writing takes over, and though it's not as florid as usual, it still causes some problems. The conflict between Sergeant Barnes and his "head" counterpart, the smart, brave Sergeant Elias (Willem Dafoe), is crudely drawn and, worse yet, symbolic: the young hero, narrating in voice-over, refers to Barnes as "our Captain Ahab," and, after all the shooting is over, speaks of "Barnes and Elias fighting for possession of my soul." That dramatic hyperbole is meant to illustrate the not very original thesis that Stone saves until the last few seconds of the movie: "The enemy," Sheen's voice intones, "was in us." There is, of course, some truth in that, but there's *some* truth in almost anything we can say about that complex war — and what's refreshing about *Platoon* up to that point is that it has mostly resisted the impulse to generalize, to make the kind of statement that, like Coppola's and Cimino's, can't possibly tell us any more than a fraction of

the truth. At its best, *Platoon* simply shows us as much as we need to know about a small patch of the territory – Stone's own experience in Vietnam – which is probably more valuable.

7   It's a little ironic, though, that after his manic, hallucinated versions of *other* people's lives – the feverishly caricatured Turks, Chinese-Americans and Miami Cubans of his previous scripts – Oliver Stone has become an honorable and scrupulous artist in dealing with the central experience of his own life. Let's hope that this strong movie isn't just an isolated episode in Stone's career, that he'll be able to carry over his new rigor and generosity from his memory to his imagination. Vietnam seems to have made him a better filmmaker – his next movies should tell us whether, in the best war-movie tradition, it's also made a man out of him.

AGENT ORANGE ON TRIAL

Fred A. Wilcox

1 On May 7, 1984, Vietnam veterans who had worked for years and invested their life's savings trying to get the Agent Orange class action suit into court learned to their dismay that the case had been settled out of court for the sum of $180 million. Reaction was swift and almost universally negative. Why, they demanded, had their attorneys failed to inform them that a settlement was imminent? How could an agreement be reached without their consent, and that contained no provisions for exactly how the money would be distributed; did not specify the kinds of illnesses that would be compensated; and did not include the wives and children of veterans exposed to defoliants? To veterans suffering from what they believed to be Agent Orange exposure, the issue had never been money. They wanted to tell the American people about the effects of toxic chemicals on human health, wanted people to see for themselves the skin rashes and cancers and birth defects. The judicial system in which they had placed such high hopes seemed to have abdicated its responsibility, leaving veterans and their families feeling angry, bitter, and bewildered.

2   In *Agent Orange On Trial*, Yale law professor Peter H. Schuck tries to unravel, perhaps one should say unveil, the complex behind-the-scenes maneuvering that led to this controversial settlement. Written primarily for those with a background in law, Schuck's work is, nevertheless, quite readable, unfolding like a vast, complex mystery novel with a cast of characters that includes:

3   *Judge Julius Weinstein*. A man the author finds simultaneously brilliant and bewildering, Machiavellian and humane, crafty and controversial. Obsessed with seeing the Agent Orange litigation settled out of court, Weinstein outmaneuvers, outsmarts, and finally outlasts the Young Turks who stroll and strut through his chambers trying in vain to persuade him to allow the case to be heard in Brooklyn Federal Court.

Fred A. Wilcox, "Agent Orange on Trial," *The Amicus Journal*, Winter 1987.

4   *Lawyers for Vietnam veterans and their families.* A consortium of flamboyant, ambitious, and often quarrelsome attorneys who fret their hour across the legal stage, jockeying for power and position arguing over procedure, firing Victor Yannacone (the one person Vietnam veterans absolutely trust), and financing the lawsuit by borrowing large sums of money from investors who see the case as merely another high stakes horse race.

5   *Special Masters.* Individuals handpicked by Weinstein to act as emissaries to the warring parties, and to articulate his labyrinthine decisions, controversial edicts, and cryptic warnings that even if a jury should rule on behalf of Agent Orange veterans he would be inclined to overturn its decision.

6   *Attorneys for Dow Chemical, Uniroyal, Monsanto, Diamond Shamrock, and Hooker.* Willing to fight a protracted trench warfare legal battle, spending $100 million to keep the case from being heard by a jury, then another $180 million to seal the courthouse doors. Yet, apparently unable to see the irony of denying that their employers bore any responsibility for the veterans' illnesses

7   Unfortunately, this is not a work of fiction. The ribald characters, bizarre events, and tumultuous ending are all too real, and the questions Schuck tries to answer extremely important to Americans who have been or will be exposed to toxic chemicals. What is really so troubling about this book is that the author, a respected authority on tort litigation, is suggesting that without substantial changes or reforms the courts are incapable of remedying or resolving mass toxic lawsuits similar to the Agent Orange litigation. To judges in the Agency Orange class action suit, writes Schuck, "the case was a legal Gordian knot, an unprecedented intellectual conundrum, an almost impossible administrative tangle that threatened to transmogrify tort litigation and deplete the court's capacity to render justice. Agent Orange fascinated them, but most of the time they wished it would go away." At the same time, Vietnam veterans and their supporters were naive in their hopes that a mass toxic tort action as complex as this could ever be resolved fairly by the courts. "The veterans," Schuck contends, "expected the law to provide the essential elements of simple justice — their day in court, with comprehensible narrative evidence, a clear determination of guilt or innocence, and a swift, straight-forward remedy." And all the while, their attorneys "knew that this view of adjudication was chimerical, the legal equivalent of the elementary civics-textbook view of politics. They knew that many of the complex, technical aspects of the Agent Orange case contradicted their clients' intuitive notions of justice and even defied common sense."

8   While *Agent Orange on Trial* is fascinating, informative, well researched, and emminently honest, Schuck's play-by-play account of how the settlement was reached may only increase Vietnam veterans' sense of betrayal and outrage .More-over, certain nagging questions remain unanswered. For example, why did Judge Weinstein insist on an early trial date? And why, if he believed the plaintiffs had no case did he not order them to take their frivolous lawsuit elsewhere? Why, indeed, did he insist one moment to the veterans' attorneys that their case was weak, then turn to the chemical companies and suggest they start gathering funds for a settle-ment? Did Judge Weinstein fully understand scientific reports and studies suggest-

ing a link between exposure to herbicides and human health problems; or the substantial amount of research demonstrating the deadly effects of TCDD-dioxin, the contaminant in Agent Orange, on laboratory animals? What might have happened to this case had he been replaced by a judge willing to allow a jury to hear the evidence and decide the case on its merits?

9   But the most urgent question to evolve from the Agent Orange class action litigation, is to whom does the nation really belong, the American people or a handful of multinational corporations with assets too great to measure? Twenty years ago, Rachel Carson wrote that our founding fathers could not have had the foresight to include a section in the Constitution guaranteeing Americans the right to a clean and healthy environment. If the out of court settlement demonstrates anything it is this: Faced with the complexities of the law and the fact that it appears to be heavily weighted to favor corporations which manufacture such chemicals, it might be time to amend the Constitution to protect future generations from the effects of dioxin, PCBs, radiation, and hundreds of other substances that inundate our environment. Carson tried to warn us, and for the past five years Vietnam veterans and their families have pleaded with Congress, the judiciary, Dow Chemical, et al., and the American people to stop for a moment and examine the horrific effects of using human beings for guinea pigs. Perhaps we do not want to acknowledge the veterans, because were we to do so we would have to look into our own toxic crystal ball. Nevertheless, Vietnam veterans are our future and, painful as that may be, the future is now.

████████████████

THE WAR IS NOT OVER
Jeff Jones

1 Janet Gardner correctly observes an increase in activity by Vietnam War veterans and activists on the issue of Agent Orange, and she also gives a good overview of the Federal government's stonewalling of Agent Orange research, which has meant that the only significant research being done is conducted through state agencies and independent scientific study ["Answers at Last?" April 11]. But while highlighting this government scandal, Gardner continues the practice of ignoring the other victims, the Vietnamese people who live in the defoliated areas. That reflects a serious problem of the anti–Agent Orange movement. The omission has a moral dimension as well as a practical one.

2   The deadly toxins used during the war have been working their way into the Vietnamese ecosystem for more than twenty-five years. During an eighteen-day trip to Vietnam last July, I visited Tu Dzu Hospital in Ho Chi Minh City. As that city's main hospital for women and as the primary-care facility for the most extreme medical complications in southern Vietnam, Tu Dzu is probably the world's leading facility for the treatment and study of Agent Orange victims. What is happening there puts the lie to any notions that the effects of Agent Orange are short-lived.

3   Dr. Le Diem Huong is the head of Tu Dzu Hospital's pediatric and neonatology departments. She told us that a retrospective study conducted by the hospital's staff found that the rate of miscarriage and birth defects among young Vietnamese women from the defoliated areas has been increasing annually. She also indicated that the hospital lacks the funds to carry out more comprehensive research.

4   The Vietnamese I spoke with consider U.S. veterans, as well as themselves, to be victims of the U.S. government's war. Dr. Huong indicated a desire to increased contact with medical and scientific workers in the United States, both because the Vietnamese experience can provide valuable research information for affected U.S. veterans, and because the Vietnamese need help. Their efforts center on young mothers and children because the toxins seem to be having their most devastating effect on those groups. A more systematic and thorough investigation of the population in the defoliated areas could, and should, be undertaken. But that would require a broader vision from those of us working on the Agent Orange issue in the United States, and a willingness to challenge the U.S. government's embargo on Vietnam.

5   Agent Orange is routinely referred to as a defoliant, used to deny the "enemy" cover. (Indeed, Gardner uses that offensive reference to the Vietnamese in explaining the name of a study by the New Jersey State Commission on Agent Orange, the Point Man Project.) But we must insist on historical accuracy. According to reports of Military Assistance Command Vietnam for 1967, the year of greatest herbicidal use, 1,486,446 acres of forest were defoliated and 221,312 acres of crops were destroyed. The poisons were also used to destroy the Vietnamese food supply. Thus, the toxin's use amounted to chemical warfare against a civilian population.

6   We need to support the work of the various state agencies and concerned scientists studying the effects of Agent Orange. It is an issue on which a coalition of Vietnam veterans and antiwar activists can be built. But let's include the Vietnamese in the effort.

IV
A NATION
OF IMMIGRANTS

Alex Haley's *Roots* (1976), which began with his search for his own "furthest-back person," motivated many Americans to think about their immigrant ancestors. Maxine Hong Kingston describes the traumas and humiliation suffered by her "Father from China." Lorna Dee Cervantes (born in San Francisco) writes of the difficulties of being caught between two cultures, living in the United States with the names and traditions of her Mexican ancestors. Their individual voices echo beneath the words of the debate, taken up here by Wayne A. Cornelius and Richard D. Lamm, about whether the United States should further restrict immigration or be a nation of open doors.

As the articles in this section make clear, immigration continues to be a central issue, both to individual Americans and to our society as a whole. As you saw in sections I, Music — Bridging Cultures, and II, Women and Film, our cultural diversity and artistic vitality have long depended on influxes of foreign ideas and people. But to many, our nation's economic resources seem to be strained by the constant flow of people demanding their piece of the American dream: work; decent food, housing, and medical care; an education for their children. How long will Americans be able and willing to pay the price of cultural plurality and the long-standing promise of freedom?

MY FURTHEST-BACK PERSON — "THE AFRICAN"

Alex Haley

1 I knew I must get to the Gambia River.

2 The first native Gambian I could locate in the U.S. was named Ebou Manga, then a junior attending Hamilton College in upstate Clinton, N.Y. He and I flew to Dakar, Senegal, then took a smaller plane to Yundum Airport, and rode a van to Gambia's capital, Bathurst. Ebou and his father assembled eight Gambia government officials. I told them Grandma's stories, every detail I could remember, as they listened intently, then reacted. "'*Kamby Bolong*' of course is Gambia River!"

From Alex Haley, "My Furthest-Back Person – 'The African,'" *The New York Times Magazine*, July 16, 1972.

I heard. "But more clue is your forefather's saying his name was '*Kinte.*'" Then they told me something I would never even have fantasized — that in places in the back country lived very old men, commonly called *griots*, who could tell centuries of the histories of certain very old family clans. As for *Kintes*, they pointed out to me on a map some family villages, Kinte-Kundah, and Kinte-Kundah Janneh-Ya, for instance.

3   The Gambian officials said they would try to help me. I returned to New York dazed. It is embarrassing to me now, but despite Grandma's stories, I'd never been concerned much with Africa, and I had the routine images of African people living mostly in exotic jungles. But a compulsion now laid hold of me to learn all I could, and I began devouring books about Africa, especially about the slave trade. Then one Thursday's mail contained a letter from one of the Gambian officials, inviting me to return there.

4   Monday I was back in Bathurst. It galvanized me when the officials said that a *griot* had been located who told the *Kinte* clan history — his name was Kebba Kanga Fofana. To reach him, I discovered, required a modified safari: renting a launch to get upriver, two land vehicles to carry supplies by a roundabout land route, and employing finally 14 people, including three interpreters and four musicians, since a *griot* would not speak the revered clan histories without background music.

5   The boat Baddibu vibrated upriver, with me acutely tense: Were these Africans maybe viewing me as but another of the pith-helmets? After about two hours, we put in at James Island, for me to see the ruins of the once British-operated James Fort. Here two centuries of slave ships had loaded thousands of cargoes of Gambian tribespeople. The crumbling stones, the deeply oxidized swivel cannon, even some remnant links of chain seemed all but impossible to believe. Then we continued upriver to the left-bank village of Albreda, and there put ashore to continue on foot to Juffure, village of the *griot.* Once more we stopped, for me to see *toubob kolong,* "the white man's well," now almost filled in, in a swampy area with abundant, tall, saw-toothed grass. It was dug two centuries ago to "17 men's height deep" to insure survival drinking water for long-driven, famishing coffles of slaves.

6   Walking on, I kept wishing that Grandma could hear how her stories had led me to the *"Kamby Bolong."* (Our surviving storyteller Cousin Georgia died in a Kansas City hospital during this same morning, I would learn later.) Finally, Juffure village's playing children, sighting us, flashed an alert. The 70-odd people came rushing from their circular, thatch-roofed, mud-walled huts, with goats bounding up and about, and parrots squawking from up in the palms. I sensed him in advance somehow, the small man amid them, wearing a pillbox cap and an off-white robe — the *griot.* Then the interpreters went to him, as the villagers thronged around me.

7   And it hit me like a gale wind: every one of them, the whole crowd, was *jet black.* An enormous sense of guilt swept me — a sense of being some kind of hybrid . . . a sense of being impure among the pure. It was an awful sensation.

8   The old *griot* stepped away from my interpreters and the crowd quickly swarmed around him — all of them buzzing. An interpreter named A. B. C. Salla

came to me; he whispered: "Why they stare at you so, they have never seen here a black American." And that hit me: I was symbolizing for them twenty-five millions of us they had never seen. What did they think of me — of us?

9   Then abruptly the old *griot* was briskly walking toward me. His eyes boring into mine, he spoke in Mandinka, as if instinctively I should understand — and A. B. C. Salla translated:

10   "Yes . . . we have been told by the forefathers . . . that many of us from this place are in exile . . . in that place called America . . . and in other places."

11   I suppose I physically wavered, and they thought it was the heat; rustling whispers went through the crowd, and a man brought me a low stool. Now the whispering hushed — the musicians had softly begun playing *kora* and *balafon*, and a canvas sling lawn seat was taken by the *griot*, Kebba Kanga Fofana, aged 75 "rains" (one rainy season each year). He seemed to gather himself into a physical rigidity, and he began speaking the *Kinte* clan's ancestral oral history; it came rolling from his mouth across the next hours . . . 17th- and 18th-century *Kinte* lineage details, predominantly what men took wives; the children they "begot," in the order of their births; those children's mates and children.

12   Events frequently were dated by some proximate singular physical occurrence. It was as if some ancient scroll were printed indelibly within the *griot's* brain. Each few sentences or so, he would pause for an interpreter's translation to me. I distill here the essence:

13   The *Kinte* clan began in Old Mali, the men generally blacksmiths ". . . who conquered fire," and the women potters and weavers. One large branch of the clan moved to Mauretania from where one son of the clan, Kairaba Kunta Kinte, a Moslem Marabout holy man, entered Gambia. He lived first in the village of Pakali N'Ding; he moved next to Jiffarong village; ". . . and then he came here, into our town village of Juffure."

14   In Juffure, Kairaba Kunta Kinte took his first wife, " . . . a Mandinka maiden, whose name was Sireng. By her, be begot two sons, whose names were Janneh and Saloum. Then he got a second wife, Yaisa. By her, he begot a son, Omoro."

15   The three sons became men in Juffure. Janneh and Saloum went off and founded a new village, Kinte-Kundah Janneh-Ya. "And then Omoro, the youngest son, when he had 30 rains, took as a wife a maiden, Binta Kebba.

16   "And by her, he begot four sons — Kunta, Lamin, Suwadu, and Madi . . . "

17   Sometimes, a "begotten," after his naming, would be accompanied by some later-occurring detail, perhaps as " . . . in time of big water (flood) he slew a water buffalo." Having named those four sons, now the *griot* stated such a detail.

18   "About the time the king's soldiers came, the eldest of these four sons, Kunta, when he had about 16 rains, went away from his village, to chop wood to make a drum . . . and he was never seen again . . . "

19   Goose-pimples the size of lemons seemed to pop all over me. In my knapsack were my cumulative notebooks, the first of them including how in my boyhood, my Grandma, Cousin Georgia and the others told of the African "*Kin-tay*" who

always said he was kidnaped near his village — while chopping wood to make a drum . . . .

20   I showed the interpreter, he showed and told the *griot*, who excitedly told the people; they grew very agitated. Abruptly then they formed a human ring, encircling me, dancing and chanting. Perhaps a dozen of the women carrying their infant babies rushed in toward me, thrusting the infants into my arms — conveying, I would later learn, "the laying on of hands . . . through this flesh which is us, we are you, and you are us." The men hurried me into their mosque, their Arabic praying later being translated outside: "Thanks be to Allah for returning the long lost from among us." Direct descendants of Kunta Kinte's blood brothers were hastened, some of them from nearby villages, for a family portrait to be taken with me, surrounded by actual ancestral sixth cousins. More symbolic acts filled the remaining day.

21   When they would let me leave, for some reason I wanted to go away over the African land. Dazed, silent in the bumping Land Rover, I heard the cutting staccato of talking drums. Then when we sighted the next village, its people came thronging to meet us. They were all — little naked ones to wizened elders — waving, beaming, amid a cacophony of crying out; and then my ears identified their words: *"Meester Kinte! Meester Kinte!"*

22   Let me tell you something: I am a man. But I remember the sob surging up from my feet, flinging up my hands before my face and bawling as I had not done since I was a baby . . . the jet-black Africans were jostling, staring . . . I didn't care, with the feelings surging. If you really knew the odyssey of us millions of black Americans, if you really knew how we came in the seeds of our forefathers, captured, driven, beaten, inspected, bought, branded, chained in foul ships, if you really knew, you needed weeping . . . .

23   Back home, I knew that what I must write, really, was our black saga, where any individual's past is the essence of the millions. Now flat broke, I went to some editors I knew, describing the Gambian miracle, and my desire to pursue the research; Doubleday contracted to publish, and Reader's Digest to condense the projected book; then I had advances to travel further.

24   What ship brought Kinte to Grandma's "'Naplis" (Annapolis, Md., obviously)? The old *griot*'s time reference to "king's soldiers" sent me flying to London. Feverish searching at last identified, in British Parliament records, "Colonel O'Hare's Forces," dispatched in mid-1767 to protect the then British-held James Fort whose ruins I'd visited. So Kunta Kinte was down in some ship probably sailing later that summer from the Gambia River to Annapolis.

25   Now I feel it was fated that I had taught myself to write in the U.S. Coast Guard. For the sea dramas I had concentrated on had given me years of experience searching among yellowing old U.S. maritime records. So now in English 18th Century marine records I finally tracked ships reporting themselves in and out to the Commandment of the Gambia River's James Fort. And then early one afternoon I found that a Lord Ligonier under a Captain Thomas Davies had sailed on the

Sabbath of July 5, 1767. Her cargo: 3,265 elephants' teeth, 3,700 pounds of beeswax, 800 pounds of cotton, 32 ounces of Gambian gold, and 140 slaves; her destination: "Annapolis."

26   That night I recrossed the Atlantic. In the Library of Congress the Lord Ligonier's arrival was one brief line in "Shipping In The Port Of Annapolis — 1748-1775." I located the author, Vaughan W. Brown, in his Baltimore brokerage office. He drove to Historic Annapolis, the city's historical society, and found me further documentation of her arrival on Sept. 29, 1767. (Exactly two centuries later, Sept. 29, 1967, standing, staring seaward from an Annapolis pier, again I knew tears.) More help came in the Maryland Hall of Records. Archivist Phebe Jacobsen found the Lord Ligonier's arriving customs declaration listing, "98 Negroes" — so in her 86-day crossing, 42 Gambians had died, one among the survivors being 16-year-old Kunta Kinte. Then the microfilmed Oct. 1, 1767, Maryland Gazette contained, on page two, an announcement to prospective buyers from the ship's agents, Daniel of St. Thos. Jenifer and John Ridout (the Governor's secretary): "from the River GAMBIA, in AFRICA . . . a cargo of choice, healthy SLAVES . . . ."

THE FATHER FROM CHINA

Maxine Hong Kingston

1 Arriving in San Francisco Bay, the legal father was detained for an indefinite time at the Immigration Station on Angel Island, almost within swimming distance of San Francisco. In a wooden house, a white demon physically examined him, poked him in the ass and genitals, looked in his mouth, pulled his eyelids with a hook. This was not the way a father ought to have been greeted. A cough tickled his chest and throat, but he held it down. The doctor demon pointed to a door, which he entered to find men and boys crowded together from floor to ceiling in bunkbeds and on benches; they stood against the walls and at the windows. These must be the hundred China Men who could enter America, he thought. But the quota was one hundred a year, not one hundred per day, and here were packed more than one hundred, nearer two hundred or three. A few people made room for him to set down his suitcases. "A newcomer. Another newcomer," they called out. A welcome

---

Maxine Hong Kingston, "The Father from China," *China Men*, Knopf, 1980.

party made its way to him. "I'm the president of the Self-Governing Association," one of them was telling him in a dialect almost like his. "The most important rule we have here is that we guard one another's chances for immigration." He also asked for dues; the father gave a few dimes toward buying newspapers and phonograph records, an invention that he had never heard before. "Now you're eligible to vote," said the president, who then said that he had won his office by having been on the island the longest, three and a half years. The legal father's heart sank, and rose again; there must be something wrong with this man, not a good man, a criminal to be jailed for so long. "Do you want to spend money on a rubber ball? Vote Yes or No." The legal father voted No. How odd it would be to say to these men, "Play ball. Go ahead. Play with it," as if they were boys and could play. Even the boys wouldn't play. Who can be that light-hearted? He wasn't really going to stay here for more than a day or two, was he? He made his way across the room. Some of the men were gambling, others exercising, cutting one another's hair, staring at their feet or folded hands or the floor. He saw two men handcuffed to each other. Readers chanted San Francisco newspapers, *Young China* and *Chinese World*. The legal father, who was skillful and lucky, joined a game and won forty silver dollars, and gave away one for the rubber ball. He learned who was being deported and who was serving a year's sentence before deportation.

2   A bell went off like a ship's alarm, but it was a dinner bell. The father followed the others to a dining hall. About ten women were coming out. They were the first women he had seen since China, and they already belonged to husbands. He did not know that he had come to a country with no women. The husbands and wives talked quickly as the guards pushed them past one another. The father saw the man ahead of him hold hands with a woman for a moment and — he saw it — pass her a note. She dropped it. She knelt and, fixing her shoe with one hand, snatched the piece of paper with the other. A big white matron grabbed her arm and took the paper. Though these people were all strangers, the father joined the men who surrounded the matron. They wrested the paper from her and tore it up. The legal father ate some of the shreds. That was the last time the men's and women's mealtimes overlapped. There seemed to be no other immediate consequences; perhaps denial of entry would be the punishment.

3   The China Men who worked in the kitchen brought food cooked and served in buckets. "Poison," the prisoners grumbled. "A couple of years ago," said the president of the Self-Governing Association, "the demons tried to starve us to death. They were taking the food money for themselves. If it weren't for us rioting, you newcomers wouldn't be eating so much today. We faced bayonets for this food." The legal father wasn't sure he would've wanted any more of the slop they were eating.

4   The men spent the long days rehearsing what they would say to the Immigration Demon. The forgetful men fingered their risky notes. Those who came back after being examined told what questions they had been asked. "I had to describe all the streets in my village." "They'll ask, 'Do you have any money?' and 'Do you

have a job?'" "They've been asking those questions all this week," the cooks and janitors confirmed. "What's the right answer?" asked the legal fathers. "Well, last week they liked 'No job' because it proves you were an aristocrat. And they liked 'No money' because you showed a willingness to work. But this week, they like 'Yes job' and 'Yes money' because you wouldn't be taking jobs away from white workers." The men groaned, "Some help." The demons did not treat people of any other race the way they did Chinese. The few Japanese left in a day or two. It was because their emperor was strong.

5   Footsteps walked across the ceiling, and bedsprings squeaked above their heads. So there were more of them locked on the second floor. "The women are up there," the father was told. Diabolical, inauspicious beginning — to be trodden over by women. "Living under women's legs," said the superstitious old-fashioned men from the backward villages. "Climbed over by women." It was bad luck even to walk under women's pants on clotheslines. No doubt the demons had deliberately planned this humiliation. The legal father decided that for a start in the new country, he would rid himself of Chinese superstitions; this curse would not count.

6   He read the walls, which were covered with poems. Those who could write protested this jailing, this wooden house (*wood* rhyming with *house*), the unfair laws, the emperor too weak to help them. They wrote about the fog and being lonely and afraid. The poets had come to a part of the world not made for honor, where "a hero cannot use his bravery." One poet was ready to ride his horse to do mighty American deeds but instead here he sat corraled, "this wooden house my coffin." The poets must have stayed long to carve the words so well. The demons were not going to free him, a scholar, then. Some were not poems exactly but statements. "This island is not angelic." "It's not true about the gold." One man blamed "the Mexican Exclusion Laws" for his imprisonment. The writers were anonymous; no official demon could trace them and penalize them. Some signed surname and village, but they were still disguised; there were many of that name from that village, many men named Lee from Toi Sahn, many a Hong of Sun Woi, and many a Three District Man and Four District No Such Man. There were dates of long stays.

7   Night fell quickly; at about four o'clock the fog poured down the San Francisco hillsides, covered the bay, and clouded the windows. Soon the city was gone, held fast by black sea and sky. The fog horns mourned. San Francisco might have been a figment of Gold Mountain dreams.

8   The legal father heard cries and thumps from someone locked in a separate shed. Words came out of the fog, the wind whipping a voice around the Island. "Let me land. Let me out. Let me land. I want to come home."

9   In the middle of one night when he was the only man awake, the legal father took out his Four Valuable Things [writing brushes, ink, inkslab, and paper], and using spit and maybe tears to mix the ink, he wrote a poem on the wall, just a few words to observe his stay. He wrote about wanting freedom. He did not sign his name; he would find himself a new American name when he landed. If the U.S. government found out his thoughts on freedom, it might not let him land. The next

morning the readers sang the new poem for the others to hear. "Who wrote this wonderful poem during the night?" they asked, but the father modestly did not say.

10   For one another's entertainment, the men rehearsed and staged skits, puppet shows, and heroic parts of operas. They juggled fruit, bottles, and the new rubber ball. The father, who was traveling with the adventures of Yüeh Fei, the Patriot, in six volumes, read aloud the part where Yüeh Fei's mother carved on his back four words: FIRST – PROTECT MY NATION. He held up for all to see the illustrations of warriors in battle. He also carried the poems of Li Po, the best poet, the Heavenly Poet, the Great White Light, Venus. The father sang about a sentry stopping Li Po from entering a city. Li Po was drunk as usual and riding a mule. He refused to give his name to the sentry, but wrote a daring poem that he was a man from whose mouth the emperor had wiped the drool; the emperor's favorite wife had held his inkslab. The impressed sentry granted him entrance. This poem heartened the men; they laughed and clapped at Li Po's cleverness and the sentry's recognition of him and poetry.

11   "What is a poem exactly?" asked an illiterate man, a Gold Mountain Sojourner who had spent twenty years in America and was on his way back to his family. "Let me give it a try," he said. "A short poem: 'On the Gold Mountain, I met black men black like coal.' Is that a poem?" The literate men were delighted. "Marvelous," they said. "Of course, it's a poem." "A simile. A simile. Yes, a poem." The legal father liked it so much, he remembered it forever.

12   The legal father learned many people's thoughts because he wrote their letters. They told their wives and mothers how wonderful they found the Gold Mountain. "The first place I came to was The Island of Immortals," they told him to write. "The foreigners clapped at our civilized magnificence when we walked off the ship in our brocades. A fine welcome. They call us "Celestials.'" They were eating well; soon they would be sending money. Yes, a magical country. They were happy, not at all frightened. The Beautiful Nation was glorious, exactly the way they had heard it would be. "I'll be seeing you in no time." "Today we ate duck with buns and plum sauce," which was true on days when the China Men in San Francisco sent gifts.

13   Every day at intervals men were called out one by one. The legal father kept himself looking presentable. He wore his Western suit and shined shoes, constantly ready.

14   One morning the barracks awoke to find a man had hanged himself. He had done it from a railing. At first he looked as if he had been tortured, his legs cut off. He had tied his legs bent at the knees like an actor or beggar playing a man with no legs, and hung himself by pushing over his chair. His body had elongated from hanging all night. The men looked through his papers and found X's across them. When new arrivals looked for beds, nobody told them that a dead, hung man had slept in that one.

15   Also, the rumor went, a woman upstairs had killed herself by sharpening a chopstick and shoving it through her ear. Her husband had sent for her, and she did not understand why he did not come to take her home.

16   At last came the legal father's turn to be interrogated. He combed his hair again. He said his good-byes. Inside the interrogation room were several white demons in formal wear; the legal father gauged by the width of lapels and ties that his own suit was not quite stylish. Standing beside the table was a Chinese-looking soldier in American uniform and a demon soldier in the same uniform. This Chinese American was the interpreter. The legal father sat opposite the interrogators, who asked his name, his village, where he was born, his birth date — easy questions.

17   "Can you read and write?" the whie demon asked in English and the Chinese American asked in Cantonese.

18   "Yes," said the legal father.

19   But the secretary demon was already writing No since he obviously couldn't, needing a translator.

20   "When did you cut off your pigtail?" asked the translator.

21   "In 1911," said the legal father. It was a safe answer, the year he would have picked anyway, not too early before the Republic nor too late, not too revolutionary nor too reactionary. Most people had cut their hair in 1911. He might have cut it for fashion as much as for revolution.

22   "Do you have relatives who are American citizens?"

23   The janitor, a China Man, who just then entered the room with dustpan and broom, nodded.

24   "Yes."

25   "Who?"

26   "My grandfather is an American. My father is an American. So I'm an American, also my three older brothers and three uncles — all Americans."

27   Then came the trap questions about how many pigs did they own in 1919, whether the pig house was made out of bricks or straw, how many steps on the back stoop, how far to the outhouse, how to get to the market from the farm, what were the addresses of the places his grandfather and father and brothers and uncles had lived in America. The interrogators liked asking questions with numbers for answers. Numbers seemed true to them. "How many times did your grandfather return to the United States?" "Twice." "Twice?" "Yes, twice. He was here once and returned twice. He was here three times altogether. He spent half his life in America and half in China." They looked into his eyes for lies. Even the Chinese American looked into his eyes, and they repeated his answers, as if doubting them. He squelched an urge to change the answers, elaborate on them. "Do you have any money?" "Yes." "How much?" He wondered if they would charge him higher fees the more money he reported. He decided to tell the truth; lying added traps. Whether or not he spoke the truth didn't matter anyway; demons were capricious. It was up to luck now.

28   They matched his answers to the ones his relatives and fellow villagers gave. He watched the hands with yellow hair on their backs turn the copies of his grandfather's and father's papers.

29   They told him to go back to the jail, where he waited for more weeks. The next time he was called to be examined — *searched* the Chinese word — they asked again, "What American relatives do you have?"

30   "My grandfather and father," he said again, "and also my three brothers and three uncles."

31   "Your grandfather's papers are illegal," the Chinese American translated. "And your father is also an illegal alien." One by one the demons outlawed his relatives and ancestors, including a Gold Rush grandfather, who had paid a bag of gold dust to an American Citizenship Judge for papers. "There are no such things as Citizenship Judges," said the Immigration Demon and put an X across the paper that had been in the family for seventy-five years. He moved on to ask more trap questions, the directions the neighbors' houses faced and the number of water buffaloes in 1920, and sent him back to the barracks.

32   He waited again. He was examined again, and since he had an accurate memory, he told them the same number of pigs as the last two times, the same number of water buffaloes (one), the same year of cutting his queue, and at last they said, "You may enter the United States of America." He had passed the American examination; he had won America. He was not sure on what basis they let him in — his diploma, his American lineage (which may have turned out to be good after all), his ability to withstand jailing, his honesty, or the skill of his deceits.

33   This legal father then worked his way across the continent to New York, the center of America.

WHEN THE DOOR IS CLOSED TO ILLEGAL ALIENS, WHO PAYS?

Wayne A. Cornelius

1 A very predictable thing happens in this country whenever the economy takes a sharp turn for the worst: The illegal alien is rediscovered. Politicians, journalists, organized labor, and other interest groups rush to blame him for every imaginable problem afflicting American society, from high unemployment to rising crime rates, escalating social-service costs, overpopulation, and balance-of-payments deficits.

Wayne A. Cornelius, "When The Door Is Closed to Illegal Aliens, Who Pays?" *The New York Times*, June 1, 1977.

2   Immigration authorities crank out ever-more-frightening "guesstimates" of the numbers of illegal aliens "simply invading" the country. The public is warned in urgent and ominous tones that illegal aliens are out to take their jobs away and add billions of dollars to their tax bills.

3   We are now witnessing yet another "rediscovery" of the illegal alien. Pressures for new restrictive measures — particularly legislation that would impose civil or criminal penalties and fines on United States employers who "knowingly" hire illegal aliens — have mounted steadily. Such restrictive measures form the core of the policy package reportedly recommended to President Carter by his cabinet-level task force on illegal aliens, and they have been proposed repeatedly by various members of Congress.

4   The case for a more restrictive immigration policy is based on three principal assumptions: that illegal aliens compete effectively with, and replace, large numbers of American workers; that the benefits to American society resulting from the aliens' contribution of low-cost labor are exceeded by the "social costs" resulting from their presence here; and that most illegal aliens entering the United States eventually settle here permanently, thus imposing an increasingly heavy, long-term burden upon the society.

5   There is as yet no direct evidence to support any of these assumptions, at least with respect to illegal aliens from Mexico, who still constitute at least 60 to 65 percent of the total flow and more than 90 percent of the illegal aliens apprehended each year.

6   Where careful independent studies of the impact of illegal immigration on local labor markets have been made, they have found no evidence of large-scale displacement of legal resident workers by illegal aliens. Studies have also shown that Mexican illegals make amazingly little use of tax-supported social services while they are in the United States, and that the cost of the services they do use is far outweighed by their contributions to Social Security and income tax revenues.

7   There is also abundant evidence indicating that the vast majority of illegal aliens from Mexico continue to maintain a pattern of "shuttle" migration, most of them returning to Mexico after six months or less of employment in the United States. In fact, studies have shown that only a small minority of Mexican illegals even aspire to settle permanently in the United States.

8   While illegal aliens from countries other than Mexico do seem to stay longer and make more use of social services, there is still no reliable evidence that they compete effectively with American workers for desirable jobs. The typical job held by the illegal alien, regardless of nationality, would not provide the average American family with more than a subsistence standard of living. In most states, it would provide less income than welfare payments.

9   Certainly in some geographic areas, types of enterprises, and job categories, illegal aliens may depress wage levels or "take jobs away" from American workers. But there is simply no hard evidence that these effects are as widespread or as serious as most policy-makers and the general public seem to believe.

10   The notion that curtailing illegal immigration will significantly reduce unemployment among the young, the unskilled, members of minority groups, and other

sectors of the United States population allegedly being displaced by illegal aliens may prove to be a cruel illusion.

11   Many of the jobs "liberated" in this way are likely to be eliminated through mechanization or through bankruptcy of the enterprises involved, and many others cannot be "upgraded" sufficiently — even with higher wages and shorter hours — to make them attractive to native workers.

12   While the benefits of a more restrictive immigration policy to the American worker have been grossly exaggerated, the costs of such a policy to both the United States and the illegal aliens' countries of origin have been consistently under-estimated.

13   The impact of "closing the door" to illegal aliens will be felt by the American consumer, in the form of higher prices for food and many other products currently produced with alien labor. Failures among small businesses — those with 25 or fewer employees, which hire more than half of the illegal aliens from Mexico — will also increase, eliminating jobs not only for illegals but for native Americans.

14   But the adverse impact of restrictive measures will be felt most intensely in Mexico, which is currently struggling to recover from its most serious economic crisis since the 1930's. At least 20 percent of the population — and a much higher proportion of the rural poor — depend upon wages earned in the United States for a large share of their cash income.

15   An employer-sanction law that is even partly effective in denying jobs to illegal aliens is likely to produce economic dislocations and human suffering on a massive scale within Mexico. This will not be simply a problem for Mexico; the implications for United States economic and foreign policy interests are obvious.

16   All available evidence indicates that employer sanctions and other restrictive measures — short of erecting a Berlin-type wall — will fail to deter economically desperate Mexicans from seeking employment in the United States.

17   In the long run, every dollar that is spent trying to enforce new restrictive policies would be much better spent on programs to reduce the "push" factors within Mexico and other sending countries that are primarily responsible for illegal immigration: rural unemployment and underemployment, low incomes, and rapid population growth.

18   For example, studies indicate that resources invested in labor-intensive, small-scale rural industries could significantly reduce the flow of illegal aliens within five to eight years.

19   In the short run, the best approach would be an expanded program of tempor-ary worker visas permitting up to six months of employment in the United States each year. A temporary-worker program that did not require a prearranged contract between the alien worker and a particular United States employer (in contrast to the former *bracero* program of contract labor) would minimize exploitation of alien workers while reducing illegal immigration and keeping open a critically important safety value for Mexico. It would also benefit United States workers, since the use of legal alien labor is likely to have a less depressing effect on wages and working conditions than the use of illegal alien labor.

20   It is ironic that a more restrictive immigration policy is being advocated by many at a point in our history when declining birth rates, the end of unlimited legal immigration, and an American labor force with more education and higher job expectations than ever before all foreshadow a shortage of workers to fill low-skill, low-wage, low-status jobs in the United States economy. When this occurs, in the not-too-distant future, the aliens who are now viewed as a burden on United States society may be seen as a highly valuable asset.

AMERICA NEEDS FEWER IMMIGRANTS

Richard D. Lamm

1 One of the major problems in making public policy is that politicians, like von Clausewitz's generals, always tend to fight the last war. It is deceptively simple to define the future in terms of our past. Abraham Lincoln said it so well: "As our case is new, so we must think and act anew. We must disenthrall ourselves."

2   Few issues facing the United States are as important as the question of immigration and in no other issue are we so blinded by our past myths.

3   As children and grandchildren of immigrants, we have made immigration such a part of our mythology and folklore that it is immensely difficult to come to grips with the new realities that face us.

4   But history plays strange tricks on civilizations. Yesterday's solutions become today's problems. The historian Arnold Toynbee said that the same elements that build up an institution eventually lead to its downfall. When the United States was an empty frontier, it needed immigrants to people an empty continent. Those days are gone, never to return, yet the myth lingers.

5   Frontier America is gone, replaced by an America of 7.6 percent unemployment, with dramatically higher unemployment in many industries and appallingly high unemployment among youth who are minority-group members. Our increasingly scarce resources, our own severe economic problems, and our own social fabric demand a rational immigration policy.

6   Immigration is already at the highest level in our history: 808,000 legal immigrants in 1980 — including the special status given to the Cubans and Haitians. That is *twice* the number of immigrants accepted by *all* the rest of the world combined.

Richard D. Lamm, "America Needs Fewer Immigrants," *The New York Times*, July 12, 1981.

7   In addition to these legal immigrants, illegal immigration is at a high, though not a quantifiable, level. We do know that we had more than one million apprehensions of illegal immigrants in the last few years — 10 times the level of apprehensions in the early 1960's with the same level of enforcement.

8   It is usually not recognized but the nation's largest number of immigrants came not in 1911 or 1893 but in 1980. Legal and illegal immigration accounts for half the United States' population-growth rate and a rising percentage of its crime and welfare statistics.

9   When Jimmy Carter ordered the Immigration and Naturalization Service to deport Iranians who had entered this country to study and then dropped out of school, the agency had to admit it had no idea how many Iranian students were in the United States, or who or where they were.

10   Whatever the pressures are now, they will soon grow dramatically worse. The demographers tell us we will add one billion people to the world's population in the next 11 years.

11   The population of Mexico has nearly tripled since 1945 and is expected to double within the next 20 years. Mexico has a labor force of 19 million people — of whom 50 percent are unemployed or seriously underemployed. And by the year 2000, it will be 45 million. Considering the great discrepancy between per-capita income in Mexico and in this country, the pull is tremendous.

12   We have to get our hearts in line with our heads and our myths in line with reality. We know we cannot accept all the people who want to come to the United States. We know our immigration policy has to be designed in the interest of the United States.

13   We hate to say "no" to that worthy individual from the poverty-stricken country who just wants to do a little better. It seems selfish to us to set limits. The Lady in the Harbor would not understand. However, I believe dramatic reform is necessary and inevitable, and that the sooner we recognize this, the better off we will be.

14   As others have observed, every year the United States is importing a new poverty class.

15   This year, with the bipartisan cooperation of Senator Alan K. Simpson, Republican of Wyoming, and Representative Romano L. Mazzoli, Democrat of Kentucky who are chairmen of subcommittees studying immigration reform, it is possible to amend our immigration laws to achieve realistic limits on legal immigration and realistic powers to curtail illegal entry.

16   America owes its first duty to our own disadvantaged, unemployed, and poor to maintain the strength of the United States.

17   We can only meet our commitments by placing realistic limits on immigration. The Lady in the Harbor symbolizes *Liberty*, not *immigration*. We must, like Abraham Lincoln, "disenthrall ourselves" from our past myths and deal with the realities of the "stormy present" — which means not overwhelming the Lady in the Harbor with more immigrants than she can absorb.

REFUGEE SHIP

Lorna Dee Cervantes

1 like wet cornstarch
  I slide past *mi abuelita's* eyes
  bible placed by her side
  she removes her glasses
  the pudding thickens

2 *mamá* raised me with no language
  I am an orphan to my spanish name
  the words are foreign, stumbling on my tongue
  I stare at my reflection in the mirror
  brown skin, black hair

3 I feel I am a captive
  aboard the refugee ship
  a ship that will never dock
  a ship that will never dock

Lorna Dee Cervantes, "Refugee Ship," *Revista Chicano-Riqueña* 3, no. 1, Winter 1975.

V
NUCLEAR
THREATS
AND ACCIDENTS

What have we learned from the two great nuclear power plant accidents of the last decade? What does it mean to live in the nuclear age? The authors in this section address these questions from a number of different perspectives. Baron Wormser's poem, "I Try to Explain to My Children . . . " captures our sense of the coldness and impersonality of life and death in the nuclear age. Edwin Diamond studies and criticizes television coverage of the Three Mile Island accident; Mary McGrory, Daniel Egger, Alice Walker and the *Wall Street Journal* editors see nuclear accidents and their aftermaths as symptoms of larger problems in our society and culture. These articles won't present you with a complete who-what-when on the accidents, but they may expose you to information and opinions you not see elsewhere. The way you react to them should help clarify your own positions on the issues.

In this section as in section VI, Medicine, Ethics, and the Law, we see that decisions once made by technicians and specialists – how to generate necessary energy, how and how long to keep a dying patient alive – have become political, ethical, and philosophical questions. The authors in this section present a challenge to us all: Will we do the work necessary to earn a voice in the decisions that affect our lives and future, or will we leave those decisions up to experts and politicians?

AN INHERENTLY DANGEROUS TECHNOLOGY

Barry Commoner

1 The accident at Three Mile Island Nuclear Power Plant in March 1979 confirmed the view that because of its very design nuclear power is an *inherently* dangerous technology. The high and growing cost of nuclear power plants is due not so much to the difficulties associated with the technology that it has in common with non-nuclear plants – that is, the conversion of energy of steam into electricity – but rather to its unique feature, the use of fission to supply the heat needed to produce steam. The accident at Harrisburg showed that a failure in the steam-to-electrcity section of the plant that would have caused very little trouble in a conventional power plant came close to producing a catastropic disaster in the nuclear one and has shut down the plant for a long time, and possibly permanently.

Barry Commoner, "An Inherently Dangerous Technology," *from* "Solar Versus Nuclear Energy: The Politics of Choice," in *The Politics of Energy*, Knopf, 1979.

2   The Three Mile Island Power Plant produced the steam needed to drive its electric turbines in a pressurized-water reactor. In such a reactor, water is circulated through the reactor's fuel core, where — because it is under pressure — it is heated far above its normal boiling point by the heat generated by the fission reaction. The superheated water flows through the reactor's "primary loop" into a heat exchanger where it brings water, which circulates in a "secondary loop," to the boiling point, and the resulting steam flows into the turbine to generate electricity. The spent steam is recondensed and pumped back to the heat exchanger, where it is again converted to steam, and so on. A third loop of cooling water is used to condense the steam, carrying off the excess heat to a cooling tower where it is finally released into the air. This arrangement is much more complex than the design of a conventional power system, where the steam generated in the boiler passes directly into the turbine. In this type of nuclear plant the water that circulates through the reactor (which is equivalent to the boiler in a conventional plant) becomes intensely radioactive, and the complex successive circulation loops are essential to keep that radioactivity from leaving the reactor.

3   On March 28, 1979, at 3:53 a.m., a pump at the Harrisburg plant failed. Because the pump failed, the reactor's heat was not drawn off in the heat exchanger and the very hot water in the primary loop overheated. The pressure in the loop increased, opening a release valve that was supposed to counteract such an event. But the valve stuck open and the primary loop system lost so much water (which ended up as a highly radioactive pool, six feet deep, on the floor of the reactor building) that it was unable to carry off all the heat generated within the reactor core. Under these circumstances, the intense heat held within the reactor could, in theory, melt its fuel rods, and the resulting "meltdown" could then carry a hugely radioactive mass through the floor of the reactor. The reactor's emergency cooling system, which is designed to prevent this disaster, was then automatically activated; but when it was, apparently, turned off too soon, some of the fuel rods overheated. This produced a bubble of hydrogen gas at the top of the reactor. (The hydrogen is dissolved in the water in order to react with oxygen that is produced when the intense reactor radiation splits water molecules into their atomic constituents. When heated, the dissolved hydrogen bubbles out of the solution.) This bubble blocked the flow of cooling water so that despite the action of the emergency cooling system the reactor core was again in danger of melting down. Another danger was that the gas might contain enough oxygen to cause an explosion that could rupture the huge containers that surround the reactor and release a deadly cloud of radioactive material into the surrounding countryside. Working desperately, technicians were able to gradually reduce the size of the gas bubble using a special apparatus brought in from the atomic laboratory at Oak Ridge, Tennessee, and the danger of a catastrophic release of radioactive materials subsided. But the sealed-off plant was now so radioactive that no one could enter it for many months — or, according to some observers, for years — without being exposed to a lethal dose of radiation.

4   Some radioactive gases did escape from the plant, prompting the Governor of Pennsylvania, Richard Thornburgh, to ask that pregnant women and children leave the area five miles around the plant. Many other people decided to leave as well,

and within a week 60,000 or more residents had left the area, drawing money from their banks and leaving state offices and a local hospital shorthanded.

5   Like the horseshoe nail that lost a kingdom, the failure of a pump at the Three Mile Island Nuclear Power Plant may have lost the entire industry. It dramatized the vulnerability of the complex system that is embodied in the elaborate technology of nuclear power. In that design, the normally benign and easily controlled process of producing steam to drive an electric generator turned into a trigger for a radioactive catastrophe.

6   Even if it is ever possible to resolve these troubles, the nuclear power industry, in its present configuration, cannot support the transition to a renewable energy system. Present (light-water) reactors are fueled with natural uranium, and can operate only as long as this fuel is available at some reasonable cost. But natural uranium is a nonrenewable fuel and recent estimates indicate that if present plans for the development of nuclear power were carried out, useful uranium supplies would be exhausted, both in the U.S. and in the world, in about twenty-five to thirty years. Nuclear power can sustain a renewable energy system capable of solving the energy crisis only if it is based on breeder reactors, in which the nuclear reaction is so arranged as to produce new fuel as the reactor generates power. If the planned-for U.S. nuclear power system is based on breeders, the supply of fuel will be enough to support appreciable nuclear power production for perhaps 1,500 to 2,000 years. But before that can happen, nuclear power will need to survive the growing challenge to both its economic and its political viability.

TWELVE DAYS OF TERROR! THE THREE MILE ISLAND STORY
Edwin Diamond

1 Press coverage of the Three Mile Island nuclear accident began offhandedly Wednesday morning, March 28, 1979, when the managing editor of the *Waynesboro* (Pennsylvania) *Record Herald* passed on to the Associated Press news service a tip that central Pennsylvania state police had been put on alert in the Harrisburg area. By the time the crisis ended, two weeks later, anchorman Walter Cronkite on CBS News would talk of "12 days of terror." The press coverage of that period was anything but casual; rather the manner in which the accident at the nuclear plant at Three Mile Island, Pennsylvania, was reported by all the media, and particularly by television, had become an issue in itself.

2   In any story different actors have different agendas and different messages to convey. This was true of the events at Three Mile Island, a nuclear power plant licensed by the federal government and operated by the Metropolitan Edison Company of Pennsylvania. There were at least three sources of messages: the press, the electric company, and the government. The press grew progressively dissatisfied with the messages of the other two, and they, in turn, grew critical of the press. By

Edwin Diamond, "Twelve Days of Terror! The Three Mile Island Story," *Sign Off: The Last Days of Television*, MIT, 1982.

the end of the crisis, the White House was spreading the word around Washington that President Carter thought the news accounts of Three Mile Island were outrageous, exaggerated, irresponsible. One distinguished nuclear scientist told me that the television coverage had been pronuclear; another equally distinguished nuclear scientist told me that it had been antinuclear. Most television viewers — ordinary people and presidents and physicists alike — tend to approve of materials that confirm their own judgments or prejudices and to disapprove of contrary information. The scientist who thought television's coverage was proindustry opposes nuclear power; the scientist who thought television was anti-industry favors it. Enough disagreement existed about what television did, and did not, show and tell viewers that our News Study Group decided to examine precisely what appeared on the three networks, from the first news tip to the final reactor shutdown. We found at Three Mile Island that

1. Television news moved with admirable responsibility initially, to the point of being cautious and slow to report developments.

2. Television news reported carefully both industry and government accounts from within the plant, though with a growing suspicion that the full story was not told.

3. Television news eventually proved to be unprepared, or unwilling, to put together the specialized analysis and detailed explanation needed to clarify the whole story; at times, in fact, it avoided promising, but risky, reporting leads in favor of more conventional, and safer, converage.

3   To back up these conclusions with specifics, we found it helpful to organize the Three Mile Island coverage into three phases.

First Alarm

4 Most news organizations had no trouble recognizing a major story in the making on March 28, and each network quickly dispatched reporters to the Three Mile Island plant, or more accurately, to the plant gates, since the state troopers were barring access to the plant itself. On Wednesday night, March 28, each network devoted a long (by network news standards) lead story to Three Mile Island. The ABC *World News Tonight* in particular was evenhanded, noncommittal. Anchorman Frank Reynolds began:

> Good evening. For many years there has been a vigorous debate in this country about the safety of the nation's 72 nuclear-energy power plants. That debate is likely to be intensified because of what happened early this morning at a nuclear-power plant in Pennsylvania.

5   On the *NBC Nightly News*, John Chancellor was also low-key. The cooling system in the nuclear-power plant had broken down, he said, but went on to stress that there was "no danger to people outside" and that the plant was shut down. Then followed reassuring reports quoting Jack Herbein, vice president for power

generation at Metropolitan Edison, as well as some state officials and Met Ed workers. Next NBC's Carole Simpson introduced some material from the Critical Mass Energy Project, a group she described as "opposed to nuclear energy." The Critical Mass spokesperson maintained that the Three Mile Island plant had been plagued with safety problems since its opening a year ago.

6   The *CBS Evening News* coverage the first night was noteworthy because there was considerable reworking of the opening words of Walter Cronkite at the beginning of the program. This is the lead, the headline, and broadcast journalists take care to strike the right tone. After what one CBS executive remembers as three or four rewrites to get the right tone, America's premiere broadcaster said to 16 million viewers tuned to the top-rated evening newscast:

> Good evening. It was the first step in a nuclear nightmare; as far as we know this hour, no worse than that. But a government official said that a breakdown in an atomic-power plant in Pennsylvania today is probably the worst nuclear accident to date. There was no apparent serious contamination of workers. But a nuclear-safety group said that radiation inside the plant is at eight times the deadly level; so strong that after passing through a three-foot-thick concrete wall, it can be measured a mile away."

7   Cronkite later in his report brought up the motion picture, *The China Syndrome*, mentioning "the current movie about a near-catastrophic nuclear meltdown" and assuring viewers that plant officials had assured the public that wasn't the situation.

8   The network reporters on the scene then offered cautious, factual accounts, but at the same time distanced themselves — sensibly, it turned out — from the story by carefully attributing the statements to officials of one sort or another. Thus Bettina Gregory on ABC said:

> . . . The NRC (Nuclear Regulatory Commission) said, "There's a hell of a lot of radiation in the reactor building . . . and [some] was detected as far as one mile away." Officials of Metropolitan Edison conceded that some workers may have been contamined, but they insisted this was not a serious accident. They said only one-tenth the amount of radiation needed for a general alarm escaped.

And with equal care, Gary Shepard of CBS News reported:

> Officials from Metropolitan Edison Company, which operates the plant, attempted to minimize the seriousness of the accident, saying the public was never in danger.

Then followed a tape of Met Ed's Herbein, who said:

> We may have some minor fuel damage, but we don't believe at this point that it's extensive . . . . We're monitoring for — for airborne contamination. The amount that we found is minimal. Very small traces of radioactivity have been released from the plant.

9 The impression the television viewer got was clear: the system had worked. As Max Robinson said on ABC News, "The plant did just what it was supposed to do, shut itself off, but not before some radioactivity escaped." Most viewers, it's fair to conclude, went to bed with little thought about Three Mile Island. When they got up the next morning, March 29, and turned on NBC's *Today Show*, they first heard a soothing reference to the malfunction at Three Mile Island, followed by Walter Creitz of Met Ed talking of the unparalleled safety record of the civilian nuclear-power industry.

10 That night Three Mile Island again was the lead story on the three network newscasts. The tone on NBC was reassuring: John Chancellor reported that the reactor was hot but normal, the system was operating. On ABC the nuclear mal-function had been moved up on the scale of seriousness to a nuclear accident. Still, ABC reported, the situation was serious but not dangerous. There was a general feeling of postmortem in the newscasts; what remained was for Met Ed to accomplish the complete cold shutdown of the reactor, to begin its extensive cleanup effort and — the thrust of the story now — the long inevitable investigations to find out what had happened. Walter Cronkite seemed to put Three Mile Island in the past tense, and as a mishap at that:

> Good evening. The questions still pour in about the nuclear accident . . . . More than 24 hours after the mishap, there is more heat than light in the confusion surrounding the incident. Critics charge "cover-up" . . . even as an industry spokesman says, "The system worked . . . . "

11 On the other networks, people stories replaced the reactor as the focus. Reporters interviewed area residents concerned about radiation as well as members of Congress who had heard from people concerned about the causes of the accident. NBC's David Brinkley described members of Congress as agitated. ABC was the most people oriented of the network news organizations; its reporters went across the road from the plant to a neat row of surburban homes for comment from a resident. By Friday morning, March 30, the *Today Show* was reporting that the danger was minimal.

12 Less than two hours later, the calm was broken. An NBC *News Update* — one of its thirty-second newsbreaks between programs — informed viewers that more radiation had been released into the atmosphere around the plant. Four hours after that, another NBC *News Update* carried word that Pennsylvania Governor Richard Thornburgh had asked for the evacuation of all pregnant women and preschool children within five miles of the plant. The story was building from low-key to high voltage.

13 The network news that Friday night jolted viewers. Each network devoted well over half of its broadcast to Three Mile Island. Frank Reynolds opened on ABC with these words:

> Good evening. The news from the Harrisburg, Pa., nuclear-energy plant is much more serious tonight. For the first time today an official of the Nuclear Regulatory Commission said there is the possibility, though not

yet the probability, of what is called a meltdown of the reactor core. That would be, in plain language, a catastrophe.

14   Walter Cronkite was even more chilling:

> We are faced with the remote but very real possibility of a nuclear melt-down at the Three Mile Island atomic-power plant. The danger faced by man for tampering with natural forces, a theme familiar from the myths of Prometheus to the story of Frankenstein, moved closer to fact from fancy through the day.

15   A young journalist I know, a New York City resident, would vividly remember the effect of Cronkite's words on her. Upset by the ominous bulletins and updates during the day, she recalls, she had hurried home to tune into CBS. After all, she thought, the calming voice of Walter Cronkite had helped us all through earlier national traumas — riots, assassinations, astronauts in tricky orbital maneuvers. He would get events in perspective. But Cronkite, she recalled, scared her more than the earlier bulletins had.

Trouble at the Source

16 With hindsight, we can see that Cronkite and CBS, along with other news organizations, were mainly reacting to the information presented by state, federal, and company officials. As these officials lost their self-assurance, television reflected this. When these officials began contradicting one another, the news began to sound contradictory. That led to confusion among the media audience. Deplorable as this might be for the formation of public opinion, it was minor compared to another area of confusion — the events taking place inside the Three Mile Island Plant. Underexperienced technicians had misread valves and contributed to the original reactor troubles, and further errors were hampering the search for corrective measures, or so we all were to learn later.

17   For example, a key clue to the damage that occurred early on Wednesday (day one) inside the reactor core was handed to operators early that afternoon. A pressure spike was clearly traced on a recorder sheet. But no one looked at the sheet until Friday, after two full days of consistent underreporting of the amount of core damage. The oversight, an NRC official later explained, may have been due to what he called the hassle factor in the control room — noise, flashing lights, people getting in one another's way.

18   In most catastrophes there is a dominant element of what might be called honest confusion. Because of it, no one needs to erect elaborate conspiracy theories to account for what is reported. In the case of Three Mile Island, we saw twin delusions develop: the initial underestimation of the mishap and the subsequent overestimation of the possibilities (what games theory people call worst-case analysis). On Friday, the day of the specter of meltdown, Joseph Hendrie, the NRC chairman, complained that he and Pennsylvania Governor Thornburgh didn't know what was going on. The governor's information, Hendrie said, was ambiguous, and

Hendrie admitted that his own information was nonexistent. These two officials, responsible for the safety of millions of Pennsylvanians, Hendrie concluded, were "like a couple of blind men staggering around making decisions." It was an apt image. Looking at the coverage, we can see that the press was dragged along as the third blind and staggering man.

The Unfilled Picture

19 Television news has the power to convey feelings, impressions, auras. In the case of Three Mile Island television first gave the feeling of nothing more than alert; next came the sense of reassurance, and then the evocation of danger. In this respect television did approximately reflect the reality of the Three Mile Island events. That is why different people saw different things. There was something to please, or displease, everybody. Television at its best should do more than hold a mirror to events. The record of the coverage of Three Mile Island shows that there were efforts to do more than repeat the official line of the moment. There were attempts by television journalists to speak in their own voices. Unfortunately, television news begins to falter when it tries analysis. Explanations, at least in the case of Three Mile Island, went by too fast, graphics were too careless, scripts radiated tabloid-think, with words too urgent — lethal, massive, dreaded, nightmarish; or too bland — mishap, malfunction.

20   Later that Friday night each network had the opportunity in special reports to give the necessary time and thought to the possibility of meltdown. How each responded reveals something about network news organizations and about television news in general. CBS News chose to do a one-hour report, immediately setting itself apart from the thirty-minute reports of ABC and NBC. On almost all counts, the CBS special report was better than the other two. Walter Cronkite and correspondent Steve Young had time to explain clearly the situation inside the reactor as of Friday. Mitchell Krauss had time to look at past nuclear-power plant accidents. Robert Schakne, who emerged as perhaps the most informed correspondent during the week, had time to raise the key question of acceptable risk-taking in the development of nuclear power.

21   The shorter ABC and NBC reports suffered by contrast. ABC's was wide but not very deep, a report touching on Three Mile Island, other reactors, the White House, Congress. On NBC John Chancellor was a model of judiciousness: he refused to scare anyone. Calmly, professorially, he showed a drawing of the plant. Chancellor achieved the best tone for television, noting the contradictions and misstatements and saying, "In terms of information, this thing is a mess . . . . " It was a good insight, and could have been used as a lead-in to an analysis of the efforts to control information at Three Mile Island. Instead it was Chancellor's sign-off. NBC opened the door but did not walk in.

22   Detailed explanations of any kind, whether about nuclear reactors or nuclear politics, appear to tax television's resources. So it was with Three Mile Island. Just as Met Ed's technicians seemed ill-prepared for their trip into the unknowns of an exposed reactor, so too did television's generalists seem over their heads in this

particular assignment. This leads to a question often put to news organizations: why not hire specialists who are at ease with scientific disciplines? The usual answer is that television can't employ full-time chemist-correspondents or physicist-correspondents or geneticist-correspondents. Where would it end? But the coverage of Three Mile Island showed the advantages of arranging for expert consultants to help out the television producers and writers. CBS News, for example, arranged for George Rathjens, one of the nation's most knowledgeable nuclear specialists, to be available for telephone consultations. Because he had no special hard line to push — he's prosafety *and* pronuclear — he helped sort out some of the confusion for CBS.

23   Three Mile Island also raised questions that had nothing to do with technical matters. The story had political and economic meanings that required analysis and explanation. For example, the push for nuclear power largely comes from the manufacturers of the equipment rather than from the utilities operators like Met Ed. An explanation of this in terms of jobs, investments, and political influence would have helped. Yet in these nontechnical, politically sophisticated areas, where the networks are supposed to be at ease, they proved to be relatively sluggish in their coverage.

24   Television was also much too diffident about looking into the causes of the accident. It didn't put authority's feet to the fire. Were there financial incentives involved in getting Three Mile Island's unit two on line before the end of calendar year 1978? Did safety get shortchanged as a result? According to a passing reference in *Time* magazine, Met Ed qualified for tax investment credits and deductions of around $40 million by meeting the year-end deadline. That aspect of the story needed development. But even when CBS News took an unhurried look back at the story in May ("Fallout from Three Mile Island"), it was remarkably gentle on the plant operators and remarkably reluctant to recreate what went on inside the plant.

25   The accident at Three Mile Island, when the record is reviewed, proved to be a triple test of competence. It tested the abilty of industry to build and operate safe, efficient nuclear plants; it tested the ability of government agencies to regulate these plants in the public interest, and it tested the ability of the press to cover complex stories in a clear, coherent, nonpanicky voice. With the benefit of critic's hindsight it is possible to see that industry, government, and press didn't quite measure up. The three institutions that should be helping the public — and the public's elected representatives — determine the future of nuclear power in the United States needed help themselves. All the bad habits the news institution has built up — overreliance on authority, grabbers, lack of memory, preoccupation with style at the expense of content — came into play at Three Mile Island. Because we've seen them so often in our other cases studies, we know the Three Mile Island coverage was no accident.

THE LESSON OF CHERNOBYL

1 Details of the Chernobyl nuclear accident have been pouring out of an international symposium in Vienna this week. Read with any discrimination, the bottom line is that no such accident is likely here. It happened, indeed, only because Soviet power reactors are designed also to produce plutonium for nuclear weapons.

2   The April 26 accident took at least 31 lives and spread radiation over a wide area. Headlines from the Vienna meeting focused on estimates of future cancer deaths from the radiation — 6,500 according to the Russians, 45,000 according to the Natural Resources Defense Council, and 24,000 according to experts at the International Atomic Energy Agency. The last figure, predicted over the next 70 years, represents a third of 1% increase in the cancer death rate in the Western part of the Soviet Union.

3   All of these figures, of course, are merely statistical extrapolations. Scientists are not especially confident of their ability to predict the cancers arising from low radiation levels, and doctors will be unable ever to say which cancers were the ones caused by Chernobyl. All other forms of energy also involve fatal accidents. For that matter, while scientists debated in Vienna, some 1,500 people were poisoned overnight by a volcanic eruption in Cameroon.

4   More important, Western scientists are now showing that the Chernobyl reactor design was inherently dangerous. They have rebutted Soviet claims that the disaster was primarily due to "silly actions" by the plant's operators. As a British expert put it, "You can make any design safe by having clever operators, but the designers of Chernobyl gave the operators too difficult a task."

5   The British government warned the Soviet Union nine years ago that the design of its graphite reactors had "serious defects," but the Russians didn't take sufficient remedial action. "We are not talking about hindsight here," said Lord Walter Marshall, the head of Britain's power industry. "This was a judgment made in advance." The Soviet design was "so unsatisfactory," Lord Marshall said, that in the West it would "have no chance to get a license."

6   Nuclear power plants in the U.S. and most other Western nations have reinforced concrete containment buildings to withstand a large explosion. Refueling is done only when the reactors are shut off. The reactors run at relatively low temperatures so that in case of a coolant loss, the fission reaction stops and the core is flooded.

7   By contrast, Soviet reactors are built like fireworks factories. They have thick walls around the core to protect workers against heat and radiation. But the reactors are covered by only an industrial-type roof. An explosion simply blows the top off, channeling the blast and debris upward into the atmosphere. That's precisely what happened at Chernobyl.

8   The primary reason for this design is that the 20 Soviet graphite reactors are intended to produce weapons-grade plutonium as well as electricity. This decision,

---

"The Lesson of Chernobyl," *The Wall Street Journal*, August 28, 1986.

made in the mid-1950s, effectively ruled out the sturdy containment and other safety measures of U.S. nuclear power plants.

9   In particular, the Soviet reactors are built for continuous, on-line refueling to provide the greatest output of plutonium. A machine is always shuttling across the top of the core, removing and replacing fuel rods among the 1,700 channels even while the reactor is operating. The size of the refueling system and the need for constant access to the core make the construction of a large steel and concrete containment building impractical, if not physically impossible.

10   Similarly, to increase plutonium production, these plants operate on a dangerous reactivity principle. As the reactor's temperature rises, fission activity increases. When coolant is lost, as happened on April 26, the reactor critically overheats, which can lead to an explosion. In addition, the Soviet graphite cores run "very, very hot, hotter than the fuel itself," said Lord Marshall. This presents the danger that any water leakage could cause a steam explosion.

11   U.S. power plants are especially designed not to produce plutonium in any large quantities. The Eisenhower administration purposely decided in the 1950s to separate civilian nuclear power from military plutonium production. All of these factors make for fundamental differences in safety-consciousness between U.S. and Soviet nuclear power planners.

12   The Chernobyl disaster clearly defines how much emphasis U.S. and other Western nuclear plant designers have placed on public health and safety. In the end, the underlying cause of the Chernobyl accident was pressure for ever greater Soviet military expansion, even at a risk to Russia's own people.

THE REAL LESSONS OF CHERNOBYL

Mary McGrory

1 Some people profess to see a silver lining in the dark cloud that rose over the crippled Soviet nuclear plant at Chernobyl. They say that the Soviet people are at last conscious of the dangers of nuclear power and will question the cavalier attitude of the authorities towards safety.

2   And if they do? Richard Pipes, Harvard history professor and former Reagan national security aide, speaking at a birthday party for dissenter Andrei Sakharov, recounted the story of a group of Soviet workers who, prior to the accident, warned of the hazards and abuses at the plant. They were promptly arrested and clapped off to the psychiatric wards for brutal cure of their "un-Soviet" attitudes.

3   It seems highly unlikely that Soviet citizens might take to the streets in protest as the funeral processions of the radiation sickness victims wind endlessly through their cities in the months and years to come.

4   The Soviet citizens have no recourse at the ballot box. Dissidents, as we all know, are simply punished, and banished. Public opinion is not a factor in Soviet

Mary McGrory, "The Real Lessons of Chernobyl," *The Washington Post*, May 25, 1986.

politics. When Mikhail Gorbachev took to television, finally, to tell what happened at Chernobyl, he was talking more to the world rather than his own people. Had it not been for the way the wind blew that day — causing the gauges of Russia's neighbors to register high radioactivity — we might not have known about Chernobyl until months later, or maybe never.

5   If there is a silver lining to be found, it is that Americans, who can march, shout and vote, may force their government to rethink all things nuclear. They may not choose to do so. They can quite easily contemplate economic ease, an amiable president and the fact that only two major nuclear accidents have occurred in the 40 years since "atoms for peace," with no debate, became a national doctrine.

6   Will there be a new surge of demands for an end to nuclear testing, for a halt in the arms race? Or will it be just another incident that fades from the public mind as the Soviets entomb their errant plant and the Soviet victims — who have not been photographed or interviewed — sicken and die in obscurity?

7   For hard-liners, Chernobyl has already produced positive fallout. While the radiation readings, all from countries outside the Soviet Union, were still high, administration officials were crowing about the superiority of U.S. plant technology and the importance of never trusting the Russians on a nuclear arms accord. They lied about their accident, and they would lie about their stockpiles of weapons, the line went.

8   Gorbachev's television address confirmed all they knew about the lamentable system — its clumsiness, rigidity, incompetence, and the Soviets' inability to deal with disaster, or with truth.

9   For the liberals, the lesson of Chernobyl is quite different. They are taking instruction from Dr. Robert Gale, the grave, fair-haired young surgeon from Los Angeles who flew to Moscow to do bone-marrow-transplants operations on Soviet victims.

10   Dr. Gale has been on television, explaining the need for international cooperation in these matters. He refuses to cast any aspersions on the quality of Soviet medical competence or facilities. He says over and over again in effect that we are all in it together, and that no one has the medical capability to deal with affliction of this magnitude. "There's no single country that could handle this kind of disaster." He and his team, which included an Israeli expert, were able to perform only 16 operations of the countless number needed. He estimated there could be 100,000 cases of radiation sickness; he does not need to add that there is no escape, no privilege when power turns lethal.

11   What he is really telling us is that in a nuclear war there would be no hope of survival. In a nuclear exchange, there would be no planes to fly in foreign doctors, no trains to take victims from explosion site to metropolitan hospitals, no hospitals, no operating rooms, no doctors, no nurses.

12   How much of this is seeping into people's minds? How they are dealing with it? How they will express their conclusions? This is all to be discovered.

13   In one corner of the world, the Chernobyl fallout can be tracked with fair exactitude. In New Hampshire, the inhabitants are in a state of near-frenzy over

being on a list of nuclear waste dump sites. Gov. John Sununu, a technology buff, is opposed to the dump but at the same time heart-and-soul for the opening of the Seabrook nuclear plant on the coast. Considered unbeatable six months ago, Sununu now faces three Democratic opponents, all of them running on a flat-out anti-nuke platform.

14   Chernobyl is an issue in the New Hampshire campaign. Maybe the silver lining is that we will at last debate the question of nuclear power — and look at the arms race while we are about it.

WEST GERMANY POURS HOT MILK

Daniel Egger

1 Late last year the state government of Bavaria quietly facilitated the sale of 252 rail-car-loads of dried milk contaminated by fallout from Chernobyl to a West German dummy corporation that sought to sell it to unsuspecting customers in Nigeria and Egypt. The 5,000 tons of milk contained amounts of radioactive cesium 137 that were eighteen times higher than the maximum level allowed by West German law.

2   Cesium emits beta rays which accumulate in human bone, tissue and organs. It can cause leukemia and other cancers, with incubation periods as long as forty years, and can be a factor in genetic damage. By conservative estimates the number of deaths in Western Europe that will result from the Chernobyl disaster, even assuming that only food with legal levels of radiation is consumed, is around 3,000. Yet less than a year after the meltdown, Europe has returned to a business-as-usual policy with regard to food exports, although radiation has not subsided to its previous levels.

3   As it happens, the Bavarian milk shipment was prevented from leaving the country when suspicious state officials in the port of Bremen and Cologne refused to grant export permits. But the case illustrates the degree to which Western European governments have been drawn into concealing the full economic and human costs of Chernobyl, dumping contaminated food on the Third World, and how easily they have evaded accountability.

4   In an emergency meeting last May, the countries of the European Community agreed to set a ceiling on permissible levels of radiation in food. For milk products and infant formula the limit is 370 becquerels per kilogram; for all other foodstuffs it is 600 Bq/kg. (A becquerel is a minute fraction of a curie and equals the release of one radioactive particle per second.) Those levels are highly controversial, as some experts believe that 60 to 200 Bq/kg is already dangerous. But the standards apply only to imports to the Common Market from nonmember countries and were designed largely to protect the member nations from Eastern European produce. The agreement places no safety limits on exports to nonmember nations.

Daniel Egger, "West Germany Pours Hot Milk," *The Nation*, March 28, 1987.

5   To avoid antagonizing the Soviet Union and to avoid setting a precedent of international legal responsibility for nuclear accidents, no Common Market country has applied to the Soviet Union for compensation. As one legal expert for the West German government put it, "We didn't want an imbroglio with the Soviet Union. We could apply directly to the district court in Kiev, but would the United States want us to apply for compensation if it had an accident?"

6   The Bavarian initiative arose because the national government was facing elections and was anxious to mollify the powerful farmers' constituency. It chose to interpret its own Atomic Law to allow financial compensation for all crops registering more than 1,850 Bq/kg — five times the Common Market level — even though technically the law does not apply to accidents that occur in the Soviet Union. The 5,000 tons of dried milk intercepted in Bremen and Cologne were produced by the Meggle corporation in Wasserberg from milk given by Bavarian cows in May, June and July of last year. At that time, on the instruction of the Bavarian government, a Federal agency paid Meggle $2 million in compensation for the tainted milk. It was then hauled by train to an unused siding in Rosenheim. Shortly afterward the Bavarian Farmers' Union measured radiation as high as 8,000 Bq/kg in some samples, and recent measurements still show the powder giving off 7,000 Bq/kg.

7   On the advice of experts at the University of Munich, Meggle arranged with the Stetten salt mine in Baden-Württemberg to entomb the milk. But last fall the mine's manager refused to go through with the deal. In November the Bavarian government tried to persuade a private incinerating firm to destroy the milk but was turned down. With precious time passing, Meggle and the Bavarian government had a common goal: to make the milk disappear any way they could.

8   So Meggle then "sold" the milk powder to the Lopex Engineering corporation for the token price of $25 a ton. No money changed hands. Lopex went bankrupt almost two years ago and is still in arrears to the West German government for more than $45,000 in taxes. Its owners have vanished. It has no assets and no address. The plan was for Lopex to dispose of the milk on unsuspecting buyers, take a cut of the profit and hand over the rest to Meggle.

9   Armin Weiss, a representative of the Green Party in the Bavarian Parliament, summed up the government's role: "Under the Atomic Law compensation is paid only when the products are either destroyed or seized by the government. Yet in this case the Bavarian state government hinted that although the firm was compensated, the government would not actually make any move against Meggle's proprietary rights over the milk." Caught red-handed, the Bavarian government has nevertheless maintained that the transaction was perfectly legal. Bavarian Minister for the Environment Alfred Dick — a kind of German James Watt — asserted, "The sale of the milk powder from one private concern to another does not require any kind of government response."

10   After Bremen and Cologne refused to accept the milk and Bavaria declined to take it back, the Federal authorities stepped in. The 252 railcars now sit behind barbed wire on a military base in Rosenheim, too hot to handle. Incinerating companies approached by the Federal government have refused to burn even a trial sack or two, quite rightly saying that incineration would only concentrate the

radiation, some of which would be bound to escape up chimneys. But another haunting question remains to be answered: What has happened to the rest of the milk produced by Meggle and other companies in Bavaria since May? Claims that contamination is no longer a problem have proved false. In February, Meggle applied for compensation for an additional 2,000 tons of highly radioactive powder made from milk produced in the last two months of 1986, even though they planned to dilute and resell it. Hans Kolo, a Social Democratic Party member on the Bavarian parliament's Environmental Committee, characterized that procedure as probable criminal fraud involving the Bavarian government as well as Meggle.

11   The Bavarian Green Party claims that in an average year 15,000 tons of dried milk are produced in the state between May and January. Therefore, approximately 8,000 tons from 1986 remain unaccounted for. Presumably they have reached foreign markets. Opposition party investigators on the trail of the lost milk say they have evidence that it made its way to Egypt, where it was sold without being identified.

12   West Germany is not alone in trying to suppress the true costs of Chernobyl. On January 7 a Brazilian Federal court disclosed that for eight months the food Brazilians had been eating from West Germany, France, Italy and at least five other Western European countries contained levels of radioactive cesium up to ten times higher than can legally be sold in Europe. The Brazilian government embargoed 5,000 tons of dried milk and turned around ships from West Germany before they could unload. In São Paulo alone, authorities pulled seventy tons of food off grocery shelves. Teams of inspectors and doctors have been dispatched to all parts of the country to locate further stocks of dangerous food. But no one knows what levels of radiation were present in the 30,000 tons of dried milk — and countless tons of other produce, including 230,000 tons of beef from the Common Market — that Brazilians unwittingly consumed before January.

13   Until last September, Brazil's legal ceiling for imports was 1,300 Bq/kg. But Federal Judge Lauro Leitao discovered that, on average, European milk imported from May through September contained double that amount. He also found that Brazil's National Commission on Nuclear Energy, at the request of the country's Finance Minister, had quietly raised the permissible level to 3,700 Bq/kg. On January 11 the head of the consumer affairs department of the São Paulo public prosecutor's office filed suit against three government agencies involved in food imports, accusing them of violating Brazilian law by allowing contaminated produce to reach consumers.

14   Brazil's nuclear industry, which was taken over by the military in early January, the same week that the food scandal became public, has especially close ties to West Germany. It is developing its own nuclear weapons capability, thanks to technology supplied by West Germany under a 1975 agreement between Bonn and the military regime then in power in Brazil. It has also invested $5 billion in two nuclear power plants of West German design, which are being built jointly with the firm Kraftwerk Union. Just two weeks after the Chernobyl disaster, West Germany promised Brazil $5 billion in joint industrial ventures, but kept the details secret.

15   At the same time an incipient antinuclear movement has begun to irritate Brazilian authorities. One senior official in the nuclear industry, expressing concern that the two reactors remain unfinished, described Chernobyl as "manna from heaven" for antinuclear activists.

16   The shadowy trade in contaminated food is only the most dramatic aspect of a campaign by several Western European governments to conceal the costs and dangers of the Chernobyl accident. One motive dominates all others: the interest these governments have in protecting their own nuclear power industries. A full accounting of the economic costs of Chernobyl might make nuclear plants uninsurable. Even more urgent is the desire to keep the lid on domestic political opposition to nuclear power by downplaying the risks.

17   The degree of evasiveness of West European governments directly reflects the degree of their financial commitment to nuclear power. Sweden, which has vowed to phase out its nuclear program by the year 2010, made a prompt and full disclosure of local contamination by Chernobyl. The French government, which has the most ambitious program in Europe, has been the most secretive. France has forty-three plants in operation; only the United States, with ninety-three, and the Soviet Union, with fifty-one, have more. It also has nineteen plants under construction and eventually aims to supply 75 percent of its electricity needs with nuclear power. But French Electrical, the agency in charge of the country's nuclear program, is $200 billion in debt and has trouble selling already available capacity.

18   French secrecy was typified by Remy Carle, director of French Electrical, who commented, "You don't tell the frogs when you are draining the marsh." France lied about background radiation levels for a week after the Chernobyl accident, refusing to admit abnormalities, although readings showed that contamination was 400 times above normal in some places. Even without eating contaminated food, which scientists believe will account for 90 percent of post-Chernobyl radiation exposure, someone absorbing fallout on that scale will take just nine days to accumulate the maximum legal yearly dose of a nuclear industry worker. Because of the government's secrecy there were instances of people picking and eating vegetables in France within sight of West German fields that had been condemned.

19   Antinuclear sentiment in Western Europe is running high. In West Germany, with nineteen plants on-line and six nearing completion, a May 1986 poll showed that 69 percent of respondents oppose the building of any further plants, and 54 percent favor phasing out existing facilities. The government is hoping to buy off the public with false assurances. Chancellor Helmut Kohl explicitly spelled out the common interests of the Soviet Union and the European nuclear industry when he wrote to General Secretary Mikhail Gorbachev immediately after Chernobyl to propose a global conference for the continued development of "safe" nuclear energy. Western governments remain so committed to a nuclear future that they are willing to lie to their own people, break their own laws and make the Third World pay for the Soviet Union's mistakes.

NUCLEAR MADNESS: WHAT YOU CAN DO

Alice Walker

1 *Nuclear Madness* is a book you should read immediately. Before brushing your teeth. Before making love. Before lunch. Its author is Helen Caldicott (with the assistance of Nancy Herrington and Nahum Stiskin), a native Australian, pediatrician, and mother of three children. It is a short, serious book about the probability of nuclear catastrophe in our lifetime, eminently thoughtful, readable, and chilling, as a book written for nuclear nonexperts, as almost all Americans are, would have to be.

2 Caldicott was six years old when the atomic bomb was dropped on Hiroshima, and calls herself a child of the atomic age. She grew up, as many of us did, under the threat of nuclear war. She recalls the fifties, when students were taught to dive under their desks at the sound of the air-raid siren and Americans by the thousands built underground fallout shelters.

3 During the sixties, political assassinations, the Civil Rights Movement, and the Vietnam War turned many people away from concern about atomic weapons and toward problems they felt they could do something about. However, as Caldicott states, the Pentagon continued resolutely on its former course, making bigger and "better" bombs every year.

4 Sometime during the sixties Robert McNamara, then Secretary of Defense, said that between the United States and the Soviet Union there already existed some four hundred nuclear bombs, enough to kill millions of people on both sides, a viable "deterrent," in his opinion, to nuclear war. The Pentagon and the Kremlin, however, apparently assumed this was not enough, and so today between the two "superpowers" there are some *fifty thousand* bombs.

5 What this means is that the U.S. and the U.S.S.R. literally have more bombs than they know what to do with: so they have targeted every city in the Northern Hemisphere with a population of at least twenty-five thousand with the number of bombs formerly set aside to wipe out whole countries. So even as you squeeze out your toothpaste, kiss your lover's face, or bite into a turkey sandwich, you are on the superpowers' nuclear hit list, a hit list made up by people who have historically been unable to refrain from showing off every new and shameful horror that they make.

6 For several years Caldicott has been on leave from her work at the Harvard Medical Center, and spends all her time practicing what she calls "preventative medicine," traveling across the Earth attempting to make people aware of the dangers we face. Like most medicine, hers is bitter, but less bitter, she believes, than watching helplessly while her child patients suffer and die from cancer and genetic diseases that are directly caused by the chemical pollutants inevitably created in the production of nuclear energy.

Alice Walker, "Nuclear Madness: What You Can Do," *In Search of Our Mothers' Gardens*, Harcourt, Brace, Jovanovich, 1983.

7   The nuclear industry, powerful, profit-oriented, totally unconcerned about our health, aided and abetted by a government that is its twin, is murdering us and our children every day. And it is up to us, each one of us, to stop it. In the event of a nuclear war all life on the planet will face extinction, certainly human beings. But even if there is no war we will face the same end — unless we put an end to the nuclear-power industry itself — only it will be somewhat slower in coming, as the air, the water, and the soil become too poisoned from nuclear waste (for which there is no known safe disposal) to support life.

8   What can we do? Like Caldicott, but even more so, I do not believe we should waste any time looking for help from our legal system. Nor do I have faith in politicians, scientists, or "experts." I have great faith, however, in individual people: you with the toothbrush, you in the sack, and you there not letting any of this shit get between you and that turkey sandwich. If it comes down to it, I know one of us *individuals* (just think of Watergate) may have to tackle the killer who's running to push the catastrophe button, and I even hope said tackle will explain why so many of us are excellent football players. (Just as I hope *something* will soon illustrate for us what our brothers learned of protecting life in Vietnam.)

9   As individuals we must join others. No time to quibble about survival being "a white issue." No time to claim you don't live here, too. Massive demonstrations are vital. Massive civil disobedience. And, in fact, massive anything that's necessary to save our lives.

10   Talk with your family; organize your friends. Educate anybody you can get your mouth on. Raise money. Support those who go to jail. Write letters to those senators and congressmen who are making it easy for the nuclear-power industry to kill us: tell them if they don't change, "cullud" are going to invade their fallout shelters. In any case, this is the big one. We must save Earth, and relieve those who would destroy it of the power to do so. Join up with folks you don't even like, if you have to, so that we may all live to fight each other again.

11   But first, read Caldicott's book, and remember: the good news may be that Nature is phasing out the white man, but the bad news is that's who She thinks we all are.

1982

I TRY TO EXPLAIN TO MY CHILDREN A NEWSPAPER ARTICLE WHICH SAYS THAT ACCORDING TO A COMPUTER A NUCLEAR WAR IS LIKELY TO OCCUR IN THE NEXT TWENTY YEARS

Baron Wormser

1 Death (I say) used to have
  Two faces — one good, one bad.
  The good death didn't like to do it,
  Kill people, dogs, insects, flowers,

Baron Wormser, "I Try to Explain to My Children . . . ," *Poetry,* March 1984.

But had to do it. It was his duty.
He would rather have been playing cards.
Without him the earth would get too crowded,
The soil would become tired, feuds would
Overtake love. That was what death
Believed — and when we thought about it
We agreed.

2   The bad death was a bully.
He would kill angels if he could.
He settled for children, poets,
All flesh increased by spirit.
He bragged and made bets and said
Disparaging things about the human race.
People made his job easy, he said.
They were full of a confusion that
Soon became hatred. He would shake
His head in wonder, but he understood.
The nations of the world offered him
Their love.

3   The new death doesn't
Have a face. He will kill us but
In the meantime he wants to kill life too.
He is calm, devoted, gradual.
He is crazy. The other two deaths
Do not like him, the way he wears
A tie as if death were an office,
The way he wants to be efficient.
Fate and fortune bore him. He has
Reasons. There cannot be enough death,
He says. You will put us out of business
The other two say, but he doesn't listen.
Things seem the same, my children, but
They aren't.

VI
MEDICINE,
ETHICS,
AND THE LAW

New advances in medicine bring us closer every day to the ability to affect radically the beginning and end of human life. Human beings can be conceived in a laboratory and carried to term by surrogate mothers. Their growth can be affected by hormones that can make them taller and may one day make them more resistant to disease. And we can keep people alive longer, even some people who beg for the mercy of death.

Because medicine is *capable* of doing so much, the question of what it *should* do has become more and more important. Medical questions are becoming legal and ethical questions. Should we let the terminally ill, suffering patient die? Should doctors tell patients the truth about how sick they are? Should we use the ability to make our children taller? And what rights does a mother have — and not have — regarding her own baby?

Faced with such questions, people will have to educate themselves about the issues and take personal stands. The educated person of the 1980s has to make choices that few could have dreamed of a half century ago. More people are questioning medical ethics, just as they are questioning the work ethic and the morality of our foreign policy. The traditional idea that human life must be preserved at all costs still prevails, but many voices are challenging it. Scientists study the medical problems of people who, exposed to man-made chemicals and radiation, have become walking guinea pigs. And every time a new carcinogen or life-extending medicine is discovered, someone has to face the toughest question: How much should we pay to avoid one case of cancer or to prolong one life?

THAT RIGHT BELONGS ONLY TO THE STATE

Mortimer Ostow, M.D.

To the Editor:

1 Nine members of the Kennedy Institute for the Study of Human Reproduction and Bioethics commented on May 18 on your May 2 editorial "Who Shall Make the Ultimate Decision?" Their assertion that it is important to establish precise criteria to guide the judgment of reasonable people cannot be faulted.

Mortimer Ostow, "That Right Belongs Only to the State," *The New York Times*, June 1, 1977.

2   I believe comment is called for, however, on your argument that vital decisions respecting life and death belong to the patient or, when he is incompetent to make them, to those who are presumed to have his best interests at heart. The members of the Kennedy Institute concur.

3   It is a basic assumption of our society that individual members possess no right to determine matters of life and death respecting other individuals, or even themselves. That right belongs only to the state. The prohibition of murder, suicide and, until recently, abortion, has rested on this assumption. The right to determine whether life-preserving efforts are to be continued or discontinued therefore belongs neither to the physician nor to the patient or his guardian, but to the state.

4   In practical terms, when such a decision is called for, the decision is to be made only by some agency or agent of the state, and it is to be made only by due process. To cede the right to the individuals involved is to license murder.

5   Aside from the philosophic argument, which not everyone will find cogent, there are two practical reasons for requiring due process in such instances. In discussion of matters of continuing or withholding life-support systems and euthanasia, the arguments usually offered relate to the best interests of the patient or to the economic cost to society. Abortion, too, is discussed in these terms. A far more important consideration, it seems to me, is what making life-and-death decisions does to the individuals who decide.

6   While most of us will doubt that having made a decision to terminate life support to a suffering relative will then incline one to commit murder, still, making such a decision does condition the unconditional respect for life, and does weaken the concept of the distinction between what is permitted and what is forbidden.

7   One can see a tendency to pass from withdrawing life support from the moribund to facilitating the death of the suffering, and from there to the neglect or even abandonment of the profoundly defective, and from there to the degradation or liquidation of any whom society might consider undesirable. The undisciplined making of life-and-death decisions tends to corrupt the individual who makes them, and corrupted individuals tend to corrupt society.

8   Second, it is not necessarily true that the individual himself has his own interests at heart. Afflicted with a painful and long-drawn-out illness, many individuals will wish for death, even when objectively there is a reasonable possibility of recovery. Permitting the patient to make the decision to die may amount to encouraging his suicide. Anyone familiar with the ambivalence which prevails in family relationships will not take it for granted that family members will necessarily represent the patient's best interests.

9   It is important for the morale and morality of our society that "the ultimate decision" be made only by a disinterested agent or agency of our society, and only by due process.

THE RIGHT TO DIE

Norman Cousins

1 The world of religion and philosophy was shocked recently when Henry P. Van Dusen and his wife ended their lives by their own hands. Dr. Van Dusen had been president of Union Theological Seminary; for more than a quarter-century he had been one of the luminous names in Protestant theology. He enjoyed world status as a spiritual leader. News of the self-inflicted death of the Van Dusens, therefore, was profoundly disturbing to all those who attach a moral stigma to suicide and regard it as a violation of God's laws.

2   Dr. Van Dusen had anticipated this reaction. He and his wife left behind a letter that may have historic significance. It was very brief, but the essential point it made is now being widely discussed by theologians and could represent the beginning of a reconsideration of traditional religious attitudes toward self-inflicted death. The letter raised a moral issue: does an individual have the obligation to go on living even when the beauty and meaning and power of life are gone?

3   Henry and Elizabeth Van Dusen had lived full lives. In recent years, they had become increasingly ill, requiring almost continual medical care. Their infirmities were worsening, and they realized they would soon become completely dependent for even the most elementary needs and functions. Under these circumstances, little dignity would have been left in life. They didn't like the idea of taking up space in a world with too many mouths and too little food. They believed it was a misuse of medical science to keep them technically alive.

4   They therefore believed they had the right to decide when to die. In making that decision, they weren't turning against life as the highest value; what they were turning against was the notion that there were no circumstances under which life should be discontinued.

5   An important aspect of human uniqueness is the power of free will. In his books and lectures, Dr. Van Dusen frequently spoke about the exercise of this uniqueness. The fact that he used his free will to prevent life from becoming a caricature of itself was completely in character. In their letter, the Van Dusens sought to convince family and friends that they were not acting solely out of despair or pain.

6   The use of free will to put an end to one's life finds no sanction in the theology to which Pitney Van Dusen was committed. Suicide symbolizes discontinuity; religion symbolizes continuity, represented at its quintessence by the concept of the immortal soul. Human logic finds it almost impossible to come to terms with the concept of nonexistence. In religion, the human mind finds a larger dimension and is relieved for the ordeal of a confrontation with nonexistence.

Norman Cousins, "The Right to Die," *Saturday Review Magazine*, 1975.

7   Even without respect to religion, the idea of suicide has been abhorrent throughout history. Some societies have imposed severe penalties on the families of suicides in the hope that the individual who sees no reason to continue his existence may be deterred by the stigma his self-destruction would inflict on loved ones. Other societies have enacted laws prohibiting suicide on the grounds that it is murder. The enforcement of such laws, of course, has been an exercise in futility.

8   Customs and attitudes, like individuals themselves, are largely shaped by the surrounding environment. In today's world, life can be prolonged by science far beyond meaning or sensibility. Under these circumstances, individuals who feel they have nothing more to give to life, or to receive from it, need not be applauded, but they can be spared our condemnation.

9   The general reaction to suicide is bound to change as people come to understand that it may be a denial, not an assertion, of moral or religious ethics to allow life to be extended without regard to decency or pride. What moral or religious purpose is celebrated by the annihilation of the human spirit in the triumphant act of keeping the body alive? Why are so many people more readily appalled by an unnatural form of dying than by an unnatural form of living?

10   "Nowadays," the Van Dusens wrote in their last letter, "it is difficult to die. We feel that this way we are taking will become more usual and acceptable as the years pass.

11   "Of course, the thought of our children and our grandchildren makes us sad, but we still feel that this is the best way and the right way to go. We are both increasingly weak and unwell and who would want to die in a nursing home?

12   "We are not afraid to die . . . . "

13   Pitney Van Dusen was admired and respected in life. He can be admired and respected in death. "Suicide," said Goethe, "is an incident in human life which, however much disputed and discussed, demands the sympathy of every man, and in every age must be dealt with anew."

14   Death is not the greatest loss in life. The greatest loss is what dies inside us while we live. The unbearable tragedy is to live without dignity or sensitivity.

TO LIE OR NOT TO LIE? – THE DOCTOR'S DILEMMA

Sissela Bok

1 Should doctors ever lie to benefit their patients – to speed recovery or to conceal the approach of death? In medicine as in law, government, and other lines of work, the requirements of honesty often seem dwarfed by greater needs: the need to shelter from brutal news or to uphold a promise of secrecy; to expose corruption or to promote the public interest.

2 What should doctors say, for example, to a forty-six-year-old man coming in for a routine physical checkup just before going on vacation with his family who, though he feels in perfect health, is found to have a form of cancer that will cause him to die within six months? Is it best to tell him the truth? If he asks, should the doctors deny that he is ill, or minimize the gravity of the prognosis? Should they at least conceal the truth until after the family vacation?

3 Doctors confront such choices often and urgently. At times, they see important reasons to lie for the patient's own sake; in their eyes, such lies differ sharply from self-serving ones.

4 Studies show that most doctors sincerely believe that the seriously ill do not want to know the truth about their condition, and that informing them risks destroying their hope, so that they may recover more slowly, or deteriorate faster, perhaps even commit suicide. As one physician wrote: "Ours is a profession which traditionally has been guided by a precept that transcends the virtue of uttering the truth for truth's sake, and that is 'as far as possible do not harm.'"

5 Armed with such a precept, a number of doctors may slip into deceptive practices that they assume will "do no harm" and may well help their patients. They may prescribe innumerable placebos, sound more encouraging than the facts warrant, and distort grave news, especially to the incurably ill and the dying.

6 But the illusory nature of the benefits such deception is meant to bestow is now coming to be documented. Studies show that, contrary to the belief of many physicians, an overwhelming majority of patients do want to be told the truth, even about grave illness, and feel betrayed when they learn that they have been misled. We are also learning that truthful information, humanely conveyed, helps patients cope with illness: helps them tolerate pain better, need less medication, and even recover faster after surgery.

7 Not only do lies not provide the "help" hoped for by advocates of benevolent deception; they invade the autonomy of patients and render them unable to make informed choices concerning their own health, including the choice of whether to *be* a patient in the first place. We are becoming increasingly aware of all that can befall patients in the course of their illness when information is denied or distorted.

Sissela Bok, "To Lie or Not to Lie? – The Doctor's Dilemma," *The New York Times*, April 18, 1978.

8   Dying patients especially — who are easiest to mislead and most often kept in the dark — can then not make decisions about the end of life: about whether or not to enter a hospital, or to have surgery; about where and with whom to spend their remaining time; about how to bring their affairs to a close and take leave.

9   Lies also do harm to those who tell them: harm to their integrity and, in the long run, to their credibility. Lies hurt their colleagues as well. The suspicion of deceit undercuts the work of the many doctors who are scrupulously honest with their patients; it contributes to the spiral of litigation and of "defensive medicine," and thus it injures, in turn, the entire medical profession.

10   Sharp conflicts are now arising. Patients are learning to press for answers. Patients' bills of rights require that they be informed about their condition and about alternatives for treatment. Many doctors go to great lengths to provide such information. Yet even in hospitals with the most eloquent bill of rights, believers in benevolent deception continue their age-old practices. Colleagues may disapprove but refrain from remonstrating. Nurses may bitterly resent having to take part, day after day, in deceiving patients, but feel powerless to take a stand.

11   There is urgent need to debate this issue openly. Not only in medicine, but in other professions as well, practitioners may find themselves repeatedly in straits where serious consequences seem avoidable only through deception. Yet the public has every reason to be wary of professional deception, for such practices are peculiarly likely to become ingrained, to spread, and to erode trust. Neither in medicine, nor in law, government, or the social sciences can there be comfort in the old saw, "What you don't know can't hurt you."

THE GROWING DANGER FROM GENE-SPLICED HORMONES

Thomas Murray

1 My son Peter is twelve, and lately the cuffs of his pants have been racing up his ankles — a sure sign that growth hormone is coursing through his body. He's on about the same growth schedule I was. By my fourteenth birthday I was already just shy of six feet, and hopeful of four or five inches more. I thought that would be enough to give me a shot at playing basketball in college. Alas, I'd reached my limit. Lacking any notable physical talents, I had to rely on guile; if you can't shoot over the guy, get him looking one way and then scurry past on the other side. (As we used to say, "Fake left, go right.") Recent happenings in genetic engineering make me wonder if something similar, albeit unintentional, is going on there: Is our attention being directed one way while what's important is slipping by on the other side?

2 At least since 1980, worries about using recombinant DNA technology to alter "human nature" have focused on gene therapy — the direct and intentional alteration of genetic material to treat disease. On June 20 of that year the general secretaries of three national organizations, for Protestants, Jews, and Catholics, wrote the President to warn: "History has shown us that there will always be those who believe it appropriate to 'correct' our mental and social structures by genetic means, so as to fit their vision of humanity. This becomes more dangerous when the basic tools to do so are finally at hand. Those who would play God will be tempted as never before."

3 Nothing garners attention as quickly as a nice little scandal; within a month of the letter, Dr. Martin Cline of UCLA provided one by experimenting on two patients with beta-zero thalassemia, a genetic condition that causes severe anemia. Cline removed some of their bone marrow, treated it with recombinant DNA containing normal hemoglobin genes, then reinserted it into the bone (after making room by killing some of the remaining marrow cells with radiation). The hope was that the treated cells would multiply and produce normal hemoglobin.

4 They didn't. Worse, Cline didn't have the approval of the UCLA committee that oversees research with human subjects. When the affair became public, the National Institutes of Health (NIH) stripped Cline of $162,000 in grant money and demanded strict supervision of his research. For those suspicious of human gene therapy, the case was proof that scientists couldn't be trusted to regulate themselves.

Thomas Murray, "The Growing Danger from Gene-Spliced Hormones, *Discover*, February 1987.

5   Since then, such work has proceeded very cautiously. A presidential commission gave its tentative blessing to gene therapy with somatic cells — those that don't pass the altered genes on to future generations. The NIH's watchdog recombinant DNA advisory committee set up a "human gene therapy subcommittee," which has suggested "points to consider" for doctors who propose to tinker with genes. Among them: whether the benefits of the treatment outweigh the risks, how to choose patients fairly, and how to publicize the results of the research. Thanks to the brouhaha over gene therapy, no great threats to humanity are likely to slip by in the near future — at least not on that side.

6   But there's another side to genetic engineering that has the power to alter us physically and socially. Rather than directly altering our genes, it can modify our bodies by supplementing the natural supply of important regulatory hormones with genetically engineered ones. A prime example is biosynthetically manufactured human growth hormone — hGH. Except for one additional amino acid — methionine (which appears to have no effect on its action) — biosynthetic hGH is identical to the hormone that promotes normal growth.

7   Produced in the pituitary gland, hGH plays a key role in determining how tall we'll become. So-called pituitary dwarfs usually lack an adequate supply of bioactive hGH. To treat them, for more than twenty years we've been harvesting pituitaries from human cadavers, each of which yields a minute quantity of hGH. Until recently the supply was barely adequate. In 1979 genetic engineers cloned the gene carrying instructions for making hGH, inserted it into a microorganism, and coaxed the bug to produce the human hormone. Just in time, it appears, because some hGH recovered from human pituitaries seems to have been contaminated with the slow virus that causes Creutzfeldt-Jakob disease (CJD), a degenerative infection of the brain. In April 1985 the Food and Drug Administration (FDA) halted the sale of natural growth hormone, and shortly thereafter approved Genentech's biosynthetic version. Since no human tissue is used in producing it, there's no danger of contamination with the CJD virus. Also, we're no longer limited by the scarcity of cadaver pituitaries, and other uses of hGH can be explored.

8   Biotechnology came to the rescue of kids deficient in growth hormone. But if hGH injections can make extremely short children a bit taller, what can it do for those who aren't dwarfs, but just shorter than average? What about the youngster who would have been only of average height? And what about the basketball player for whom a couple of inches more might mean the difference between the schoolyard and the NBA? In short (no pun intended), why not use hGH to give your child the advantages that come with being tall?

9   Years ago, at an FDA hearing, I speculated that once biosynthetic hGH was approved, people would want to use it for all sorts of non-therapeutic purposes. One member of the FDA committee told me that several parents had already asked her if they could get the drug for their kids, who weren't hGH-deficient. All, she recalled, were physicians. Rebecca Kirkland, who does clinical trials of biosyntheic hGH at the Baylor College of Medicine, recently said she's had inquiries from five parents wanting to get hGH for their normal children.

10   Why would parents want to go to such expense (treatment with biosynthetic hGH costs roughly $10,000 a year), cause their children pain (the shots hurt a bit), and risk unknown long-term side effects? Quite simply, because it's advantageous to be tall — within limits. A modest body of scientific evidence supports the commonsense observation that taller people often get the nod over their shorter counterparts, because they're perceived as more intelligent, good-looking, likable, extroverted, and attractive. Being very much taller than average is a mixed blessing, to be sure. But being a few inches above average seems to help.

11   A survey at the University of Pittsburgh in 1968 found that starting salaries for graduates varied with height: roughly $300 an inch up to six feet two inches. In a study of men whose heights had been recorded twenty-five years earlier, a graduate student at Washington University in St. Louis demonstrated a "height bonus" of approximately $400 per inch.

12   When a researcher at Eastern Michigan University presented two hypothetical job candidates to recruiters, one eight inches taller than the other, 72 per cent preferred the taller one, 27 per cent said there was no difference, and only one chose the shorter applicant. And much has been made of the fact that the taller candidate for President usually wins. Only two presidents — Madison and Benjamin Harrison — were shorter than the average American male of their eras.

13   If some parents want to give their child the edge that height seems to confer, what's wrong with that? If it's O.K. to spend $2,500 on orthodontics, to buy your kid private tennis and music lessons, or to spend $10,000 a year and up for prep school and private college, what's a few thousand bucks more to buy a couple of inches? The kid could turn out to be a klutz at tennis, have a tin ear, and major in Michelob, but taller is taller.

14   In this century, we make a strong presumption in favor of liberty. Before we interfere with the right of parents to bring up their children as they judge best, we demand strong reasons for doing so. Can we find them in the case of hGH?

15   Let me ask a skeptical question: What's the disease for which human growth hormone is the cure? Philosophers have a difficult time agreeing on the definition of disease, but most would recognize a physiological deficiency in hGH as a genuine disease, and hGH injections as a reasonable treatment. There are some kids, though, who aren't measurably deficient in hGH but who are very short. Their shortness can be a consequence of any one of numerous medical problems, or they may fall into the category of "familial short stature" — that is, short like mom or pop. Either way, can their shortness ever be a disability? A disability is a condition that interferes with the tasks of daily living. If people are so short that they qualify for the elevator riddle,* their shortness may well be a disability. Disabilities usually justify medical intervention. But what if a person isn't suffering from a disease, and isn't so short that the lack of height becomes a disability? What if it's merely a disadvantage?

---

*Why did the man always take the elevator to the sixth floor, then walk up four more flights to his apartment? Because he could only reach the button for the sixth floor.

16 Even if hGH turns out to be physiologically harmless — some experts have warned of possible effects on glucose regulation, as well as an increased risk of athero-sclerosis and high blood pressure — there may be psychological consequences to treating children with the hormone. The unmistakable message given to a child is that shortness is a grave enough problem to justify the considerable expense, inconvenience, and discomfort of hGH treatment. It's likely to increase the child's self-consciousness about height. And since children rarely grow as much with the hormone as they or their parents hope, disappointment is likely.

17   A study of hGH-deficient children and their families found that the most psychologically mature kids weren't those who grew the most but those whom parents and other adults had treated appropriately for their age rather than their size. Kids who were encouraged to pursue interests where their height wasn't a disadvantage were much happier with themselves.

18   People differ in so many ways: in intelligence, charm, quickness of hand and foot, facility with words, wit, etc. But when we put children through hGH treatments, we focus almost entirely on their height (where they don't "measure up") and ignore their other talents and abilities. Understandably, short kids receiving hGH may come to feel that they're inadequate and inferior.

19 All other things being equal, taller basketball players are more effective than shorter ones. Height is an advantage in basketball and some other sports. In almost all other realms of human endeavor, though, height bears no relationship to the ability to do a job well. But in a culture that regularly imputes desirable characteristics to tall people and undesirable ones to short ones, shortness is surely a disadvantage. (Even our language is laden with "heightisms": we look up to people we admire, look down on those we don't.)

20   Like other "isms," such as racism and sexism, heightism involves making unwarranted judgments about people based on irrelevant criteria. Does anyone believe the solution to racism is to find a drug that lightens black skin? The mind boggles at the possible biotechnological remedies for sexism. And yet those who want to give their kids hGH are proposing just this sort of technological end-run around heightism.

21   If we choose to allow hGH to be used for non-disease, non-disabling shortness, then we must make a choice. Either we let those who can afford to buy it for their children, or we make it available at public expense to all children whose parents want it.

22   Suppose we let it be sold. The children of rich parents will have one more leg up, so to speak, on their peers. You could ask, what's one more advantage in light of all the others available to people with means? But the prospect of two classes — one tall and monied, the other short and poor — is ugly and disquieting. It would allow injustice to be piled upon injustice.

23   Suppose we take the other route and provide hGH to anyone who wants it. If all parents (short and tall alike) rushed out to get hGH shots for their kids, the average height of the entire population might increase. But in all likelihood the distribution of height in the population wouldn't change much, if at all. There would

still be the taller and the shorter, and since we're doing nothing to diminish heightism, discrimination against the shorter would continue. Some people would benefit, of course — for example, the stockholders in Genentech (which holds a patent for making biosynthetic hGH) and those who produce fabrics (since everyone will be wearing bigger sizes). Meanwhile, at considerable social expense, kids would get their three shots a week with a little pain and, we hope, minimal side effects.

24   Inevitably, a few eager parents would want to regain the edge for their kids and try to get bigger doses of hGH, like those athletes who take increasing amounts of anabolic steroids in the hope of obtaining an advantage over their rivals. In both cases, individuals pursue their own interests, only to make everyone worse off.

25   Whether hGH is available just to those who can pay for it or to everyone, the results would be unfortunate. In one instance, we use biotechnology to reinforce the advantages of wealth; in the other, we incur enormous expense and unknown risks without making anyone better off. The wisest course is to restrict hGH to cases of disease and disability.

26   Although hGH may be the first biosynthetic hormone to tempt us to improve on human nature, it won't be the last. Imagine what we might do with a hormone that prompted damaged nerves to regenerate. Someone would wonder whether it would also stimulate growth in the brain. And soon we'd be trying to enlarge our brains, however misguided that might be, scientifically or morally.

27   It also occurs to me that simply by writing this article I may spur some parents to seek out growth hormone for their child of normal height. I fervently hope not. But the temptation posed by hGH, and by other fruits of biotechnology as yet unripened, will be great. And it will require all our collective common sense to use them wisely.

MOTHERHOOD IS POWERLESS

Judith Levine

1 "Surrogate parenting has been on trial," announced a gleeful Noel Keane last Tuesday at the end of the first leg of the Baby M case. "By upholding the contract, Judge Sorkow has vindicated it." Keane, director of the Infertility Center of New York and the self-styled "father" of surrogate motherhood, is only partly right. On trial in Judge Harvey Sorkow's courtroom was not only surrogate motherhood, but one defiant surrogate mother. And vindicated was not surrogate motherhood in its entirety, but Noel Keane, William Stern, and everyone who profits from the paid gestation of babies.

2   Everyone, of course, except the mothers. After excluding a good deal of testimony supporting Mary Beth Whitehead, Judge Harvey Sorkow issued an often inconsistent, sometimes vitriolic 121-page decision that upheld and enforced the contract and terminated her parental rights altogether. Stunning all but the most unabashed supporters of surrogate motherhood, he stampeded over Whitehead's constitutional rights, maligned her gratuitously, and punished her cruelly and unusually. If feminists do not make themselves heard — and fast — the biases revealed in this Bergen County courtroom will become law in many states. And surrogate mothering will be, legally, a nasty and unfair business for women.

3 The Baby M case has muddled the issues of surrogate motherhood beyond recognition. The muddle seems intrinsic to debating public policy within the forum of one idiosyncratic trial. The real people get in the way of the abstractions. Whitehead is not pure enough to make a good heroine, and her plight is too tragic for a villain's. Stern is too nice to be a bad guy, but his righteousness and genetic hubris disqualify him as a hero. Nobody, least of all Judge Sorkow, seems able to separate the merits, flaws, and errors of these individuals from those of the contracts they signed.

4   Viewed most cynically, or perhaps realistically, the judge shouldn't be expected to make that separation. His decisions, both on custody and on the contract, represent the class and sex biases of people who are likely to be judges against people who are likely to be surrogate mothers. The outcome of the case was practically built into its players and the nature of custody battles. The Sterns, middle-class professionals, got the best lawyer for the job — Gary Skoloff, whose stock in trade is skewering one parent to win a child for the other. He brought in an arsenal of evidence that the Whitehead home was plagued by alcoholism and violence and that Mary Beth was selfish and crazy, especially during crises. The Whiteheads apparently cast around at random; their attorneys, Harold Cassidy et al.,

Judith Levine, "Motherhood Is Powerless," *The Village Voice*, April 14, 1987.

stumbled through the case, hardly touching on the Sterns' fitness as parents and focusing instead on the potential harm to the Whitehead family should they lose the baby. This merely inflamed the judge, who had ruled that he would admit only evidence about the baby's best interest. Moreover, Cassidy insulted his client and ultimately undermined her case by stressing that she was "nothing" without Sara, leaving her open to attacks that she was needy and overidentified with her children.

5   The fact is, Skoloff did a "good job" and Cassidy (who, interestingly, was more intelligent out of the courtroom than in it) didn't. Even putting aside questions of the two families' finances, if I were Judge Sorkow, ruling on the evidence before me and understanding that joint custody would be unworkable, I would probably have awarded custody of Baby M to the Sterns.

6   But the judge went way beyond placing the child in a family that appears even-keeled instead of one that is allegedly troubled. He showed his contempt for Whitehead throughout the trial and in his final statement. He quoted at length the testimony of the psychologists who damned her most, even one whose qualifications he doubted. But his epithets — "impulsive," "manipulative," "exploitive" of her children, "narcissistic," "a woman without empathy" who exhibits a "fundamental inability to speak the truth" — did not add up to proof that Mary Beth Whitehead abused or neglected her child, so far the only legal justification for terminating parental rights.

7   Still, against the admonitions of Lorraine Abraham, the child's court-appointed guardian, Judge Sorkow "terminated" Mary Beth Whitehead anyway. Abraham, who recommended granting the Sterns custody, nonetheless testified that severing all contact between mother and child would be "inhuman" and "irrevocable," "so awesome a step that we cannot, in all conscience, take it."

8   Sorkow's tongue-lashing was generally regarded as excessive. One lawyer suggested that perhaps he overstated his case to ensure that the custody determination would be upheld by the appellate court. But what about the termination? To me, it looks like fury.

9   At what? The judge seems especially disturbed that Whitehead "dominates" her husband, and (he returns to this theme several times) disrespects professionals. She overrode a recommendation by her son's school authorities (!) and, of course, didn't make good on her promise to the Sterns. Equally important, *she defied the court.* Instead of handing over her baby to the police, she "eloped" with her family across state lines. Instead of bowing to her betters, this uppity woman disobeyed them all.

10 Sorkow, a man who feels deeply the pain of the infertile and keeps lollipops on his desk for children, could not muster sympathy for a powerless woman who made a tragic mistake, then turned to more and more irrational and desperate steps to try to get out of it. Instead, while congratulating the Sterns on their grace under pressure, he reveals only disgust for Whitehead's powerlessness and desperation. Indeed, he is punishing her for it. Judge Sorkow's justification for this cruelty is simple: a deal is a deal. On its face, the logic of his decision is mind-boggling: He starts out by

saying that all considerations beyond the best interest of the child are merely "commentary." But he upholds giving Stern the baby because the contract says the father gets the baby. Breach of contract, in fact, is one of Whitehead's dishonorable deeds. And because the Sterns "deserve" the baby, the contract is good. What if the mother had proven to be the better parent? Would the contract then be invalid?

11   The details of Sorkow's reasoning are equally screwy. He asserts that since surrogate arrangements were not imagined when laws governing adoption or termination of parental rights evolved, adapting them to surrogate cases would require the courts to "tortuously reason to their conclusions." But contract law, equally ignorant of these arrangements, is applicable, he says. He voids the contract's clause abrogating the surrogate's constitutionally protected option to abort her fetus, yet he implicitly abrogates her right to rear a child she bears, addressing only Stern's right to procreate. He side-steps the argument that surrogate arrangements allow the rich to pay the poor to make their babies by saying that "the *desire* to propagate the species . . . is within the souls of all men and women regardless of economic status."

12   Talk about tortuous reasoning: Harvey Sorkow appears to have had a conclusion in mind from the start. He allowed only the evidence that would support that conclusion, and when the law didn't fit, he twisted it until it did. Immediately after reading his statement, he whisked Elizabeth Stern into his chambers and performed a record-speed adoption. He knew that appellate courts almost always uphold adoption decrees — they trust that the trial judge knew the evidence and the people involved in the dispute. So he must have known that once Stern was the legal mother, Cassidy would have little chance of obtaining a stay of Whitehead's parental-rights termination.

13   But if trial courts are entrusted with the facts, appellate courts interpret the law, and Sorkow's stupid and biased ruling on the termination and the contract have good odds of being overturned. It is one of the comforts of American law that a person cannot sign her fundamental rights away. If Mary Beth Whitehead entered a contract to sell herself as a gestational slave or sell a baby against her will, no court can force her to "make good." An unconstitutional deal is not a deal.

14   Still, the Constitution is in highly political hands these days, and new laws on surrogacy are yet to be written. Proposals are proliferating around the country, many of which seem more concerned with avoiding lawsuits than protecting surrogate mothers or children. Two are circulating in New York State. The Senate bill, introduced by John Dunne and Mary Goodhue, stipulates that, upon signing the preconception agreement, a surrogate mother would surrender all parental rights. It reinforces heterosexual, profamily prejudices by allowing only married, infertile couples to enter such contracts. Assemblyman Patrick Halpin's bill, which would give the woman 20 days after birth to request custody but would prohibit pay for her services, is better, but not great.

15 While the legislators try to codify the rules of surrogate motherhood, feminists have begun to articulate their feelings and express their outrage at the proceedings in Hackensack. A petition signed by over 100 feminists denounced the expert

witnesses' standards of parental "fitness" — making the correct interpretation of a baby's whimper, for instance, or playing pattycake correctly. Such standards would disqualify all of us, the petition said; a woman doesn't have to be "perfect" to be a good mother. A group calling itself the Committee for Mary Beth Whitehead and led by Phyllis Chesler, Karen Malpede, and Kathleen Lahey has demonstrated in front of the courthouse and the Infertility Center protesting the indictment of Whitehead as a working-class person, a woman, and a mother and calling for an end to profiteering in the baby trade.

16   Beyond anger over the vilification of Mary Beth Whitehead, feminist consensus ends. But as pressure mounts to take sides, those whose sentiments can be expressed most plainly on a placard start to represent all of us: "Feminists" believe that babies belong to mothers and surrogate contracts exploit unwitting poor women, so Whitehead should get Baby M and surrogate motherhood should be outlawed.

17   I, too, have been unnerved and chastened by the Baby M debacle. I've watched the court and the media — as usual — pit woman against woman. A few weeks ago, the cover of *People* magazine pictured Mary Beth Whitehead and Elizabeth — not Bill — Stern. Whitehead, not having noticed that full-time, full-energy motherhood has gone out of vogue, has been branded as pathologically overinvolved in her children's lives. She irons her son's T-shirts and blow-dries her daughter's hair. Although she's had only four hours a week with Baby M, she's accused of crowding the baby. Elizabeth Stern, the modern woman, is too modern: She postponed pregnancy to finish her medical training, then refused to risk her health by bearing her own child. When the Whiteheads' lawyer suggested that Stern's work schedule would make her a bad mother, she decided not to put the baby in child care and to work part-time. And while I'm not surprised by the revelations of Noel Keane's quick and shoddy business practices, I am dismayed by the readiness with which most surrogate mothers are ganging up against Mary Beth. Understandably, they're threatened by her "defection"; they fear their employers will be wary of them, and, I suspect, that they may experience an unforeseen change of heart too.

18   But I think it's unwise and unrealistic to try to outlaw surrogate motherhood. The practice, as one California broker triumphantly put it, is here to stay. Criminalizing it, like prostitution, would only punish the women selling their services on the black market that demand would inevitably create. I don't even think babies automatically "belong" to their mothers. I believe Stern, as Baby M's father, had a right to seek custody.

19   Still, I'd never characterize myself as a "supporter" of surrogate motherhood. Certain contradictions continue to assert themselves: If feminism stands for women's freedom to do what they want with their lives and their bodies, how do we protect women from the exploitation they're likely to encounter in a male-dominated, often misogynist world? Can we keep all our options open — and our eyes, too?

20   And if we want to minimize the inequities that have been justified by biological sex differences, how do we recognize, and should we ever privilege, those differences? Gestating a baby for nine months obviously cannot be compared to

donating sperm. But does that mean, necessarily, that at birth mothers have more claim to children than fathers? Can we open up the definitions of "family" — and of men's obligations within them — without abolishing "mother right?"

21   The Baby M case cannot resolve these dialectics, fundamental to all feminist debate. It is tempting to try to deny ambiguity and form single-issue alliances with our enemies in the belief that some activist progress can be made there. But that will only backfire. We can't retreat to the haven of protectionism and biological determinism as Chesler's group is doing. That corner is already crowded with religious officials, misogynists, and family chauvinists. Nor can we wish surrogate motherhood away by mewing for laws that would sweep it into the back alleys. Rather, we must fight for legislation that establishes fair pay and working conditions for women who choose to gestate babies for a fee; paramount among those conditions must be a grace period after birth to decide whether or not to surrender the child.

22   Surrogate motherhood is a stopgap solution to the more profound problems of infertility and the unmeshed needs of parentless children and childless adults. The Stern-Whitehead contract turned out to be more than they — or perhaps anybody — bargained for. Unless feminists make some intelligent noise, surrogate motherhood will be no bargain at all for women.

VII
GOING
INTO
BUSINESS

What does "going into business" mean today? What is it like to "be in business"? The five authors in this section show us the business world from radically different perspectives. Calvin Trillin takes the matter lightly; Michael Korda calls it "blood sport." Peter Drucker's article is over thirty-five years old, yet you hear his ideas echoed daily in universities and corporate boardrooms. Susan Fraker's article is disturbing for women who have ascended the lower rungs of the business world's ladder and who think, therefore, that they will eventually get to the top.

These selections reveal the complexity of the decision to become a business person, as well as the relationship that decision bears to others about the conduct of life. What preparations, including formal education, are most useful? What are realistic expectations for career advancement? How do we deal with discrimination based on age, sex, or race? And how can business people exert moral responsibility in a world that seems to reward self-assertion and the pursuit of self-interest? These considerations, which reverberate through many of the readings in other sections, can provide focuses for your thinking and theses for your writing.

WHEN BUSINESS BECOMES BLOOD SPORT

Michael Korda

1 The word survival, because of its most recent connotations, has come to be associated with those pessimistic souls who are convinced that a Communist-inspired world economic collapse ("It"), an urban uprising ("Them") or some other catastrophe is going to force middle-class white Americans to the hills, where they will have to live off the land and defend themselves against whoever the enemy turns out to be, domestic or foreign, according to their ideology. Judging from the voluminous literature of "survivalists" (as they call themselves to show they're not just passive survivors), Armageddon is going to be like a homicidal boy-scout outing.

2 But surviving the eighties may well turn out to be not so very different from surviving the seventies or the sixties, or even the forties. The key weapon will not be a handmade dagger or a roll of gold coins strapped to your waist but, as usual, smarts, quick thinking, a keen sense of competition and the cultivation of basic survival instincts. The battleground will not be in the hills, mountains, and urban street, but where it has always been: right here in the office, where you're trying to hold on to your job or work your way up to a better-paying one.

3 And with good reason. When corporations talk about running lean and cutting out the fat, when interest rates soar and business stagnates, when corporate

---

From Michael Korda, "When Business Becomes Blood Sport," *Playboy*, June 1981.

America hunkers down, *they mean you*, as several million of your fellow citizens have already discovered. As the economy falters, as more women enter the work force, as companies tighten up in the face of foreign competition, the race to the top is going to be harder, tougher and faster. What's more, even those who *do* survive are going to have to get themselves promoted at a rapid rate if they're going to stay ahead of inflation.

4   It's no longer enough just to do your job. You have to do it better than your competitors or, at any rate *be seen* as doing it better. Born survivors don't have problems in this area. Nobody has to tell *them* to look out for number one. They've been doing it for a lifetime. They can step into a revolving door behind you and come out ahead. It's in their blood. Nothing personal, but if you're in the way, too bad.

5 "The fast track is getting faster all the time," my friend Hal Grieff says, as he nurses a Perrier with lime in the grillroom of The Four Seasons, casing the house. Architect Philip Johnson is here; Sy Newhouse, the financier who has just bought Random House, is here; Morton Janklow, the lawyer-agent who represents Judith Krantz, is here; Douglas Fairbanks, Jr., is having lunch with theatrical superlawyer Arnold Weissberger; Irving Lazar is table-hopping from Truman Capote to John Chancellor. Grieff looks content, or as content as a 24-hour-a-day survivor can look. He's among winners.

6   Actually, Grieff is more at home in "21," where there's a less glitzy group of winners – David Mahoney, reputedly one of the highest-paid corporate C.E.O.s in the country; Roy Cohn, the lawyer whose very name strikes terror in the hearts of opposing counsel; Michael Burke of Madison Square Garden, the Rangers and the Knicks. It's essential to Grieff that he isn't surrounded by losers, nonentities, *schleps*. He can breathe.

7   Grieff stares at a plump, elderly man seated across from us with a ravishing young woman, pulling on a Davidoff Monte Cristo Individuale, while watching the maître de spoon out caviar. There is a bottle of Dom Pérignon champagne in a silver ice bucket beside the table. The elderly man's eyes resemble the caviar. They are black and very, very cold.

8   "Gunther Kleinfeld," Grieff says with approval. "A *real* survivor."

9   Kleinfeld, it so happens, has survived being a concentration-camp inmate, a displaced person, a penniless refugee; he has made and lost several fortunes, survived innumerable bankruptcies, divorces, mergers, acquisitions and lawsuits to emerge as a heavyweight hotel and resort developer. Who else, Grieff asks rhetorically, could have persuaded Saudi investors to put their petrodollars into an Israeli hotel?

10   Grieff's eyes sparkle with admiration. He relishes survival stories. He himself has danced from network to network and back again, always leaping one step up in salary and title while leaving behind him a trail of disaster. He knows exactly when to ask for a raise (when his numbers are up), when to move to a new job (when he knows his numbers are down but before the company has found out), when to say yes, when to say no; when, as they say, to play his hand and when to fold.

11   When Grieff worked at CBS ("Black Rock"), he outfitted himself with a dark suit from Morty Sills, black Gucci loafers, capped teeth (a $10,000 investment in success), brown hair — the CBS hard-edged look. At NBC (more *haimish*, particularly under Fred Silverman), he switched to tweed suits from Dunhill Tailors, brown brogues from Peal & Co., knitted ties. At ABC, he adopted what he called his "off-the-rack" look, the fighting underdog image. Grieff's talent for camouflage is impeccable.

12   He himself is a connoisseur of survival techniques. He tells how he was invited to lunch by the chairman of the board of a major corporation. Grieff was in one of his periodic slumps — "kamikaze time" he calls it — when, every so often, he runs something into the ground. And when he does, he's off to a new job before the news is out on the street. He buys a few new suits, eats out at expensive restaurants, puts on a show. He doesn't believe in waiting around glumly for the ax to fall; he's off and running in time for it to descend on his former subordinates who stayed behind.

13   The chairman's secretary suggests lunch the next day at one in Biarritz. Grieff knows most of the restaurants in New York, but Biarritz doesn't ring a bell. "Which Biarritz is it, honey?" he asks, hoping to conceal his ignorance.

14   "Biarritz, France," the secretary says.

15   A lesser man would express surprise, or ask for a ticket, but Grieff is a survivor. He charges a Concorde round-trip ticket to his American Express card, flies to Paris, rents a car, drives to Biarritz, and at one the next day, he's having lunch with the legendary tycoon, who shows no surprise that Grieff has flown the Atlantic to see him.

16   "You staying in France long?" he asks Grieff after picking his brain for two hours, between telephone calls.

17   Grieff doesn't hesitate. "No," he says, "I'm going back to New York tonight. I have a heavy day tomorrow."

18   "Tomorrow is Saturday."

19   Grieff shrugs. "I get my best work done on weekends. It's the only time the office is quiet."

20   A look of respect crosses his host's face. "You flew here just to see me?" he asks.

21   Grieff nods.

22   "At your *own* expense?"

23   Grieff hesitates, but he knows his man. "No," he says, "at *yours.* I'm billing you for the whole thing."

24   His host smiles with relief and shakes Grieff's hand. "Good!" he says. "You want the job, you got it. For a moment there, I thought you were a schmuck!"

25   Grieff laughs as he tells the story. Hell, that's nothing. Gunther Kleinfeld once rented an apartment in Aristotle Onassis' building and rode up and down in the elevator for days so that he could meet Ari "by accident" and pitch him a hot investment. What's more, he persuaded Onassis to put up $13,000,000 between the 24th floor and the lobby, and got a lift downtown in Onassis' limousine afterward.

26   Grieff studies people like that. He's a fast learner for a boy from the Bronx, for a boy from *anywhere*. He has his shoes polished twice a day, at his desk. He carries no money in his pockets. He doesn't own an overcoat, gloves, a raincoat, galoshes or an umbrella. A guy who goes everywhere in a limo doesn't need them, and Grieff knows that owning any one of those objects stamps you as a nonlimo person.

27   Grieff gets a limo written into his contracts for starters, though he's too shrewd to make a point of it, which might suggest that his limo status was a matter for negotiation. During his discussions, he merely alludes to the world-famous entertainment company that was just about to hire a major executive at $250,000 a year and lost him because it refused to give him a limo. Chintzy!

28   Everybody laughs; nobody wants to be thought chintzy. Grieff's limo slips in without argument. After all, if a guy is worth a quarter of a mil a year, he's worth a limo. And a cost-of-living clause, and half a mil of life insurance, and first-class travel.

29   Grieff dismisses those things as unimportant. He knows how to sell himself — he's money in the bank. He talks about what *he* can do for them. In a gentlemanly way, he takes it for granted that they're going to look after him. No demands, no specifics, no shopping list of perks. Grieff talks about profits, bottom line, the dazzling future. He lets *them* suggest what they'll offer him, nodding his head impatiently, almost with embarrassment, as if those details were of no interest to him compared with the challenge and excitement of the job at hand.

30   They almost think he'd pay them to let him do the job. By the time he's through, they're throwing limos, stock options and health-club memberships at him, and he's shrugging — sure, that's fine, whatever you guys want. I'll take whatever you think is fair. Shit, I don't care if I ride the *subway*, except it's a waste of time, but let me tell you how I can turn this area around for you . . . .

31 It's easy to overlook the fact that success is not a question of ego, because most successful people are egomaniacs, self-involved to an extraordinary degree. But (and it's the 24-kt. but) they have their ego firmly under control. Survivors know that pride and ego are heavy burdens to carry on the way up. As the late Harry Cohn, the foulmouthed, tough, genius boss of Columbia Studios, used to say, "I need a guy, I'll kiss his ass in Macy's window at high noon. I'm not proud."

32   You want the deep respect of your peers; you don't want to demean yourself; your self-image is important to you? Congratulations; you're a wonderful human being. But that sudden pain between the shoulder blades just may be a knife. Survivors believe in getting what they want. As one successful executive thoughtfully said, "I need to feel good about myself 24 hours a day. And I feel good about myself when I've *won*." . . .

33 Survivors never fall on their faces. They don't show pain, fear, resentment or defeat. They have, to use the basic word, *balls*. Also, *chutzpah*, realism and a sense of self-interest as highly developed as a bat's sonar. Plus a certain degree of inevitable ruthlessness. If you already have all those qualities, and are using them to the maximum degree, you're in good shape for the Eighties, whatever form the

apocalypse takes. If there's the slightest fear in your mind that maybe, just *maybe*, you're not moving as fast as you'd like to, or as fast as the guy (or gal) next to you, there are a number of things you should learn about survival. In fact, if your salary isn't increasing by 20 percent a year, given the current rate of inflation, you'd better start learning *fast*.

34   Survival *can* be learned. Start by recognizing that the days of the organization man (or woman) are gone, partly because organizations themselves are becoming more flexible, less hierarchic, forced to change at a rapid pace because of new technology and unimaginable financial conditions. Organizations no longer "look after" their people. Stay on long enough and you'll find your boss is a man (or woman) 20 years younger than you are, who can't even remember your name. This is not the age for putting in 40 years and retiring with a gold watch. People who put their faith in the Chrysler Corporation for job security, for example, have recently found out (1) that no matter how large a corporation is, it can turn bottoms up in the age of OPEC; and (2) that when a corporation is in big trouble, it doesn't hesitate to shed even its oldest and most loyal employees, while those at the top, who made the original decisions that led to disaster, stay on, with stiff upper lips and six-figure salaries.

35   In business, the usual practice is to reverse maritime tradition. When the ship hits an iceberg, the captain and the officers take to the boats and the passengers and crew go down with the ship. The lesson to be learned from that is: The higher up you are, the safer your job is. At the *very* top, those who have screwed up go to the International Monetary Fund, or are co-opted into government, or step up to become chairman of the board, or run a foundation. There, it is assumed, since they can do no good, they will find it difficult to do any harm. Even at a less exalted level, the senior executives of a company have the advantage of being better informed (they know when it's time to jump ship) and are in a better position to blame other people (you, for example) for what went wrong.

36   The trick is to understand the organization the way you understand a woman you love. You don't have to think she's without faults, you may be aware that she has certain secrets in her past, but you have to accept them and understand them. Blindly believing she's perfect is not the best way to survive a love affair or a marriage. It's the employees who are always telling you "This is a great place to work" who usually get canned first in times of trouble. The realists stay on, unless things are so bad it pays to go elsewhere. In the same way, you have to commit yourself to the organization's goals without becoming a company man and trusting that Big Brother, whether it's G.M., Chrysler, CBS or Bankers Trust, will take care of you. Big Brother, you may be sure of it, is looking out for number one.

37   The first step is to identify the immediate power elite — the men and women who are insiders, who not only participate in the crucial decisions (at whatever level you're involved) but also influence the way in which more senior managers rate their subordinates. This is where survival training pays off. Where there's an "in" group, you have to become part of it, while keeping your eyes open for ways to outflank the group. If the "in" group wears dark-blue suits, buy a dark-blue suit (even if you're a woman). If they're interested in football, learn to talk football

(even if you're a woman). The main thing is to be seen as part of the company's basic inner circle, even if it's at some inconvenience to yourself. When the ax falls, it's better to be among those who are busy deciding who gets axed than among the axed. Basic survival . . . .

38 It is five A.M. and it's dark inside Kleinfeld's plane, as he flies back from Los Angeles, where he has been putting together a deal. Kleinfeld puffs on his cigar as the plane descends toward New York at nearly 600 mph. He is almost, but not quite, relaxed, his legs stretched out with his feet on a leather ottoman, his shoes off. Kleinfeld is in his element.

39   "What time do we arrive?" he asks, pushing the button on his intercom.

40   "We'll be landing pretty soon, Mr. Kleinfeld, don't worry," the pilot replies.

41   A spasm of anger crosses Kleinfeld's plump face. "I didn't *ask* that," he says. "I asked *what time*."

42   A pause. The pilot clears his throat. "E.T.A. is exactly 5:45, Eastern standard time, Mr. Kleinfeld."

43   Kleinfeld nods. "Thank you," he says, switching off the intercom. "A new boy," he points out. "He hasn't learned yet. Well, we all learn."

44   What has Kleinfeld learned?

45   He stares out the window, thinks for a moment. "To keep moving. When I used to work for other people, I discovered that if you sat for more than a year at the same job or the same salary, you were dead. Get out. Move. Switch jobs. Success is an escalator. If it stops, you're stuck between floors. What do you do if the escalator stops? You get off, take the elevator, take the stairs. Right? You don't just stand there, waiting for it to start up again."

46   Is that true even when business is bad?

47   Kleinfeld nods. "Business is bad? So what else is new? There are always problems. Listen, in a plague, you sell coffins, yes? In a drought, you sell water. In a flood?"

48   "You sell boats."

49   He smiles "Or water wings."

50   How has he always managed to survive?

51   A moment of thought. "I kept in mind the simple fact that you can only survive by understanding the world as it is. Most people think it ought to be some other way or, worse yet, they hope it really is, despite what they see every day with their own eyes. What you see is what there is. It isn't going to be any better. So you say to yourself, OK, that's the way it is; now" — Kleinfeld pantomimes rolling up his sleeves — "let's get down to it!"

52   Isn't he ever depressed by that Manichaean point of view?

53   He laughs. "No. I'm not depressed. Not ever. I survived the Nazis. I survived being a refugee. I survived working for people who were real monsters. I know what matters is to be honest about oneself. I'm ambitious. Fine. I admit it. I'm greedy. OK, so *nu*? I live by my wits. Who doesn't? I'll tell you something. The first time I was ever sent out to negotiate a big deal, I went to England, and I met with these guys in their Savile Row suits and their accents, and I was *impressed*. So we get to dealing, and I realize that I'm brighter than these people, even if they do have old-

school ties and handsome shoes. When we get to the end, we settle on two million, and I'm delighted. I was figuring a million five tops. We all shake hands. The guys stand up to leave, and the chief negotiator for the other side suddenly looks as if he'd forgotten something. "Oh, Mr. Kleinfeld,' he says, 'dollars or pounds?' Well, in those days, the pound was worth four bucks. I thought for a moment and I said, 'Pounds.' He nodded as if that was what he expected, and we shook hands. I couldn't belive it. I was willing to settle for $1,500,000, and here I just got $8,000,000 by *keeping my mouth shut*! It taught me a lesson."

54   What lesson? The plane banks over Manhattan, as the lights begin to turn off in the dark below. The flaps and wheels go down with a subdued hum. Somewhere down there, Kleinfeld's limo is waiting; somewhere in his cooperative apartment, coffee is being brewed for his return. He stared at the SEAT BELTS sign as it lights up and pushes a button to turn it off.

55   "A guy can land without a seat belt on his own airplane," he says. "I told them to take the sign out . . . . What lesson? If you want to survive in business, even in life, *listen before you talk*. Let the other guy suggest the price. Let the other guy say what he's going to do. Let the other guy mention a number."

56   The plane lands smoothly, draws to a stop, the stairs descend with a low whine. Outside, Kleinfeld's chauffeur waits in the damp dawn with an umbrella. The limo is parked under the wing. Kleinfeld yawns and makes his way to the door. "Survival," he says, as the copilot helps him into his suit jacket, "is like getting laid — it's just a question of self confidence and opportunity."

57   And desire?

58   Kleinfeld stands on the steps, while the chauffeur holds the umbrella as high as he can to shelter him. "Of course, desire," he says. "The rest you can fake, but the desire to survive — that's the bottom line."

59   He gets into the car, slams the door, picks up the telephone. Rain is beading the windows. He looks up, pushes a button, his window goes down.

59   "Hey," he says, "it's raining. You want a lift?"

60   I nod.

61   "You know," Kleinfeld remarks, "a real survivor would have stepped into the limo right after me, without asking. I once did that to Onassis, and you know what he said to me? He said, 'You could get shot for that. I have bodyguards.' So I told him, 'I'm not worried.' 'Why not?' he asked. 'Because then you'd never find out what my deal is!'"

62   Kleinfeld sits back in the limo. He is silent for a moment. "I *liked* Onassis," he says, like a man offering an unpopular opinion. "He was a real survivor." Kleinfeld looks almost sympathetic in the gray dawn light. He is thinking of Onassis. "He taught me another valuable lesson," he remarks in a quiet voice.

63   I ask what it was.

64   "Nobody's ever too big to listen to a deal. If you want to survive, you've got to look as if you're *giving*, not getting, *offering*, not asking. A survivor seduces the world. Losers try to rape it, or don't even give it a try, but a survivor believes in *all* the possibilities. He's an eternal optimist about himself — and a pessimist about other people."

Not a bad combination, I suggest.

65   "Not bad." Kleinfeld looks out at the grimy rows of houses, the rusting el, the potholed streets. "Life teaches you survival," he says. "It's just that most people don't want to learn. They want to believe in organizations, companies, rules, friends, lovers, wives, brothers-in-law. In the end, you want to survive, you got to learn to trust only one person."

67   He pulls a curtain down to close off his view of Queens — you've seen one pothole, you've seen them all.

68   "Yourself."

IT'S FAILURE, NOT SUCCESS

Ellen Goodman

1 I knew a man who went into therapy about three years ago because, as he put it, he couldn't live with himself any longer. I didn't blame him. The guy was a bigot, a tyrant and a creep.

2   In any case, I ran into him again after he'd finished therapy. He was still a bigot, a tyrant and a creep, *but* . . . he had learned to live with himself.

3   Now, I suppose this was an accomplishment of sorts. I mean, nobody else could live with him. But it seems to me that there are an awful lot of people running around and writing around these days encouraging us to feel good about what we should feel terrible about, and to accept in ourselves what we should change.

4   The only thing they seem to disapprove of is disapproval. The only judgment they make is against being judgmental, and they assure us that we have nothing to feel guilty about except guilt itself. It seems to me that they are all intent on proving that I'm OK and You're OK, when in fact, I may be perfectly dreadful and you may be unforgivably dreary, and it may be — gasp! — *wrong.*

5   What brings on my sudden attack of judgmentitis is success, or rather, *Success!* — the latest in a series of exclamation-point books all concerned with How to Make it.

6   In this one, Michael Korda is writing a recipe book for success. Like the other authors, he leapfrogs right over the "Shoulds" and into the "Hows." He eliminates value judgments and edits our moral questions as if he were Fanny Farmer and the subject was the making of a blueberry pie.

7   It's not that I have any reason to doubt Mr. Korda's advice on the way to achieve success. It may very well be that successful men wear handkerchiefs stuffed neatly in their breast pockets, and that successful single women should carry suitcases to the office on Fridays whether or not they are going away for the weekend.

8   He may be realistic when he says that "successful people generally have very low expectations of others." And he may be only slightly cynical when he writes:

Ellen Goodman, "It's Failure, Not Success," *Close to Home*, The Washington Post Company, 1979.

"One of the best ways to ensure success is to develop expensive tastes or marry someone who has them."

9   And he may be helpful with his handy hints on how to sit next to someone you are about to overpower.

10   But he simply finesses the issues of right and wrong — silly words, embarrassing words that have been excised like warts from the shiny surface of the new how-to books. To Korda, guilt is not a prod, but an enemy that he slays on page four. Right off the bat, he tells the would-be successful reader that:

■ It's OK to be greedy.

■ It's OK to look out for Number One.

■ It's OK to be Machiavellian (if you can get away with it).

■ It's OK to recognize that honesty is not always the best policy (provided you don't go around saying so).

■ And it's always OK to be rich.

11   Well, in fact, it's not OK. It's not OK to be greedy, Machiavellian, dishonest. It's not always OK to be rich. There is a qualitative difference between succeeding by making napalm or by making penicillin. There is a difference between climbing the ladder of success, and macheteing a path to the top.

12   Only someone with the moral perspective of a mushroom could assure us that this was all OK. It seems to me that most Americans harbor ambivalence toward success, not for neurotic reasons, but out of a realistic perception of what it demands.

13   Success is expensive in terms of time and energy and altered behavior — the sort of behavior he describes in the grossest of terms: "If you can undermine your boss and replace him, fine, do so, but never express anything but respect and loyalty for him while you're doing it."

14   This author — whose *Power!* topped the best-seller list last year — is intent on helping rid us of that ambivalence which is a signal from our conscience. He is like the other "Win!" "Me First!" writers, who try to make us comfortable when we should be uncomfortable.

15   They are all Doctor Feelgoods, offering us placebo prescriptions instead of strong medicine. They give us a way to live with ourselves, perhaps, but not a way to live with each other. They teach us a whole lot more about "Failure!" than about success.

WHY WOMEN AREN'T GETTING TO THE TOP

Susan Fraker

1 Ten years have passed since U.S. corporations began hiring more than token numbers of women for jobs at the bottom rung of the management ladder. A decade
into their careers, how far up have these women climbed? The answer: not as far
as their male counterparts. Despite impressive progress at the entry level and in
middle management, women are having trouble breaking into senior management.
"There is an invisible ceiling for women at that level," says Janet Jones-Parker,
executive director of the Association of Executive Search Consultants Inc. "After
eight or ten years, they hit a barrier."

2   The trouble begins at about the $75,000 to $100,000 salary level, and seems to
get worse the higher one looks. Only one company on *Fortune*'s list of the 500
largest U.S. industrial corporations has a woman chief executive. That woman,
Katharine Graham of the Washington Post Co. (No. 342), readily admits she got the
job because her family owns a controlling share of the corporation.

3   More surprising, given that women have been on the ladder for ten years, is
that none currently seems to have a shot at the top rung. Executive recruiters,
asked to identify women who might become presidents or chief executives of
Fortune 500 companies, draw a blank. Even companies that have women in senior
management privately concede that these women aren't going to occupy the chairman's office.

4   Women have only four of the 154 spots this year at the Harvard Business
School's Advanced Management Program — a prestigious 13-week conclave to
which companies send executives they are grooming for the corridors of power. The
numbers aren't much better at comparable programs at Stanford and at Dart-
mouth's Tuck School. But perhaps the most telling admission of trouble comes
from men at the top. "The women aren't making it," confessed the chief executive
of a *Fortune* 500 company to a consultant. "Can you help us find out why?"

5   All explanations are controversial to one faction or another in this highly
charged debate. At one extreme, many women — and some men — maintain that
women are the victims of blatant sexism. At the other extreme, many men — and a
few women — believe women are unsuitable for the highest managerial jobs: they
lack the necessary assertiveness, they don't know how to get along in this rarefied
world, or they have children and lose interest in — or time for — their careers.
Somewhere in between is a surprisingly large group of men and women who see
"discrimination" as the major problem, but who often can't define precisely what
they mean by the term.

6   The discrimination they talk about is not the simple-minded sexism of dirty
jokes and references to "girls." It is not born of hatred, or indeed of any ill will that
the bearer may be conscious of. What they call discrimination consists simply of

Susan Fraker, "Why Women Aren't Getting to the Top," *Fortune*, April 16, 1984.

treating women differently from men. The notion dumbfounds some male managers. You mean to say, they ask, that managerial women don't want to be treated differently from men in any respect, and that by acting otherwise — as I was raised to think only decent and gentlemanly — I'm somehow prejudicing their chances for success? Yes, the women respond.

7   "Men I talk to would like to see more women in senior management," says Ann Carol Brown, a consultant to several *Fortune* 500 companies. "But they don't recognize the subtle barriers that stand in the way." Brown thinks the biggest hurdle is a matter of comfort, not competence. "At senior management levels, competence is assumed," she says. "What you're looking for is someone who fits, someone who gets along, someone you trust. Now that's subtle stuff. How does a group of men feel that a woman is going to fit? I think it's very hard."

8   The experience of an executive at a large Northeastern bank illustrates how many managerial women see the problem. Promoted to senior vice president several years ago, she was the first woman named to that position. But she now believes it will be many years before the bank appoints a woman executive vice president. "The men just don't feel comfortable," she says. "They make all sorts of excuses — that I'm not a banker [she worked as a consultant originally], that I don't know the culture. There's a smoke screen four miles thick. I attribute it to being a woman." Similarly, 117 of 300 women executives polled recently by UCLA's Graduate School of Management and Korn-Ferry International, an executive search firm, felt that being a woman was the greatest obstacle to their success.

9   A common concern among women, particularly in law and investment banking, is that the best assignments go to men. "Some departments — like sales and trading or mergers and acquisitions — are considered more macho, hence more prestigious," says a woman at a New York investment bank. "It's nothing explicit. But if women can't get the assignments that allow them to shine, how can they advance?"

10   Women also worry that they don't receive the same kind of constructive criticism that men do. While these women probably overestimate the amount of feedback their male colleagues receive, even some men acknowledge widespread male reluctance to criticize a woman. "There are vast numbers of men who can't do it," says Eugene Jennings, professor of business administration at Michigan State University and a consultant to a dozen large companies. A male banking executive agrees: "A male boss will haul a guy aside and just kick ass if the subordinate performs badly in front of a client. But I heard about a woman here who gets nervous and tends to giggle in front of customers. She's unaware of it and her boss hasn't told her. But behind her back he downgrades her for not being smooth with customers."

11   Sometimes the message that has to be conveyed to a woman manager is much more sensitive. An executive at a large company says he once had to tell a woman that she should either cross her legs or keep her legs together when she sat. The encounter was obviously painful to him. "She listened to me and thanked me and expressed shock at what she was doing," he recalls, with a touch of agony in his voice. "My God, this is something only your mother tells you. I'm a fairly direct person and a great believer in equal opportunity. But it was damn difficult for me to say this to a woman whom I view to be very proper in all other respects."

12   Research by Anne Harlan, a human resource manager at the Federal Aviation
Administration, and Carol Weiss, a managing associate of Charles Hamilton Associ-
ates, a Boston consulting firm, suggests that the situation doesn't necessarily improve
as the number of women in an organization increases. Their study, conducted at
the Wellesley College Center for Research on Women and completed in 1982,
challenges the theory advanced by some experts that when a corporation attained a
"critical mass" of executive women — defined as somewhere between 30% and 35%
— job discrimination would vanish naturally as men and women began to take each
other for granted.

13   Harlan and Weiss observed the effects of different numbers of women in an
organization during a three-year study of 100 men and women managers at two
Northeastern retailing corporations. While their sample of companies was not large,
after their results were published, other companies said they had similar experiences. Harlan and Weiss found that while overt resistance drops quickly after the
first few women become managers, it seems to pick up again as the number of
women reaches 15%. In one company they studied, only 6% of the managers were
women, compared with 19% in the second company. But more women in the
second company complained of discrimination, ranging from sexual harassment to
inadequate feedback. Could something other than discrimination — very different
corporate cultures, say — have accounted for the result? Harlan and Weiss say no,
that the two companies were eminently comparable.

14   Consultants and executives who think discrimination is the problem tend to
believe it persists in part because the government has relaxed its commitment to
affirmative action, which they define more narrowly than some advocates do.
"We're not talking about quotas or preferential treatment," says Margaret Hennig
who, along with Anne Jardim, heads the Simmons College Graduate School of
Management. "That's stupid management. We just mean the chance to compete
equally." Again, a semantic chasm separates women and men. Women like Hennig
and Jardim think of affirmative action as a vigorous effort on the part of companies
to ensure that women are treated equally and that sexist prejudices aren't permitted
to operate. Men think the term means reverse discrimination, giving women preferential treatment.

15   Legislation such as the Equal Employment Opportunity Act of 1972 prohibits
companies from discriminating against women in hiring. The laws worked well —
indeed, almost too well. After seven or eight years, says Jennings of Michigan State,
the pressure was off and no one pushed hard to see that discrimination was eliminated in selecting people for senior management. Jennings thinks the problem began
in the latter days of the Carter Administration, when the economy was lagging and
companies worried more about making money than about how their women managers were doing. The Reagan Administration hasn't made equal opportunity a
priority either.

16   What about the belief that women fall behind not because of discrimination,
but because they are cautious, unaggressive, and differently motivated than men —
or less motivated? Even some female executives believe that women derail their
careers by choosing staff jobs over high-risk, high-reward line positions. One

woman, formerly with a large consumer goods company and now president of a market research firm, urges women to worry less about sexism and more about whether the jobs they take are the right route to the top. "I spent five years thinking the only reason I didn't become a corporate officer at my former company was because of my sex," she says. "I finally had to come to grips with the fact that I overemphasized being a woman and underemphasized what I did for a living. I was in a staff function — the company didn't live and die by what I did."

17 Men and women alike tend to believe that because women are raised differently they must manage differently. Research to support this belief is hard to come by, though. The women retail managers studied by Harlan and Weiss, while never quarterbacks or catchers, had no trouble playing on management teams. Nor did they perform less well on standardized tests measuring qualities like assertiveness and leadership. "Women don't manage differently," Harlan says flatly.

18 In a much larger study specifically addressing management styles, psychologists Jay Hall and Susan Donnell of Teleometrics International Inc., a management training company, reached the same conclusion. They matched nearly 2,000 men and women managers according to age, rank in their organization, kind of organization, and the number of people they supervised. The psychologists ran tests to assess everything from managerial philosophies to the ability to get along with people, even quizzing subordinates on their views of the boss. Donnell and Hall concluded, "Male and female managers do not differ in the way they manage the organization's technical and human resources."

19 Data on how women's expectations — and therefore, arguably, their performance — may differ from men's are more confusing. Stanford Professor Myra Strober studied 150 men and 26 women who graduated from the Stanford Business School in 1974. When she and a colleague, Francine Gordon, polled the MBAs shortly before graduation, they discovered that the women had much lower expectations for their peak earnings. The top salary the women expected during their careers was only 60% of the men's. Four years later the ratio had fallen to 40%.

20 Did this mean that women were less ambitious or were willing to take lower salaries to get management jobs? Strober doesn't think so. She says a major reason for the women's lower salary expectations was that they took jobs in industries that traditionally pay less, but which, the women thought, offered opportunities for advancement. Almost 20% of the women in her sample went into government, compared with 3% of the men. On the other hand, no women went into investment banking or real estate development, which each employed about 6% of the men. Strober points out, however, that investment banking and big-time real estate were all but closed to women in the early 1970s. "One way people decide what their aspirations are," she says, "is to look around and see what seems realistic. If you look at a field and see no women advancing, you may modify your goals."

21 Some of what Mary Anne Devanna found in her examination of MBAs contradicts Strober's conclusions. Devanna, research coordinator of the Columbia Business School's Center for Research in Career Development, matched 45 men and 45 women who graduated from the Columbia Business School from 1969 to 1972.

Each paired man and woman had similar backgrounds, credentials, and marital status. The starting salaries of the women were 98% of the men's. Using data collected in 1980, Devanna found a big difference in the salaries men and women ultimately achieved, though. In manufacturing, the highest paying sector, women earned $41,818 after ten years vs. $59,733 for the men. Women in finance had salaries of $42,867 vs. $46,786 for the men. The gap in the service industries was smallest: $36,666 vs. $38,600. She then tested four hypotheses in seeking to explain the salary differences: (1) that women are less successful because they are motivated differently than men, (2) that motherhood causes women to divert attention from their careers, (3) that women seek jobs in low-paying industries, and (4) that women seek types of jobs — in human resources, say — that pay less.

22   Devanna found no major differences between sexes in the importance they attached to the psychic or monetary rewards of work. "The women did not expect to earn less than the men," she says. Nor did she find that motherhood led women to abandon their careers. Although several women took maternity leaves, all returned to work full time within six months. Finally, Devanna found no big differences in the MBAs' choice of industry or function, either when they took their first jobs or ten years later.

23   Devanna concluded that discrimination, not level of motivation or choice of job, accounted for the pay differences. Could the problem simply have been performance — that the women didn't manage as well as men? Devanna claims that while she couldn't take this variable into account specifically, she controlled for all the variables that should have made for a difference in performance — from family background to grades in business school.

24   In their discussions with male executives, researchers like Devanna hear a recurrent theme — a conviction that women don't take their careers seriously. Even though most female managers were regarded as extremely competent, the men thought they would eventually leave — either to have children or because the tensions of work became too much. Both are legitimate concerns. A woman on the fast track is under intense pressure. Many corporate types believe that she gets much more scrutiny than a man and must work harder to succeed. The pressures increase geometrically if she has small children at home.

25   Perhaps as a result, thousands of women have careers rather than husbands and children. In the UCLA-Korn/Ferry study of executive women, 52% had never married, were divorced, or were widowed, and 61% had no children. A similar study of male executives done in 1979 found that only 5% of the men had never married or were divorced and even fewer — 3% — had no children.

26   Statistics on how many women bear children and then leave the corporation are incomplete. Catalyst, a nonprofit organization that encourages the participation of women in business, studied 815 two-career families in 1980. It found that 37% of the new mothers in the study returned to work within two months; 68% were back after 4½ months; 87% in eight months. To a company, of course, an eight-month absence is a long time. Moreover, the 10% or so who never come back — most males are convinced the figure is higher — represent a substantial capital

investment lost. It would be naive to think that companies don't crank this into their calculation of how much the women who remain are worth.

27   Motherhood clearly slows the progress of women who decide to take long maternity leaves or who choose to work part time. But even those committed to working full time on their return believe they are sometimes held back — purposely or inadvertently. "Men make too many assumptions that women with children aren't free to take on time-consuming tasks," says Gene Kofke, director of human resources at AT&T. Karen Gonçalves, 34, quit her job as a consultant when she was denied challenging assignments after the birth of her daughter. "I was told clearly that I couldn't expect to move ahead as fast as I had been," she says. Later, when Gonçalves began working at the consulting firm of Arthur D. Little Inc. in Cambridge, Massachusetts, she intentionally avoided discussions of family and children: "I didn't keep a picture of my daughter in the office, and I would travel anywhere, no matter how hard it was for me."

28 Sometimes pregnancy is more of an issue for the men who witness it than for the women who go through it. Karol Emmerich, 35, now treasurer of Dayton Hudson Corp., was the first high-level woman at the department-store company to become pregnant. "The men didn't really know what to do," she recalls. "They were worried when I wanted to take three months off. But they wanted to encourage me to come back. So they promoted me to treasurer when I was seven months pregnant. Management got a lot of good feedback." Emmerich's experience would please Simmons Dean Anne Jardim, who worries that most organizations aren't doing enough to keep women who want to have children. "It's mind-boggling," she argues. "Either some of the brightest women in this country aren't going to reproduce or the companies are going to write off women in whom they have a tremendous investment."

29   To the corporation it may seem wasteful to train a woman and then be unable to promote her because she won't move to take the new job. The Catalyst study found that 40% of the men surveyed had moved for their jobs, vs. only 21% of the women. An argument can be made that an immobile executive is worth less to the corporation — and hence may be paid less.

30   Where women frequently do go is out of the company and into business for themselves. "When the achievements you want aren't forthcoming, it makes going out on your own easier," says a woman who has set up her own consultancy. "I was told I wouldn't make it into senior management at my bank. Maybe I just didn't have it. But the bank never found any woman who did. They were operating under a consent decree and they brought in a lot of women at the vice president level. Every single one of them left." Karen Gonçalves left Arthur D. Little to do part-time teaching and consulting when she was pregnant with her second child. "I didn't think I would get the professional satisfaction I wanted at ADL," she says.

31   From 1977 to 1980, according to the Small Business Administration, the number of businesses owned by women increased 33%, compared with an 11% increase for men — though admittedly the women's increase started from a much

smaller base. While it's not clear from the numbers that women are entering the entrepreneurial ranks in greater numbers than they are joining corporations, some experts think so. "It's ironic," says Strober of Stanford. "The problem of the 1970s was bringing women into the corporation. The problem of the 1980s is keeping them there."

32   A few companies, convinced that women face special problems and that it's in the corporation's interest to help overcome them, are working hard at solutions. At Penn Mutual Life Insurance Co. in Philadelphia, where nearly half the managers are women, executives conducted a series of off-site seminars on gender issues and sex-role stereotypes. Dayton Hudson provides support (moral and financial) for a program whereby women in the company trade information on issues like personal financial planning and child care.

33 What women need most, the experts say, are loud, clear, continuing statements of support from senior management. Women have come a long way at Merck, says B. Lawrence Branch, the company's director of equal employment affairs, because Chairman John J. Horan insisted that their progress be watched. Merck has a program that identifies 10% of its women and 10% of minorities as "most promising." The company prepares a written agenda of what it will take for them to move to the next level. Progress upward may mean changing jobs or switching functions, so Merck circulates their credentials throughout the company. "We have a timetable and we track these women carefully," says Branch. Since 1979 almost 40% of the net growth in Merck's managerial staff has been women.

34   Sensitive to charges of reverse discrimination, Branch explains that Merck has for years singled out the best employees to make sure they get opportunities to advance. Women, he notes, were consistently underrepresented in that group. In his view the tracking program simply allows women to get into the competition with fast-track men. Others might not be so charitable. Any company that undertakes to do something on behalf of its managerial women leaves itself open to the charge that it too is discriminating — treating women and men differently.

35   What everyone may be able to agree on is that opening corporations to competition in the executive ranks is clearly good for performance and profits. But how can a company do this? It can try to find productive part-time work for all employees who want to work part time — even managers. It can structure promotions so that fewer careers are derailed by an absence of a few months or the unwillingness to relocate. It can make sure that the right information, particularly on job openings, reaches everyone. Perhaps most importantly, it can reward its managers for developing talent of all sorts and sexes, penalize them if they don't, and vigilantly supervise the process.

THE BASIC SKILL

Peter Drucker

1 Most of you . . . will be employees all your working life, working for somebody else and for a pay check. And so will most, if not all, of the thousands of other young Americans . . . in all the other schools and colleges across the country.

2 Ours has become a society of employees. A hundred years or so ago only one out of every five Americans at work was employed, i.e., worked for somebody else. Today only one out of five is not employed but working for himself. And where fifty years ago "being employed" meant working as a factory laborer or as a farm-hand, the employee of today is increasingly a middle-class person with a substantial formal education, holding a professional or management job requiring intellectual and technical skills. Indeed, two things have characterized American society during these last fifty years: the middle and upper classes have become employees; and middle-class and upper-class employees have been the fastest-growing groups in our working population — growing so fast that the industrial worker, that oldest child of the Industrial Revolution, has been losing in numerical importance despite the expansion of industrial production.

3 This is one of the most profound social changes any country has ever under-gone. It is, however, a perhaps even greater change for the individual young person about to start. Whatever he does, in all likelihood he will do it as an employee; wherever he aims, he will have to try to reach it through being an employee.

4 Yet you will find little if anything written on what it is to be an employee. You can find a great deal of very dubious advice on how to get a job or how to get a promotion. You can also find a good deal on work in a chosen field, whether it be metallurgy or salesmanship, the machinist's trade or bookkeeping. Every one of these trades requires different skills, sets different standards, and requires a differ-ent preparation. Yet they all have employeeship in common. And increasingly, especially in the large business or in government, employeeship is more important to success than the special professional knowledge or skill. Certainly more people fail because they do not know the requirements of being an employee than because they do not adequately possess the skills of their trade; the higher you climb the ladder, the more you get into administrative or executive work, the greater the emphasis on ability to work within the organization rather than on technical com-petence or professional knowledge.

5 Being an employee is thus the one common characteristic of most careers today. The special profession or skill is visible and clearly defined; and a well-laid-out sequence of courses, degrees, and jobs leads into it. But being an employee is the foundation. And it is much more difficult to prepare for it. Yet there is no recorded information on the art of being an employee.

Peter Drucker, "The Basic Skill," from "How to Be an Employee," *Fortune*, May 1952.

6 The first question we might ask is: what can you learn in college that will help you in being an employee? The schools teach a great many things of value to the future accountant, the future doctor, or the future electrician. Do they also teach anything of value to the future employee? The answer is: "Yes — they teach the one thing that it is perhaps most valuable for the future employee to know. But very few students bother to learn it."

7 This one basic skill is the ability to organize and express ideas in writing and in speaking.

8 As an employee you work with and through other people. This means that your success as an employee — and I am talking of much more here than getting promoted — will depend on your ability to communicate with people and to present your own thoughts and ideas to them so they will both understand what you are driving at and be persuaded. The letter, the report or memorandum, the ten-minute spoken "presentation" to a committee are basic tools of the employee.

9 Of course . . . if you work on a machine your ability to express yourself will be of little importance. But as soon as you move one step up from the bottom, your effectiveness depends on your ability to reach others through the spoken or the written word. And the further away your job is from manual work, the larger the organization of which you are an employee, the more important it will be that you know how to convey your thoughts in writing or speaking. In the very large organization, whether it is the government, the large business corporation, or the military, this ability to express oneself is perhaps the most important of all the skills a [person] can possess.

10 Of course, skill in expression is not enough by itself. You must have something to say in the first place. The popular picture of the engineer, for instance, is that of a man who works with a slide rule, T square, and compass. And engineering students reflect this picture in their attitude toward the written word as something quite irrelevant to their jobs. But the effectiveness of the engineer — and with it his usefulness — depends as much on his ability to make other people understand his work as it does on the quality of the work itself.

11 Expressing one's thoughts is one skill that the school can really teach, especially to people born without natural writing or speaking talent. Many other skills can be learned later — in this country there are literally thousands of places that offer training to adult people at work. But the foundations for skill in expression have to be laid early: an interest in and an ear for language; experience in organizing ideas and data, in brushing aside the irrelevant, in wedding outward form and inner content into one structure; and above all, the habit of verbal expression. If you do not lay these foundations during your school years, you may never have an opportunity again.

12 If you were to ask me what strictly vocational courses there are in the typical college curriculum, my answer — now that the good old habit of the "theme a day" has virtually disappeared — would be: the writing of poetry and the writing of short stories. Not that I expect many of you to become poets or short-story writers — far from it. But these two courses offer the easiest way to obtain some skill in expression. They force one to be economical with language. They force one to

organize thought. They demand of one that he give meaning to every word. They train the ear for language, its meaning, its precision, its overtones — and its pitfalls. Above all they force one to write.

13   I know very well that the typical employer does not understand this as yet, and that he may look with suspicion on a young college graduate who has majored, let us say, in short-story writing. But the same employer will complain — and with good reason — that the young [people] whom he hires when they get out of college do not know how to write a simple report, do not know how to tell a simple story, and are in fact virtually illiterate. And he will conclude — rightly — that the young [people] are not really effective, and certainly not employees who are likely to go very far.

INVESTMENT OPPORTUNITIES

Calvin Trillin

1 Those who think that our family is a bit listless about looking after our financial affairs are apparently unaware of the sort of effort we put into the Publishers Clearing House Sweepstakes every year. We really go for it. We do our homework. We play hardball. We keep our eyes on the bottom line. We always lose.

2   "I think this year we should leverage our options," I said when the Publishers Clearing House Million Dollar Sweeps entry arrived in the mail a couple of months ago.

3   "What does that mean?" my younger daughter, Sarah, asked.

4   "Your mother can explain the details," I said. "I'm strictly an idea man."

5   I'm the one who had the idea about entering sweepstakes in the first place. Sarah, who is eleven, hasn't come up with any sound investment strategies since she got stymied trying to fill out the entry form for a drawing some beer company was holding for a new Pontiac Trans Am ("What should I put for business phone?"). It's natural for me to have a lot of ideas about these matters because I know a number of Wall Street millionaires. As it happens, every single person in the lower third of my college class — every single person, that is, except Blinko Moshler, who's a prominent lawyer in Toledo, and Dalt Durfee, who is the Deputy Under-secretary of State for Asian Economic Affairs — is a Wall Street Millionaire. I occasionally run into one of them, usually at some restaurant I can't really afford. They're always talking about leveraging their options, or maybe optioning their leverages; ask my wife if you want the details.

6   They also talk a lot about what they're getting out of and what they're getting into. "I just got out of the market and into shrimp boats," one of the millionaires said when I came across a brace of them at an East Side nouvelle cuisine joint that seemed to be charging the price of a shrimp boat for three cold shrimp and a heart-shaped raspberry.

Calvin Trillin, "Investment Opportunities," *With All Disrespect*, Ticknor & Fields, 1985.

7   "I just got out of shrimp boats and into boxcars," said the other one, someone I'll call Martin G. Cashflow. In his crowd, Cashflow is known for having just got out of whatever it is that everyone else is about to get into. Cashflow also happens to be one of those trendy millionaires who gets in and out of fads at the same time he's getting in and out of investments, so sometimes he's getting out of backgammon and into cattle ranches or into Sufism and out of discount plumbing supplies. Cashflow is the person who told me a long time ago that my problem was that writers are labor in a labor-intensive industry.

8   "I just got out of the New York State Instant Lotto and into the Reader's Digest Sweepstakes," I said. When they looked unimpressed, I assured them that I was savvy enough to have marked my entry form in a way that kept my name in the sweepstakes without obligating me to sign up at the special sweepstakes rate for a subscription to *Reader's Digest* for life plus ninety-nine years. I don't subscribe to any magazines. Some time after Cashflow told me that my problem was being labor in a labor-intensive industry, he told me that the smart money got out of magazines and into software years ago, at around the same time he got out of silver futures and into the Maharaj Ji. ("I don't think I want to get into software," I said at the time, thinking that it had something to do with flannel pajamas. "Kid, you *are* software," Cashflow replied. "That's your problem.") I figured there was nothing much I could do about writing for magazines — unless, of course, the big New Jersey Lottery number does turn out one year to be my Army serial number with the last two digits reversed for good luck — but I was at least smart enough not to subscribe to any.

9 This year, we had a family meeting about the Publishers Clearing House Sweepstakes. We sat at the dining room table, with sharpened pencils and clean white memo pads in front of us. "How's the little-bitty sticker end holding up, Sarah?" I asked. In our operation, Sarah is the specialist in how to figure out which little-bitty sticker is supposed to be pasted where on the entry blank.

10   "Piece of cake," Sarah said.

11   With Sarah trouble-shooting the little-bitty sticker end, I figured, the decision we had facing us was which of the three superprizes we wanted — a certified check for $250,000, a $250,000 custom-built dream home, or $40,000 a year for ten years.

12   "How do the numbers look on that one, Abigail?" I asked my older daughter.

13   "Ten times forty thousand is four hundred thousand, Daddy," Abigail said. "Don't you remember what I told you about just adding a zero on the tens table?"

14   "But the question is whether we want to go for the ten-year payout or get the two-fifty up front and put that money to work for us," I said.

15   "I'd rather have a Pontiac Trans Am," Sarah said.

16   "O.K., we'll meet again as soon as I figure out which option gives us the most leverage," I said, trying to imagine how Martin Cashflow would end a meeting. "I'll have my girl get back to your girl."

17   "But Daddy," Abigail said, "we *are* your girls."

18   I spent the next weeks trying to answer the questions that would allow us to eyeball a ballpark figure on the bottom line, or something like that. Is a $250,000 custom-built dream home the sort of thing Cashflow has in mind when he goes on about shelters? Aren't all $250,000 dream homes custom-built, or do some people have prefabricated dreams? In ten years, will $40,000 buy a Pontiac Trans Am? How about a Mars bar? I was thinking about such questions when Alice pointed out that entries to the Publishers Clearing House Sweepstakes had been due four days before ("You forgot to assign someone the deadline end"). I still had questions. If we decided to take the up-front cash and get it working for us, how many Instant Lotto tickets would $250,000 buy? What could "leverage your options" possibly mean?

VIII THE WORK ETHIC TODAY

We read a lot about our growing leisure time and how we can or should use it, but we don't generally pay as much attention to what's changing in our work lives. What's the status of the work ethic today? Does work contribute to our identities and our feelings about ourselves, or do we work only to make money? In four essays, a poem, and interviews with two American workers, six authors in this section find that Americans still value work, perhaps as highly as ever. Unfortunately, that doesn't mean all American workers are happy.

Unlike the selections in section VII, the readings in this section focus not on careers or on one kind of work but on the act of working, the drive to do something productive, whether it is to make an ox cart or to write a newspaper story. The work ethic has long been considered part of the American cultural heritage, yet some have charged that American workers no longer believe in it, and that consequently their productivity and the quality of their work are falling behind those of foreign workers. These and other related issues such as the effectiveness of education versus training and the equitable allocation of resources and responsibility recur in many of the readings in this book. They affect all areas of our culture and society.

THE WORK ETHIC IS UNDEREMPLOYED

Daniel Yankelovich

1 Americans hold two beliefs about why the Japanese are outdoing us in autos, steel, appliances, computer chips, and even subway cars. The first is that our productivity has become stagnant. The second is that this has happened because our work ethic has deteriorated badly.

2   The first belief is, alas, true. Since 1965, the country's productivity has improved at ever smaller rates. It now shows no growth at all, and may even be falling. But despite these signs and additional evidence that people are not working as hard as they once did, it is emphatically not true that our work ethic has become weaker. If by work ethic — very slippery term — we mean endowing work with intrinsic moral worth and believing that everyone should do his or her best possible job irrespective of financial reward, then recent survey research shows that the work ethic in the United States is surprisingly sturdy, and growing sturdier.

3   To understand the findings, we need to keep in mind the sharp distinction between work *behavior* — what we actually do in the work place — and the work *ethic* — set of psychological and moral beliefs.

Daniel Yankelovich, "The Work Ethic Is Underemployed," *Psychology Today*, May 1982.

4   A 1980 Gallup study for the United States Chamber of Commerce shows that an overwhelming 88 percent of all working Americans feel that it is personally important to them to work hard and do their best on the job. (This should not be confused with Gallup findings that fewer Americans are enjoying their work — a separate issue). The study concludes that a faulty work ethic is *not* responsible for the decline in our productivity; quite the contrary, the study identifies "a widespread commitment among U.S. workers to improve productivity" and suggests that "there are large reservoirs of potential upon which management can draw to improve performance and increase productivity."

5   In a subtler examination of American attitudes toward work, a 1982 pilot study for the nonprofit Public Agenda Foundation explores three conceptions of what might be called the "unwritten work contract" — the assumptions that each individual makes about what he or she will give to the job and expects to get in return. The first conception is one that historians recognize as the dominant attitude toward work throughout human history: the view that people labor only because they would not otherwise have the resources to sustain themselves. A second conception regards work as a straight economic transaction in which people relate effort to financial return: The more money they get, the harder they work; the less money they receive, the less effort they give. The third conception views work as carrying a moral imperative to do one's best apart from practical necessity or financial remuneration. The Public Agenda considers the implications of its findings so important that it intends to replicate the pilot study — from which national figures can only be surmised — among a larger cross-section of the work force within the next few months.

6   The study found that nearly four out of five people in the work force (78 percent) embrace the third conception aligning themselves with the statement: "I have an inner need to do the very best job I can regardless of pay." Fewer than one out of 10 working Americans (7 percent) embrace the idea of work as a mere "business transaction" whereby one regulates one's effort according to the size of one's paycheck, and an additional 15 percent regard work as a necessary but disagreeable chore ("Working for a living is one of life's necessities. I would not work if I did not have to").

7   Other surveys reveal similar findings. In 1977, for example, the respected Quinn and Staines Quality of Employment Survey conducted by the University of Michigan's Survey Research Center discovered that three out of four Americans (75 percent) would prefer to go on working even if they could live comfortably without working for the rest of their lives. It is revealing of the expanding commitment to the value of work that eight years earlier, significantly fewer Americans (67 percent) had expressed the same attitude.

8   Yet at the same time that the work ethic, in the sense defined above, has actually been growing stronger, most Americans also believe that people are working less. A 1981 Harris study for Sentry Insurance reveals that:

■ 78 percent of all working Americans feel that "people take less pride in their work than they did 10 years ago."

■ 73 percent believe that "the motivation to work hard is not as strong today as it was a decade ago."

■ 69 percent feel that our workmanship is worse than it was.

■ 63 percent simply believe that"most people do not work as hard today as they did 10 years ago."

9   Polls by Harris and Gallup, and my own research firm, show that business leaders hold similar views.

10   These beliefs do not prove that Americans are actually working less effectively than in the past. But it is difficult to discount such widespread impressions among both working people and business leaders. One bit of direct evidence on the declining performance of American workers allows us to go beyond these impressions. For a number of years, the University of Michigan asked a sample of workers to keep a diary of activities on the job. Analysis of these diaries reveals that between 1965 and 1975 the amount of time workers actually worked declined by more than 10 percent. If extrapolated to all American workers, the researchers say, this one factor alone, quite apart from such considerations as insufficient investments or aging equipment, could account for the slowed tempo of productivity growth in the decade from 1965 to 1975.

11   How, then, are we to reconcile these two sets of seemingly incompatible facts? Why do Americans endorse the ideal of giving one's best to the job while their actual performance reveals a slackening effort? What forces have produced this self-defeating situation at the precise moment when economic competition from Japan, Korea, Taiwan, Germany, and other nations threatens to outpace us and drag down our standard of living?

12   The answer lies, I believe, in the deeply flawed reward system, both psychological and financial, that now rules the American work place. To grasp this argument, we need to understand just what most work is like today. The Public Agenda study asked people the amount of control they exercised over how hard they worked and over the quality of the products they made or services they performed. A huge majority (82 percent) stated that they had some degree of discretion and control over the effort they gave to their job, and an even larger majority (88 percent) said that they had control over the quality of the work or service they performed (72 percent, a great deal of control; 16 percent, moderate control). This finding illuminates a little-noted but important fact about the modern work place: most working Americans have it in their power to decide whether they will satisfy only the minimum requirements of the job or exert the extra effort that makes the difference between ordinariness and high quality, between adequacy and excellence.

13   When the Public Agenda asked people whether they were using this freedom of choice to fulfill their "inner need to do the very best job" they can, fewer than one out of five (16 percent) said they were. All others acknowledged that they could improve their effectiveness — if they really wanted to. And many claimed that they could be twice as effective as they are now.

14   Why aren't they? The answer could hardly be plainer. When Gallup's Chamber of Commerce study asked workers whom they thought would benefit from the improvements in their productivity, only 9 percent felt that they, the workers, would. Most assumed that the beneficiaries would be others — consumers or stockholders or management. This finding accords with the finding of Yankelovich, Skelly, and White several years ago that a majority of college students no longer believe that working hard pays off. Some interpreted this finding to mean that the work ethic was eroding. It signifies, rather, the growing doubt that hard work will bring the rewards people have come to cherish. When Gallup's Chamber of Commerce study asked people whether they would work harder and do a better job if they were more involved in decisions relating to their work, an overwhelming 84 percent said they would. One need not take this finding literally to appreciate the vast sea of yearning that underlies it.

15   We arrive, then, at the heart of the matter. The questions of who benefits from increased productivity, and how, are the critical factors, not the work ethic. If the American work ethic has gone to seed, there is not much anyone can do about the problem of productivity. But if, as I contend, our work *ethic* is actually thriving while our work *behavior* falters, then the prognosis for action is excellent — once we grasp the reasons for the discrepancy and confront the task of remedying it.

16   In principle, most Americans are willing to work harder and turn out a higher-quality product; indeed, their self-esteem demands that they do so. That they are not doing it points directly to a serious flaw in management and in the reward system under which they perform their jobs. Why should workers make a greater effort if (a) they don't have to and (b) they believe that others will be the beneficiaries of such efforts? It is ironic that a political administration so finely tuned to encouraging the business community should pay such scant attention to stimulating the average American to work harder.

17   As our competitive posture in traditional industries such as steel and automobiles grows ever more grim, workers and trade unions are starting to pay more attention to productivity. But in many labor circles productivity is still regarded as a code term for speedups that benefit management and threaten job security. The mismatch between the national goal of improved productivity and the inadequate system of rewards now in operation could hardly be more obvious.

18   Lest anyone dismiss the idea that a more thoughtful approach to rewards can pay off, a large body of experimental data proves otherwise. Psychologist Raymond Katzell has reviewed 103 experiments designed to test whether an improved incentive system — including both money and greater control over one's work — would lead to higher individual productivity. It did in 85 of the experiments.

19   Perhaps more to the point is the Japanese experience in this country. The Japanese distinguish between the "soft" factors of production (the dedication of the work force) and such "hard" factors as technology, capital investment, and research and development. They recognize that the soft factors are just as important as the hard ones and that, indeed, the two are interdependent. It is this understanding that underlies Japan's spectacular success not only in their homeland but also in the plants they own and manage in the United States. One Japanese strategy, for

example, is to bring together both workers and managers to solve the problem of how new technology can be introduced to the advantage of both. Such participation does not just assure workers of job security; it enables them to devise with management a system that also provides job satisfaction. The Japanese success in this country is evidence that the American belief in the work ethic is not just rhetoric. Without the work ethic, the Japanese would have had to rely solely on the hard factors, by themselves not enough to spur productivity.

20   Ironically, the Japanese seem to have a better grasp of how to capitalize on our work ethic than we do. In the American approach to work, the relevant institutions – business management, labor unions, government, professional economists – do not have a firm grasp of the soft factors and how they interact with the hard ones. Unwittingly, most "experts" hold an obsolete image of the work force as a pool of "labor" responsive solely to economic imperatives, driven by the fear of unemployment, and inspired by the promise of consumer goods – the familiar carrot-and-stick psychology that worked in the past when workers and work were different. The leaders who run our institutions do not really understand today's work force: tens of millions of well-educated Americans, proud of their achievements, zealous of their freedoms, motivated by new values, with substantial control over their own production, and ready to raise their level of effort if given the proper encouragement.

WORK, LABOR, AND PLAY
W. H. Auden

1 So far as I know, Miss Hannah Arendt was the first person to define the essential difference between work and labor. To be happy, a man must feel, firstly, free and, secondly, important. He cannot be really happy if he is compelled by society to do what he does not enjoy doing, or if what he enjoys doing is ignored by society as of no value or importance. In a society where slavery in the strict sense has been abolished, the sign that what a man does is of social value is that he is paid money to do it, but a laborer today can rightly be called a wage slave. A man is a laborer if the job society offers him is of no interest to himself but he is compelled to take it by the necessity of earning a living and supporting his family.

2   The antithesis to labor is play. When we play a game, we enjoy what we are doing, otherwise we should not play it, but it is a purely private activity, society could not care less whether we play it or not.

3   Between labor and play stands work. A man is a worker if he is personally interested in the job which society pays him to do; what from the point of view of society is necessary labor is from his own point of view voluntary play. Whether a job is to be classified as labor or work depends, not on the job itself, but on the tastes of the individual who undertakes it. The difference does not, for example

W. H. Auden, "Work, Labor, and Play," *A Certain World: A Commonplace Book*, Viking, 1970.

coincide with the difference between a manual and a mental job; a gardener or a cobbler may be a worker, a bank clerk a laborer. Which a man is can be seen from his attitude toward leisure. To a worker, leisure means simply the hours he needs to relax and rest in order to work efficiently. He is therefore more likely to take too little leisure than too much; workers die of coronaries and forget their wives' birthdays. To the laborer, on the other hand, leisure means freedom from compulsion, so that it is natural for him to imagine that the fewer hours he has to spend laboring, and the more hours he is free to play, the better.

3   What percentage of the population in a modern technological society are, like myself, in the fortunate position of being workers? At a guess I would say sixteen per cent, and I do not think that figure is likely to get bigger in the future.

4   Technology and the division of labor have done two things: by eliminating in many fields the need for special strength or skill, they have made a very large number of paid occupations which formerly were enjoyable work into boring labor, and by increasing productivity they have reduced the number of necessary laboring hours. It is already possible to imagine a society in which the majority of the population, that is to say, its laborers, will have almost as much leisure as in earlier times was enjoyed by the aristocracy. When one recalls how aristocracies in the past actually behaved, the prospect is not cheerful. Indeed, the problem of dealing with boredom may be even more difficult for such a future mass society than it was for aristocracies. The latter, for example, ritualized their time; there was a season to shoot grouse, a season to spend in town, etc. The masses are more likely to replace an unchanging ritual by fashion which it will be in the economic interest of certain people to change as often as possible. Again, the masses cannot go in for hunting, for very soon there would be no animals left to hunt. For other aristocratic amusements like gambling, dueling, and warfare, it may be only too easy to find equivalents in dangerous driving, drug-taking, and senseless acts of violence. Workers seldom commit acts of violence, because they can put their aggression into their work, be it physical like the work of a smith, or mental like the work of a scientist or an artist. The role of aggression in mental work is aptly expressed by the phrase "getting one's teeth into a problem."

THE IMPORTANCE OF WORK
Gloria Steinem

1 Toward the end of the 1970s, *The Wall Street Journal* devoted an eight-part, front-page series to "the working woman" — that is, the influx of women into the paid-labor force — as the greatest change in American life since the Industrial Revolution.

Gloria Steinem, "The Importance of Work," *Outrageous Acts and Everyday Rebellions*, Holt, Reinhart and Winston, 1983.

2   Many women readers greeted both the news and the definition with cynicism. After all, women have always worked. If all the productive work of human maintenance that women do in the home were valued at its replacement cost, the gross national product of the United States would go up by 26 percent. It's just that we are now more likely than ever before to leave our poorly rewarded, low-security, high-risk job of homemaking (though we're still trying to explain that it's a perfectly good one and that the problem is male society's refusal both to do it and to give it an economic value) for more secure, independent, and better-paid jobs outside the home.

3   Obviously, the real work revolution won't come until all productive work is rewarded — including child rearing and other jobs done in the home — and men are integrated into so-called women's work as well as vice versa. But the radical change being touted by the *Journal* and other media is one part of that long integration process: the unprecedented flood of women into salaried jobs, that is, into the labor force as it has been male-defined and previously occupied by men. We are already more than 41 percent of it — the highest proportion in history. Given the fact that women also make up a whopping 69 percent of the "discouraged labor force" (that is, people who need jobs but don't get counted in the unemployment statistics because they've given up looking), plus an official female unemployment rate that is substantially higher than men's, it's clear that we could expand to become fully half of the national work force by 1990.

4   Faced with this determination of women to find a little independence and to be paid and honored for our work, experts have rushed to ask: "Why?" It's a question rarely directed at male workers. Their basic motivations of survival and personal satisfaction are taken for granted. Indeed, men are regarded as "odd" and therefore subjects for sociological study and journalistic reports only when they *don't* have work, even if they are rich and don't need jobs or are poor and can't find them. Nonetheless, pollsters and sociologists have gone to great expense to prove that women work outside the home because of dire financial need, or if we persist despite the presence of a wage-earning male, out of some desire to buy "little extras" for our families, or even out of good old-fashioned penis envy.

5   Job interviewers and even our own families may still ask salaried women the big "Why?" If we have small children at home or are in some job regarded as "men's work," the incidence of such questions increases. Condescending or accusatory versions of "What's a nice girl like you doing in a place like this?" have not disappeared from the workplace.

6   How do we answer these assumptions that we are "working" out of some pressing or peculiar need? Do we feel okay about arguing that it's as natural for us to have salaried jobs as for our husbands — whether or not we have young children at home? Can we enjoy strong career ambitions without worrying about being thought "unfeminine"? When we confront men's growing resentment of women competing in the work force (often in the form of such guilt-producing accusations as "You're taking men's jobs away" or "You're damaging your children"), do we simply state that a decent job is a basic human right for everybody?

7   I'm afraid the answer is often no. As individuals and as a movement, we tend to retreat into some version of a tactically questionable defense: "Womenworkbecause-wehaveto." The phrase has become one word, one key on the typewriter — an economic form of the socially "feminine" stance of passivity and self-sacrifice. Under attack, we still tend to present ourselves as creatures of economic necessity and familial devotion. "Womenworkbecausewehaveto" has become the easiest thing to say.

8   Like most truisms, this one is easy to provide with statistics. Economic need *is* the most consistent work motive — for women as well as men. In 1976, for instance, 43 percent of all women in the paid-labor force were single, widowed, separated, or divorced, and working to support themselves and their dependents. An additional 21 percent were married to men who had earned less than ten thousand dollars in the previous year, the minimum then required to support a family of four. In fact, if you take men's pensions, stocks, real estate, and various forms of accumulated wealth into account, a good statistical case can be made that there are more women who "have" to work (that is, who have neither the accumu-lated wealth, nor husbands whose work or wealth can support them for the rest of their lives) than there are men with the same need. If we were going to ask one group "Do you really need this job?" we should ask men.

9   But the first weakness of the whole "have to work" defense is its deceptive-ness. Anyone who has ever experienced dehumanized life on welfare or any other confidence-shaking dependency knows that a paid job may be preferable to the dole, even when the handout is coming from a family member. Yet the will and self-confidence to work on one's own can diminish as dependency and fear increase. That may explain why — contrary to the "have to" rationale — wives of men who earn less than three thousand dollars a year are actually *less* likely to be employed than wives whose husbands make ten thousand dollars a year or more.

10   Furthermore, the greatest proportion of employed wives is found among families with a total household income of twenty-five to fifty thousand dollars a year. This is the statistical underpinning used by some sociologists to prove that women's work is mainly important for boosting families into the middle or upper middle class. Thus, women's incomes are largely used for buying "luxuries" and "little extras": a neat double-whammy that renders us secondary within our families, and makes our jobs expendable in hard times. We may even go along with this interpretation (at least, up to the point of getting fired so a male can have our job). It preserves a husbandly ego-need to be seen as the primary breadwinner, and still allows us a safe "feminine" excuse for working.

11   But there are often rewards that we're not confessing. As noted in *The Two-Career Couple*, by Francine and Douglas Hall: "Women who hold jobs by choice, even blue-collar routine jobs, are more satisfied with their lives than are the full-time housewives."

12   In addition to personal satisfaction, there is also society's need for all its members' talents. Suppose that jobs were given out on only a "have to work" basis to both women and men — one job per household. It would be unthinkable to lose the unique abilities of, for instance, Eleanor Holmes Norton, the distinguished

chair of the Equal Employment Opportunity Commission. But would we then be forced to question the important work of her husband, Edward Norton, who is also a distinguished lawyer? Since men earn more than twice as much as women on the average, the wife in most households would be more likely to give up her job. Does that mean the nation could do as well without millions of its nurses, teachers, and secretaries? Or that the rare man who earns less than his wife should give up his job?

13   It was this kind of waste of human talents on a society-wide scale that traumatized millions of unemployed or underemployed Americans during the Depression. Then, a one-job-per-household rule seemed somewhat justified, yet the concept was used to displace women workers only, create intolerable dependencies, and waste female talent that the country needed. That Depression experience, plus the energy and example of women who were finally allowed to work during the manpower shortage created by World War II, led Congress to reinterpret the meaning of the country's full-employment goal in its Economic Act of 1946. Full employment was officially defined as "the employment of those who want to work, without regard to whether their employment is, by some definition, necessary. This goal applies equally to men and to women." Since bad economic times are again creating more need for women to be employed — we need such a goal more than ever. Women are again being caught in a tragic double bind: We are required to be strong and then punished for our strength.

14   Clearly, anything less than government and popular commitment to this 1946 definition of full employment will have the less powerful groups, whoever they may be, in danger. Almost as important as the financial penalty paid by the powerless is the suffering that comes from being shut out of paid and recognized work. Without it, we lose much of our self-respect and our ability to prove that we are alive by making some difference in the world. That's just as true for the suburban woman as it is for the unemployed steel worker.

15   But it won't be easy to give up the passive defense of "weworkbecausewe-haveto."

16   When a woman who is struggling to support her children and grandchildren on welfare sees her neighbor working as a waitress, even though that neighbor's husband has a job, she may feel resentful; and the waitress (of course, not the waitress's husband) may feel guilty. Yet unless we establish the obligation to provide a job for everyone who is willing and able to work, that welfare woman may herself be penalized by policies that give out only one public-service job per household. She and her daughter will have to make a painful and devisive decision about which of them gets that precious job, and the whole household will have to survive on only one salary.

17   A job as a human right is a principle that applies to men as well as women. But women have more cause to fight for it. The phenomenon of the "working woman" has been held responsible for everything from an increase in male impotence (which turned out, incidentally, to be attributable to medication for high blood pressure) to the rising cost of steak (which was due to high energy costs and beef import restrictions, not women's refusal to prepare the cheaper, slower-cooking cuts).

Unless we see a job as part of every citizen's right to autonomy and personal ful-fillment, we will continue to be vulnerable to someone else's idea of what "need" is, and whose "need" counts the most.

18   In many ways, women who do not have to work for simple survival, but who choose to do so nonetheless, are on the frontier of asserting this right for all women. Those with well-to-do husbands are dangerously easy for us to resent and put down. It's easier still to resent women from families of inherited wealth, even though men generally control and benefit from that wealth. (There is no Rockefeller Sisters Fund, no J. P. Morgan & Daughters, and sons-in-law may be the ones who really sleep their way to power.) But to prevent a woman whose husband or father is wealthy from earning her own living, and from gaining the self-confidence that comes with that ability, is to keep her needful of that unearned power and less willing to disperse it. Moreover, it is to lose forever her unique talents.

19   Perhaps modern feminists have been guilty of a kind of reverse snobbism that keeps us from reaching out to the wives and daughters of wealthy men; yet it was exactly such women who refused the restrictions of class and financed the first wave of feminist revolution.

20   For most of us, however, "womenworkbecausewehaveto" is just true enough to be seductive as a personal defense.

21   If we use it without also staking out the larger human right to a job, however, we will never achieve that right. And we will always be subject to the false argu-ment that independence for women is a luxury affordable only in good economic times. Alternatives to layoffs will not be explored, acceptable unemployment will always be used to frighten those with jobs into accepting low wages, and we will never remedy the real cost, both to families and to the country, of dependent women and a massive loss of talent.

22   Worst of all, we may never learn to find productive, honored work as a natural part of ourselves and as one of life's basic pleasures.

OX CART MAN

Donald Hall

1 In October of the year,
   he counts potatoes dug from the brown field,
   counting the seed, counting
   the cellar's portion out,
   and bags the rest on the cart's floor.

2 He packs wool sheared in April, honey
   in combs, linen, leather
   tanned from deerhide,
   and vinegar in a barrel
   hooped by hand at the forge's fire.

3 He walks by ox's head, ten days
   to Portsmouth Market, and sells potatoes,
   and the bag that carried potatoes,
   flaxseed, birch brooms, maple sugar, goose
   feathers, yarn.

4 When the cart is empty he sells the cart.
   When the cart is sold he sells the ox,
   harness and yoke, and walks
   home, his pockets heavy
   with the year's coin for salt and taxes,

5 and at home by fire's light in November cold
   stitches new harness
   for next year's ox in the barn,
   and carves the yoke, and saws planks
   building the cart again.

Donald Hall, "Ox Cart Man," *Kicking Leaves*, Harper and Row, 1978.

WHO BUILT THE PYRAMIDS? MIKE LEFEVRE

1 Who built the seven towers of Thebes?
The books are filled with the names of kings.
Was it kings who hauled the craggy blocks of stone? . . .
In the evening when the Chinese wall was finished
Where did the masons go? . . .

— Bertolt Brecht

Studs Terkel

2 *It is a two-flat dwelling, somewhere in Cicero, on the outskirts of Chicago. He is thirty-seven. He works in a steel mill. On occasion, his wife Carol works as a waitress in a neighborhood restaurant; otherwise, she is at home, caring for their two small children, a girl and a boy.*

3   *At the time of my first visit, a sculpted statuette of Mother and Child was on the floor, head severed from body. He laughed softly as he indicated his three-year-old daughter: "She Doctor Spock'd it."*

4 I'm a dying breed. A laborer. Strictly muscle work . . . pick it up, put it down, pick it up, put it down. We handle between forty and fifty thousand pounds of steel a day. (Laughs) I know this is hard to believe — from four hundred pounds to three-and four-pound pieces. It's dying.

5   You can't take pride any more. You remember when a guy could point to a house he built, how many logs he stacked. He built it and he was proud of it. I don't really think I could be proud if a contractor built a home for me. I would be tempted to get in there and kick the carpenter in the ass (laughs), and take the saw away from him. 'Cause I would have to be part of it, you know.

6   It's hard to take pride in a bridge you're never gonna cross, in a door you're never gonna open. You're mass-producing things and you never see the end result of it. (Muses) I worked for a trucker one time. And I got this tiny satisfaction when I loaded a truck. At least I could see the truck depart loaded. In a steel mill, forget it. You don't see where nothing goes.

7   I got chewed out by my foreman once. He said, "Mike, you're a good worker but you have a bad attitude." My attitude is that I don't get excited about my job. I do my work but I don't say whoopee-doo. The day I get excited about my job is the day I go to a head shrinker. How are you gonna get excited about pullin' steel? How are you gonna get excited when you're tired and want to sit down?

8   It's not just the work. Somebody built the pyramids. Somebody's going to build something. Pyramids, Empire State Building — these things just don't happen. There's hard work behind it. I would like to see a building, say, the Empire State,

Studs Terkel, "Who Built the Pryamids? Mike Lefevre," *Working*, Random House, 1975.

I would like to see on one side of it a foot-wide strip from top to bottom with the name of every bricklayer, the name of every electrician, with all the names. So when a guy walked by, he could take his son and say, "See, that's me over there on the forty-fifth floor. I put the steel beam in." Picasso can point to a painting. What can I point to? A writer can point to a book. Everybody should have something to point to.

9   It's the not-recognition by other people. To say a woman is *just* a housewife is degrading, right? Okay. *Just* a housewife. It's also degrading to say *just* a laborer. The difference is that a man goes out and maybe gets smashed.

10   When I was single, I could quit, just split. I wandered all over the country. You worked just enough to get a poke, money in your pocket. Now I'm married and I got two kids . . . (trails off). I worked on a truck dock one time and I was single. The foreman came over and he grabbed my shoulder, kind of gave me a shove. I punched him and knocked him off the dock. I said, "Leave me alone. I'm doing my work, just stay away from me, just don't give me the with-the-hands business."

11   Hell, if you whip a damn mule he might kick you. Stay out of my way, that's all. Working is bad enough, don't bug me. I would rather work my ass off for eight hours a day with nobody watching me than five minutes with a guy watching me. Who you gonna sock? You can't sock General Motors, you can't sock anybody in Washington, you can't sock a system.

12   A mule, an old mule, that's the way I feel. Oh yeah. See. (Shows black and blue marks on arms and legs, burns.) You know what I heard from more than one guy at work? "If my kid wants to work in a factory, I am going to kick the hell out of him." I want my kid to be an effete snob. Yeah, mm-hmm. (Laughs.) I want him to be able to quote, Walt Whitman, to be proud of it.

13   If you can't improve yourself, you improve your posterity. Otherwise life isn't worth nothing. You might as well go back to the cave and stay there. I'm sure the first caveman who went over the hill to see what was on the other side — I don't think he went there wholly out of curiosity. He went there because he wanted to get his son out of the cave. Just the same way I want to send my kid to college.

THE MASON: CARL MURRAY BATES

Studs Terkel

1 Stone's my life. I daydream all the time, most times it's on stone. Oh, I'm gonna build me a stone cabin down on the Green River. I'm gonna build stone cabinets in the kitchen. The stone door's gonna be awful heavy and I don't know how to attach the hinges. I've got to figure out how to make a stone roof. That's the kind of thing. All my dreams, it seems like it's got to have a piece of rock mixed in it.

2   If I got some problem that's bothering me, I'll actually wake up in the night and think of it. I'll sit at the table and get a pencil and paper and go over it, makin' marks on paper or drawin' or however . . . this way or that way. Now I've got to work this and I've only got so much. Or they decided they want it that way when you already got it fixed this way. Anyone hates tearing his work down. It's all the same price but you still don't like to do it.

3   These fireplaces, you've got to figure how they'll throw out heat, the way you curve the fireboxes inside. You have to draw a line so they reflect heat. But if you throw too much of a curve, you'll have them smoke. People in these fine houses don't want a puff of smoke coming out of the house.

4   The architect draws the picture and the plans, and the draftsman and the engineer, they help him. They figure the strength and so on. But when it comes to actually makin' the curves and doin' the work, you've got to do it with your hands. It comes right back to your hands.

5   When you get into stone, you're gettin' away from the prefabs, you're gettin' into the better homes. Usually at this day and age they'll start into sixty to seventy thousand and run up to about half a million. We've got one goin' now that's mighty close, three or four hundred thousand. That type of house is what we build.

6   The lumber is not near as good as it used to be. We have better fabricating material, such as plywood and sheet rock and things of that sort, but the lumber itself is definitely inferior. Thirty, forty years ago a house was almost entirely made of lumber, wood floors . . . Now they have vinyl, they have carpet, everything, and so on. The framework wood is getting to be of very poor quality.

7   But stone is still stone and the bricks are actually more uniform than they used to be. Originally they took a clay bank . . . I know a church been built that way. Went right on location, dug a hole in the ground and formed bricks with their hands. They made the bricks that built the building on the spot.

8   Now we've got modern kilns, modern heat, the temperature don't vary. They got better bricks now than they used to have. We've got machines that make brick, so they're made true. Where they used to, they were pretty rough. I'm buildin' a big fireplace now out of old brick. They run wide, long, and it's a headache. I've been two weeks on that one fireplace.

Studs Terkel, "The Mason: Carl Murray Bates," *Working*, Random House, 1975.

9   The toughest job I ever done was this house, a hundred years old plus. The lady wanted one room left just that way. And this doorway had to be closed. It had deteriorated and weathered for over a hundred years. The bricks was made out of broken pieces, none of 'em were straight. If you lay 'em crooked, it gets awful hard right there. You spend a lifetime trying to learn to lay bricks straight. And it took a half-day to measure with a spoon, to try to get the mortar to match. I'd have so much dirt, so much soot, so much lime, so when I got the recipe right I could make it in bigger quantity. Then I made it with a coffee cup. Half a cup of this, half a cup of that . . . I even used soot out of a chimney and sweepin's off the floor. I was two days layin' up a little doorway, mixin' the mortar and all. The boss told the lady it couldn't be done. I said, "Give me the time, I believe I can do it." I defy you to find where that door is right now. That's the best job I ever done.

10   There's not a house in this country that I haven't built that I don't look at every time I go by. (Laughs.) I can set here now and actually in my mind see so many that you wouldn't believe. If there's one stone in there crooked, I know where it's at and I'll never forget it. Maybe thirty years, I'll know a place where I should have took that stone out and redone it but I didn't. I still notice it. The people who live there might not notice it, but I notice it. I never pass that house that I don't think of it. I've got one house in mind right now. (Laughs.) That's the work of my hands. 'Cause you see, stone, you don't prepaint it, you don't camouflage it. It's here, just like I left it forty years ago.

11   I can't imagine a job where you go home and maybe go by a year later and you don't know what you've done. My work, I can see what I did the first day I started. All my work is set right out there in the open and I can look at it as I go by. It's something I can see the rest of my life. Forty years ago, the first blocks I ever laid in my life, when I was seventeen years old. I never go through Eureka — a little town down here on the river — that I don't look thataway. It's always there.

12   Immortality as far as we're concerned. Nothin' in this world lasts forever, but did you know that stone — Bedford limestone, they claim — deteriorates one-sixteenth of an inch every hundred years? And it's around four or five inches for a house. So that's gettin' awful close. (Laughs.)

IX
PAYING
FOR AN
EDUCATION

Every year, it seems, college tuition costs go up, federal money for education goes down, and college gets even harder to pay for. In this section, Caroline Bird and Gary Becker debate whether college is worth all the expense. *Business Week* calls on the government to be more generous in financing education, while Steven Madoff focuses on co-op programs that mix paid work with school. In what may be the most controversial selection, Norman Ellenberger discusses the goals that bring some athletes to — but do not always get them through — college.

The issue extends beyond the financial strain on individual families. Many educators in the 1960s felt that colleges should open their doors to anyone who wanted to come. Now, with the cost of a year at some colleges nearing $20,000, college is seen again as a privilege, and it becomes increasingly difficult for the unprivileged to break in and get an education. The question of how to pay for college affects all of society and leads to many additional questions. Who will get an education? Who will get the best jobs? Who will have the chance to take full benefit of the American way of life? And who will have the power to make the decisions that affect all our futures?

EDUCATION HAS BEEN NEGLECTED LONG ENOUGH
Business Week

1 Following World War II, millions of U.S. veterans went to college under the GI Bill, which paid the cost of tuition and books plus a modest living allowance. Vastly popular, the program was seen as compensation to young people whose lives had been interrupted by war. It was also an enormous investment in human capital that proved of incalculable benefit to America. Now no comparable educational effort seems conceivable. The Reagan Administration's new fiscal 1988 budget continues the trend of cutting federal grants for education. This illustrates once again that a particularly damaging fallout from the budget deficit is to distract attention from the country's legitimate needs.

2 Can anybody doubt that improving education is a crucial need? Study after study documents U.S. deficiencies in teaching science, mathematics, languages, and other vital subjects. Recently the U.S. and Japan reported on each other's educatonal systems. Not surprisingly, the U.S. found more to admire about Japan's secondary education than the Japanese found to praise in this country's.

3 Americans are wedded to local control of education — and that should not change. But the result is an educational system radically uneven in quality. That is where Washington should be playing a role: encouraging and pointing the way to

"Education Has Been Neglected Long Enough," *Business Week*, February 2, 1987.

improved standards. For the Administration to trim severely even its modest financial support for education sends the wrong message. Leaving education firmly in
local hands, the national government could use a variety of techniques — matching
grants, for example — to fortify local interest in specific projects. It also could
focus grants, say, to prepare college students to go into teaching, as is already done
to lure doctors to rural areas. A report on education from the Committee for
Economic Development last year underscored business' concern about education
and its readiness to play its part in upgrading it. It is up to the federal government
to forge an effective nationwide commitment to make U.S. education second
to none.

WHERE COLLEGE FAILS US

Caroline Bird

1 The case *for* college has been accepted without question for more than a generation. All high school graduates ought to go, says Conventional Wisdom and statistical evidence, because college will help them earn more money, become "better"
people, and learn to be more responsible citizens than those who don't go.

2   But college has never been able to work its magic for everyone. And now that
close to half our high school graduates are attending, those who don't fit the
pattern are becoming more numerous, and more obvious. College graduates are
selling shoes and driving taxis; college students sabotage each other's experiments
and forge letters of recommendation in the intense competition for admission to
graduate school. Others find no stimulation in their studies, and drop out — often
encouraged by college administrators.

3   Some observers say the fault is with the young people themselves — they are
spoiled, stoned, overindulged, and expecting too much. But that's mass character
assassination, and doesn't explain all campus unhappiness. Others blame the state
of the world, and they are partly right. We've been told that young people have to
go to college because our economy can't absorb an army of untrained eighteen-
year-olds. But disillusioned graduates are learning that it can no longer absorb an
army of trained twenty-two-year-olds, either.

4   Some adventuresome educators and campus watchers have openly begun to
suggest that college may not be the best, the proper, the only place for every young
person after the completion of high school. We may have been looking at all those
surveys and statistics upside down, it seems, and through the rosy glow of our own
remembered college experiences. Perhaps college doesn't make people intelligent,
ambitious, happy, liberal, or quick to learn new things — maybe it's just the other
way around, and intelligent, ambitious, happy, liberal, and quick-learning people are
merely the ones who have been attracted to college in the first place. And perhaps

Caroline Bird, "Where College Fails Us," *Signature Magazine*, Diners Club Inc., 1975.

all those successful college graduates would have been successful whether they had gone to college or not. This is heresy to those of us who have been brought up to believe that if a little schooling is good, more has to be much better. But contrary evidence is beginning to mount up.

5   The unhappiness and discontent of young people is nothing new, and problems of adolescence are always painfully intense. But while traveling around the country, speaking at colleges, and interviewing students at all kinds of schools — large and small, public and private — I was overwhelmed by the prevailing sadness. It was as visible on campuses in California as in Nebraska and Massachusetts. Too many young people are in college reluctantly, because everyone told them they ought to go, and there didn't seem to be anything better to do. Their elders sell them college because it's good for them. Some never learn to like it, and talk about their time in school as if it were a sentence to be served.

6   Students tell us the same thing college counselors tell us — they go because of pressure from parents and teachers, and stay because it seems to be an alternative to a far worse fate. It's "better" than the Army or a dead-end job, and it has to be pretty bad before it's any worse than staying at home.

7 College graduates say that they don't want to work "just" for the money: They want work that matters. They want to help people and save the world. But the numbers are stacked against them. Not only are there not enough jobs in world-saving fields, but in the current slowdown it has become evident that there never were, and probably never will be, enough jobs requiring higher education to go around.

8   Students who tell their advisers they want to help people, for example, are often directed to psychology. This year the Department of Labor estimates that there will be 4,300 new jobs for psychologists, while colleges will award 58,430 bachelor's degrees in psychology.

9   Sociology has become a favorite major on socially conscious campuses, but graduates find that social reform is hardly a paying occupation. Male sociologists from the University of Wisconsin reported as gainfully employed a year after graduation included a legal assistant, sports editor, truck unloader, Peace Corps worker, publications director, and a stockboy — but no sociologist per se. The highest paid worked for the post office.

10   Publishing, writing, and journalism are presumably the vocational goal of a large proportion of the 104,000 majors in Communications and Letters expected to graduate in 1975. The outlook for them is grim. All of the daily newspapers in the country combined are expected to hire a total of 2,600 reporters this year. Radio and television stations may hire a total of 500 announcers, most of them in local radio stations. Nonpublishing organizations will need 1,100 technical writers, and public-relations activities another 4,400. Even if new graduates could get all these jobs (they can't, of course), over 90,000 of them will have to find something less glamorous to do.

11   Other fields most popular with college graduates are also pathetically small. Only 1,900 foresters a year will be needed during this decade, although schools of

forestry are expected to continue graduating twice that many. Some will get sub-professional jobs as forestry aides. Schools of architecture are expected to turn out twice as many as will be needed, and while all sorts of people want to design things, the Department of Labor forecasts that there will be jobs for only 400 new industrial designers a year. As for anthropologists, only 400 will be needed every year in the 1970s to take care of all the college courses, public-health research, community surveys, museums, and all the archaeological digs on every continent. (For these jobs graduate work in anthropology is required.)

12   Many popular occupations may seem to be growing fast without necessarily offering employment to very many. "Recreation work" is always cited as an expanding field, but it will need relatively few workers who require more special training than life guards. "Urban planning" has exploded in the media, so the U.S. Department of Labor doubled its estimate of the number of jobs to be filled every year in the 1970s – to a big, fat 800. A mere 200 oceanographers a year will be able to do all the exploring of "inner space" – and all that exciting underwater diving you see demonstrated on television – for the entire decade of the 1970s.

13   Whatever college graduates *want* to do, most of them are going to wind up doing what *there is* to do. During the next few years, according to the Labor Department, the biggest demand will be for stenographers and secretaries, followed by retail-trade salesworkers, hospital attendants, bookkeepers, building custodians, registered nurses, foremen, kindergarten and elementary-school teachers, receptionists, cooks, cosmetologists, private-household workers, manufacturing inspectors, and industrial machinery repairmen. These are the jobs which will eventually absorb the surplus archaeologists, urban planners, oceanographers, sociologists, editors, and college professors.

14   Vocationalism is the new look on campus because of the discouraging job market faced by the generalists. Students have been opting for medicine and law in droves. If all those who check "doctor" as their career goal succeed in getting their MDs, we'll immediately have ten times the target ratio of doctors for the population of the United States. Law schools are already graduating twice as many new lawyers every year as the Department of Labor thinks we will need, and the oversupply grows annually.

15   Specialists often find themselves at the mercy of shifts in demand, and the narrower the vocational training, the more risky the long-term prospects. Engineers are the classic example of the "Yo-Yo" effect in supply and demand. Today's shortage is apt to produce a big crop of engineering graduates after the need has crested, and teachers face the same squeeze.

16   Worse than that, when the specialists turn up for work, they often find that they have learned a lot of things in classrooms that they will never use, that they will have to learn a lot of things on the job that they were never taught, and that most of what they have learned is less likely to "come in handy later" than to fade from memory. One disillusioned architecture student, who had already designed and built houses, said, "It's the degree you need, not everything you learn getting it."

17   A diploma saves the employer the cost of screening candidates and gives him a predictable product: He can assume that those who have survived the four-year ordeal have learned how to manage themselves. They have learned how to budget their time, meet deadlines, set priorities, cope with impersonal authority, follow instructions, and stick with a task that may be tiresome without direct supervision.

18   The employer is also betting that it will be cheaper and easier to train the college graduate because he has demonstrated his ability to learn. But if the diploma serves only to identify those who are talented in the art of schoolwork, it becomes, in the words of Harvard's Christopher Jencks, "a hell of an expensive aptitude test." It is unfair to the candidates because they themselves must bear the cost of the screening — the cost of college. Candidates without the funds, the academic temperament, or the patience for the four-year obstacle race are ruled out, no matter how well they may perform on the job. But if "everyone" has a diploma, employers will have to find another way to choose employees, and it will become an empty credential.

19   (Screening by diploma may in fact already be illegal. The 1971 ruling of the Supreme Court in *Griggs* v. *Duke Power Co.* contended that an employer cannot demand a qualification which systemically excludes an entire class of applicants, unless that qualification reliably predicts success on the job. The requiring of a high school diploma was outlawed in the *Griggs* case, and this could extend to a college diploma.)

20 The bill for four years at an Ivy League college is currently climbing toward $25,000; at a state university, a degree will cost the student and his family about $10,000 (with taxpayers making up the difference).

21   Not many families can afford these sums, and when they look for financial aid, they discover that someone else will decide how much they will actually have to pay. The College Scholarship Service, which establishes a family's degree of need for most colleges, is guided by noble principles: uniformity of sacrifice, need rather than merit. But families vary in their willingness to "sacrifice" as much as the bureaucracy of the CSS thinks they ought to. This is particularly true of middle-income parents, whose children account for the bulk of the country's college students. Some have begun to rebel against this attempt to enforce the same values and priorities on all. "In some families, a college education competes with a second car, a color television, or a trip to Europe — and it's possible that college may lose," one financial-aid officer recently told me.

22   Quite so. College is worth more to some middle-income families than to others. It is chilling to consider the undercurrent of resentment that families who "give up everything" must feel toward their college-age children, or the burden of guilt children must bear every time they goof off or receive less than top grades in their courses.

23   The decline in return for a college degree within the last generation has been substantial. In the 1950s, a Princeton student could pay his expenses for the school year — eating club and all — on less than $3,000. When he graduated, he entered a

job market which provided a comfortable margin over the earnings of his agemates who had not been to college. To be precise, a freshman entering Princeton in 1956, the earliest year for which the Census has attempted to project lifetime earnings, could expect to realize a 12.5 percent return on his investment. A freshman entering in 1972, with the cost nearing $6,000 annually, could expect to realize only 9.3 percent, less than might be available in the money market. This calculation was made with the help of a banker and his computer, comparing college as an investment in future earnings with other investments available in the booming money market of 1974, and concluded that in strictly financial terms, college is not always the best investment a young person can make.

24   I postulated a young man (the figures are different with a young woman, but the principle is the same) whose rich uncle would give him, in cash, the total cost of four years at Princeton — $34,181. (The total includes what the young man would earn if he went to work instead of to college right after high school.) If he did not spend the money on Princeton, but put it in the savings bank at 7.5 percent interest compounded daily, he would have, at retirement age sixty-four, more than five times as much as the $199,000 extra he could expect to earn between twenty-two and sixty as a college man rather than a mere high school graduate. And with all that money accumulating in the bank, he could invest in something with a higher return than a diploma. At age twenty-eight, when his nest egg had reached $73,113, he could buy a liquor store, which would return him well over 20 percent on his investment, as long as he was willing to mind the store. He might get a bit fidgety sitting there, but he'd have to be dim-witted to lose money on a liquor store, and right now we're talking only about dollars.

25   If the young man went to a public college rather than Princeton, the investment would be lower, and the payoff higher, of course, because other people — the taxpayers — put up part of the capital for him. But the difference in return between an investment in public and private colleges is minimized because the biggest part of the investment in either case is the money a student might earn if he went to work, not to college — in economic terms, his "foregone income." That he bears himself.

26 Rates of return and dollar signs on education are a fascinating brain teaser, and, obviously, there is a certain unreality to the game. But the same unreality extends to the traditional calculations that have always been used to convince taxpayers that college is a worthwhile investment.

27   The ultimate defense of college has always been that while it may not teach you anything vocationally useful, it will somehow make you a better person, able to do anything better, and those who make it through the process are initiated into the "fellowship of educated men and women." In a study intended to probe what graduates seven years out of college thought their colleges should have done for them, the Carnegie Commission found that most alumni expected the "development of my abilities to think and express myself." But if such respected educational psychologists as Bruner and Piaget are right, specific learning skills have to be acquired very early in life, perhaps even before formal schooling begins.

28   So, when pressed, liberal-arts defenders speak instead about something more encompassing, and more elusive. "College changed me inside," one graduate told us fervently. The authors of a Carnegie Commission report, who obviously struggled for a definition, concluded that one of the common threads in the perceptions of a liberal education is that it provides "an integrated view of the world which can serve as an inner guide." More simply, alumni say that college should have "helped me to formulate the values and goals of my life."

29   In theory, a student is taught to develop these values and goals himself, but in practice, it doesn't work quite that way. All but the wayward and the saintly take their sense of the good, the true, and the beautiful from the people around them. When we speak of students acquiring "values" in college, we often mean that they will acquire the values — and sometimes that means only the tastes — of their professors. The values of professors may be "higher" than many students will encounter elsewhere, but they may not be relevant to situations in which students find themselves in college and later.

30   Of all the forms in which ideas are disseminated, the college professor lecturing a class is the slowest and most expensive. You don't have to go to college to read the great books or learn about the great ideas of Western Man. Today you can find them everywhere — in paperbacks, in the public libraries, in museums, in public lectures, in adult-education courses, in abridged, summarized, or adapted form in magazines, films, and television. The problem is no longer one of access to broadening ideas; the problem is the other way around: how to choose among the many courses of action proposed to us, how to edit the stimulations that pour into our eyes and ears every waking hour. A college experience that piles option on option and stimulation on stimulation merely adds to the contemporary nightmare.

31   What students and graduates say that they did learn on campus comes under the heading of personal, rather than intellectual, development. Again and again I was told that the real value of college is learning to get along with others, to practice social skills, to "sort out my head," and these have nothing to do with curriculum.

32   For whatever impact the academic experience used to have on college students, the sheer size of many undergraduate classes in the 1970s dilutes faculty-student dialogue, and, more often than not, they are taught by teachers who were hired when colleges were faced with a shortage of qualified instructors, during their years of expansion and when the big rise in academic pay attracted the mediocre and the less than dedicated.

33   On the social side, colleges are withdrawing from reponsibility for feeding, housing, policing, and protecting students at a time when the environment of college may be the most important service it could render. College officials are reluctant to "intervene" in the personal lives of the students. They no longer expect to take over from parents, but often insist that students — who have, most often, never lived away from home before — take full adult responsibility for their plans, achievements, and behavior.

34   Most college students do not live in the plush, comfortable country-clublike surroundings their parents envisage, or, in some cases, remember. Open dorms, particularly when they are coeducational, are noisy, usually overcrowded, and often

messy. Some students desert the institutional "zoos" (their own word for dorms) and move into run-down, overpriced apartments. Bulletin boards in student centers are littered with notices of apartments to share and the drift of conversation suggests that a lot of money is dissipated in scrounging for food and shelter.

35 Taxpayers now provide more than half of the astronomical sums that are spent on higher education. But less than half of today's high school graduates go on, raising a new question of equity: Is it fair to make all the taxpayers pay for the minority who actually go to college? We decided long ago that it is fair for childless adults to pay school taxes because everyone, parents and nonparents alike, profits by a literate population. Does the same reasoning hold true for state-supported higher education? There is no conclusive evidence on either side.

36   Young people cannot be expected to go to college for the general good of mankind. They may be more altruistic than their elders, but no great numbers are going to spend four years at hard intellectual labor, let alone tens of thousands of family dollars, for "the advancement of human capability in society at large," one of the many purposes invoked by the Carnegie Commission report. Nor do any considerable number of them want to go to college to beat the Russians to Jupiter, improve the national defense, increase the Gross National Product, lower the crime rate, improve automobile safety, or create a market for the arts — all of which have been suggested at one time or other as benefits taxpayers get for supporting higher education.

37   One sociologist said that you don't have to have a reason for going to college because it's an institution. His definition of an institution is something everyone subscribed to without question. The burden of proof is not on why you should go to college, but why anyone thinks there might be a reason for not going. The implication — and some educators express it quite frankly — is that an eighteen-year-old high school graduate is still too young and confused to know what he wants to do, let alone what is good for him.

38   Mother knows best, in other words.

39   It had always been comfortable for students to believe that authorities, like Mother, or outside specialists, like educators, could determine what was best for them. However, specialists and authorities no longer enjoy the credibility former generations accorded them. Patients talk back to doctors and are not struck suddenly dead. Clients question the lawyer's bills and sometimes get them reduced. It is no longer self-evident that all adolescents must study a fixed curriculum that was constructed at a time when all educated men could agree on precisely what it was that made them educated.

40   The same with college. If high school graduates don't want to continue their education, or don't want to continue it right away, they may perceive more clearly than their elders that college is not for them.

41   College is an ideal place for those young adults who love learning for its own sake, who would rather read than eat, and who like nothing better than writing research papers. But they are a minority, even at the prestigious colleges, which recruit and attract the intellectually oriented.

42   The rest of our high school graduates need to look at college more closely and critically, to examine it as a consumer product, and decide if the cost in dollars, in time, in continued dependency, and in future returns is worth the very large investment each student — and his family — must make.

WHY SHOULDN'T COLLEGE BE A SMART INVESTMENT?

Gary S. Becker

1 The beginning of a new school year reminds many families of the financial sacrifice required to send children through college. At elite private universities, tuition runs about $12,000 a year. Expenditures on room, board, and travel, as well as forgone earnings while in school, add at least $8,000 a year, raising the total cost of four years of education to more than $80,000.

2   Tuition averages only about $1,500 a year at public colleges and universities, but students at public schools, as well as private ones, must also settle for lower-paying and usually part-time jobs. And many public-school students also pay room and board. In addition, an increasing number of students have the added expense of postgraduate education at law, business, and other professional schools.

3   In the past, the cost of higher education was less a problem because mainly wealthy families sent their children to college. Nowadays, well over half of all high school graduates continue their education; blacks, Hispanics, and other minorities account for almost 20% of all college students. To add to the burden, college tuition and fees have almost doubled since 1980.

No Downpayments

4 Yet when placed in perspective, the cost of college education does not seem so daunting. Four years at an elite university are no more expensive than, say, buying a nice home. Most college graduates eventually own their own homes, and the median price of single-family dwellings purchased recently exceeds the $80,000 that a college education cost them. Moreover, owner-occupied housing does not yield financial returns, except sometimes a real capital gain, whereas higher education usually greatly raises lifetime earnings. The average financial rate of return on the cost of a typical investment in a four-year college education is 7% to 10%.

5   True, attending college is a risky investment. Yet if an elite higher education is no more expensive than good housing and if college is a profitable investment, why do individuals who must pay all or part of their own education have more difficulty in financing a college education than in financing the purchase of a house? One reason is that most college students are young and have not had much time to save

Gary S. Becker, ''Why Shouldn't College Be a Smart Investment?'' *Business Week*, September 8, 1986.

for a downpayment on their investment in education. More important, housing can be used as collateral for a mortgage, but a college education cannot serve as a collateral for an education loan. If a mortgage holder defaults, a lender takes possession of the house. Obviously, a lender cannot take possession of a college education without somehow requiring the defaulter to engage in involuntary servitude, which would be illegal.

6   To help pay for their college education, many students work during the summer and part-time while in school. Further, most parents help out with gifts or loans, and all colleges provide scholarships and employment opportunities. In recent years, the federal government has taken an active role in financing college education with Pell grants, direct loans, guaranteed student loans, college work-study programs, and educational-opportunity grants. More than half of all freshmen entering college now receive some form of direct federal assistance.

It's A Gift

7 Since education is poor collateral for strictly commercial loans, I believe that the federal government should help students. But the present programs are badly flawed. They subsidize college students with taxpayers' money, even though most taxpayers earn less than the typical college-educated person. These subsidies take the forms of loans at below-market interest rates, outright gifts, and allowing borrowers to default even when they can easily afford to pay. The current default rate on guaranteed student loans exceeds 10%.

8   To eliminate the subsidy, effective interest rates on student loans should equal the rate of return on business investments with similar risks. Students who default should be energetically prosecuted so that student loans would no longer be a free ride at the taxpayers' expense.

9   With few exceptions, interest rates charged students have not been related to their eventual earnings. One way a loan program could take into account the uncertainty about financial returns from a college education would be to require student borrowers who were later financially successful to pay back more than unsuccessful borrowers. A pilot program might require borrowers to pay a fixed percentage of their income for a specified period of time. In effect, the government would share the risk of college investments by buying nonvoting common stock in student borrowers. Stocks are usually the appropriate way to finance risky investments like a college education. Low returns from loans to students who do not do well would be balanced by high returns from loans to students who end up earning a lot.

10   Federal assistance can help college students finance the large and rising cost of higher education without imposing the burden on taxpayers. Student loans with appropriate fixed interest rates and with paybacks contingent on the financial success of borrowers would achieve this worthwhile purpose.

WE HAVE TO MAKE MONEY

Norman Ellenberger

1 We should be clear that we are not talking about athletics in general, we are talking about football and basketball. And football and basketball have no effect on education. Oh, professors might complain about the athletic budget and that they don't have enough money for research, but we are kidding ourselves if we say that athletics are running the colleges. Athletics are not what we are talking about. We are talking about money, a survival situation, and let's-be-number-one.

2   What is wrong if a young man pursues a career in professional athletics? We say that people must have goals in life. If the only possible goal for a young man is professional athletics, what is wrong with that? Why degrade that drive within a young man? It is not how many reach the goal that counts. So only two or three percent make it. Well, big deal! How many make it to the top of RCA? How many make it to the top in any profession? It isn't how many make it. It's what they are exposed to along the way, and what kind of people they become as a result.

3   There is no difference between pursuing athletics and pursuing art, or modern dance, or marching band.

4   The worship that we have for the athlete is healthy and universal. We can go clear back to the Greeks and the Olympics to find the origin of that. The monies now involved are a modern development. It is said that football and basketball programs are for physical activity. But how much physical activity is there for the hundred thousand people in a stadium watching twenty-two guys play football? We also hear that the program is to give us such values as fair play, the purity of competition, an exemplification of the American way of life, ethics, morality. Well, I watch Saturday afternoon college football on television, and I see the NCAA's thirty- or sixty-second spot at halftime, where the virtues of football and basketball are expounded as if they were like motherhood, apple pie, and the flag. And I giggle. It just ain't there. Sports are the way they are because of the almighty dollar. We have to make money. Somebody, for God's sake, say it!

5   People don't want to know what's going on. I've lived it first-hand; and I refer not just to my most recent experience in court. I am not here as a martyr. I have lived it through being involved for fifteen years in the college sports scene on all levels. People say, I know something is happening, but don't tell me. So, we turn our heads. Then we get caught up in it, and at that point we say, "It's the system." All right, but let's define that system.

6   It is said that we "use" the poor kid we recruit for sports. He has his athletic career, but he never graduates. Still, is the only individual we want to educate in the United States the brainy person, the one who has a direction in life, a mother and father, books, a home? If so, then we will have a very limited society.

Norman Ellenberger, "We Have to Make Money," *from* "Tell It Like It Is: We Have to Make Money," *The Center Magazine*, January/February 1982.

7   Somewhere along the line the young man who does not have these advantages has to have help. Who cares whether that person graduates from college? It is not that important. He did not want to go to college in the first place. He is performing a service. He is doing what he is supposed to do. That does not make him a bad person. And when he is through, sure, we would like to graduate him, but we can't. There is no program in any university that he can handle. But he is one hell of an athlete. He can run up and down the basketball court for you. He will bring you money. He will do all these things that people say are so dastardly. But don't you know that that young man is benefiting, that he is learning to be a person, that he is developing, that he is becoming a member of society? Some of the greatest young men whom I have ever been fortunate to coach never graduated. But they have jobs, they have families, and they are not in the breadlines. The reason: they came and put on a pair of short pants and sneakers and ran up and down the basketball court.

8   The NCAA has a book of rules and regulations that every coach in the United States is supposed to follow, but the coaches don't even understand that book. You can take two or three hundred college coaches who are violating rules, fire them, and find two or three hundred replacements tomorrow. The next day, they will all be violating the rules, not because they want to, but partly because they do not even understand the rules. So, we add more rules and hire more investigators. The NCAA can hire as many investigators as it wants, but it still will not work.

9   I stand before you a convicted felon. I was indicted by our state grand jury in New Mexico on twenty-two counts of felony. I was convicted of twenty-one of them.* But don't view me as a martyr. I am not asking for your sympathy. I don't need that. I am far above that. I am simply trying to represent the coaches in a profession that I dearly love, and that I will probably never again have an opportunity to pursue.

10   But if we ever come out from under the hypocrisy and the myopia, and if we will just define where we are and what we want, and then get the rules and regulations that can be administered by the system, we can solve this problem.

---

*Ellenberger, a basketball coach, was convicted of fraud for doctoring academic transcripts in favor of student athletes.

A WAY TO PAY THAT'S NOT JUST ACADEMIC
Steven H. Madoff

1 Back when annual college bills ran to three figures, a few schools started something called cooperative education — alternating semesters of off-campus jobs with semesters of study. For decades it was looked on as an eccentric way to spend your undergraduate years. Now, with the average annual cost of tuition, room and board running close to $9,000 at private colleges, co-op education has been discovered for what it is — part cost cutter, part career builder.

Steven H. Madoff, "A Way to Pay That's Not Academic," *Money*, June 1984.

2   From 1970 to 1983, the number of colleges and universities offering such programs grew from 200 to about 1,000; last year alone, 200,000 students enrolled in them earned $1.5 billion. And the federal government, despite its sharp cuts in financial aid for higher education in general, is considering increasing co-op funding from $14.4 million to as much as $20 million next year.

3   Co-op education has nothing to do with conventional work-study programs, under which colleges provide part-time on-campus jobs for undergraduates. In a typical co-op arrangement, a student takes a responsible job, often as a trainee in his chosen field, at a company that has formally agreed to cooperate with a school in providing off-campus employment. On average, co-op students earn $6,000 for half a year's work. These earnings, minus income taxes, are usually figured into the student's financial aid package back at college, thus decreasing his need for grants and loans.

4   Co-oping is a powerful help to the graduate job seeker too. It often leads to full-time employment with the same company and at a higher salary than a less experienced applicant could expect. The federal government, the largest co-op employer of all, put about 13,000 students to work in 1983 — chiefly in the military services, the National Aeronautics and Space Administration, the Treasury and the Department of Agriculture. And the U.S. holds on to 75% of these students after graduation.

5   In fact, the experience often turns out to be of far more lasting value than money. Notes Sam Sovilla, director of the University of Cincinnati's co-op program: "Once students get into their co-op jobs, the financial benefits have become a given. Then the students start focusing on career development."

6   Preparation for entering a co-op program doesn't begin until at least freshman year. During the first term, the student can talk to the school's co-op counselors, look through job lists and decide on which jobs to apply for. He also states what subject he plans to major in, but he can change his mind later. While it's possible to begin off-campus work during the spring term of freshman year, generally a student waits until he has experienced a full year of campus life. To be accepted and to continue in many co-op programs, a student must maintain a grade-point average of at least 2.5 on a 4.0 scale.

7   The next steps are job applications and interviews. For government work, you fill out Standard Form 171 — the Personal Qualifications Statement — which asks for a listing of work experience and courses completed. After being accepted for a job, a student typically begins alternating work and academic terms, including summers, until his senior year, when many co-op programs require that he return to school full time.

8   Though students may receive some academic credit for their work, they complete most of their degree requirements in the classroom. Co-op students usually make up for lost academic time in summer school. Some take five years to get their baccalaureates, but they almost always pay only minimum enrollment fees, sometimes nothing, for semesters when they're off working.

9   A free brochure that answers virtually any question you might have on the subject is *Undergraduate Programs of Cooperative Education in the United States and*

Canada (National Commission for Cooperative Education, 360 Huntington Ave., Boston, Mass. 02115). It lists participating schools, length of work terms, type of credit given and the most popular kinds of jobs. Another helpful guide is *Earn and Learn: Cooperative Education Opportunities Offered by the Federal Government* (Octameron Press, P.O. Box 3437, Alexandria, Va. 22302; $2.25 including postage.).

10   Co-oping isn't everyone's ideal college education. Most co-op students are in business administration, computer science, engineering and the hard sciences. Humanities students are in less demand for co-op jobs, and those who participate in cooperative programs don't fare as well as more technical graduates. The median starting salary for 1983 co-op grads in mechanical engineering was $26,000; for graduates with B.A.s in the humanities, it was exactly half that.

11   Lance Goodmon, 20, a junior majoring in aerospace mechanical engineering at the University of Central Florida in Orlando, is among the lucky ones. "I've always liked tinkering, figuring out mechanical devices," he says. "I wanted the same kind of experience in school, directly applying what I learned." In his senior year of high school, Goodmon heard of the co-op program that the university maintained with NASA. "I knew that's what I wanted to do," he recalls.

12   Goodmon had a foretaste of job competition when he first applied to the NASA program: there were no positions available. He reapplied and beat out 14 other applicants for a six-month stint on a crew helping systems engineers to build equipment for Spacelab at the Kennedy Space Center.

13   Since then Goodmon has been able to get through school mostly on his own. Like many co-op students who seek jobs near their home towns, Goodmon lives with his parents — 15 miles from the space center and 30 miles from campus. So he could scratch room and board costs. He calculated his expenses last year at $4,700, including tuition, books, entertainment and the 1981 Datsun 200SX that he's paying off over 36 months. During work terms, he pays $25 for registration. His earnings were $7,200, leaving him savings of $2,500.

14   Peter Watson, 24, a junior in physics at Antioch College in Yellow Springs, Ohio, has helped to test the currents where the Indian and Atlantic oceans meet. It happened on an oceanographic cruise off South Africa last fall.

15   Co-oping actually drew Watson back to higher education. After an unhappy first year at Rensselaer Polytechnic in Troy, N.Y., he dropped out for four years and worked as a forklift operator in Birmingham, Ala., his home town. Then he heard about Antioch's co-op program and was attracted by its practical, untheoretical approach. Through a Guaranteed Student Loan, two college grants, part-time work as a teaching assistant and his co-op earnings, he's been able to pay the $9,290 annual total cost of tuition, room and board, save a bit and, as he says, "live humbly."

16   Antioch and other centers of cooperative education — notably Drexel University in Philadelphia, Georgia Tech in Atlanta, Northeastern University in Boston and the University of Cincinnati — are best known for offering varied job possibilities. It's a major benefit of their long-established relations with business and the scientific community.

17   Yet you don't always have to go to these schools to find a broad variety of job opportunities. Robert Kahn, 21, a junior in economics and international relations at Macalester College in St. Paul, has found work related to his major that has given him a taste of Europe as well as helped to pay his college bills. Unlike typical co-op programs, Macalester's doesn't operate on alternating terms. Students work in the summer, again during a six-week winter break and up to 20 hours a week while studying on campus.

18   Medtronic Inc., a medical-equipment manufacturer in Minneapolis, hired Kahn for an internship in international finance. He was kept on as a senior financial clerk and set up a computer data base for foreign-currency fluctuations. At a salary of $285 a week, he earned $4,500, saved half and put the other half toward Macalester's $9,350 annual costs. He paid the rest with scholarships, a residence assistantship in his dorm and $4,500 from his parents.

19   During his winter break, Kahn finished up his project in Medtronic's Paris office and then began studying economics for a term at the Center for European Studies in Toulon. In June he'll rejoin Medtronic for the summer, traveling among its offices in France, Belgium and Spain. Says Kahn: "Now I want to apply to graduate business schools and specialize in international finance."

20   Cyndi Carr, 20, decided on her career objective halfway through high school. She wants to go into food-processing management. A junior in the Food Science and Technology Department at Oregon State University in Corvallis, she is enrolled in what fellow students call a six-pack program: six months at school and six months at work. Carr started co-oping last fall at General Foods' Birdseye division in Woodburn, about an hour's drive from campus. A quality-control supervisor for frozen foods, she directed a staff of up to 20 workers. She earned $7,200 during her first term at Birdseye and was easily able to cover her $3,600 living expenses. She explains: "I didn't want to go to college and find out after four years that I didn't like what I was doing."

21   Mitzi Canavit, 20, gets a chance to see things from a decidedly uncampuslike perspective. Sitting in the cockpit of an F-15 fighter, she reads the position of a distant jet on her instrument panel, accelerates, pulls up next to it, then drops down, does a loop and signs off.

22   Her F-15 cockpit is actually MACS-5, the Manned Air Combat Simulator at McDonnell Douglas' St. Louis headquarters. There Canavit, a junior electrical engineering major at the University of Missouri, is in her third work term, helping to develop software programs for several types of flight simulators. Besides earning $7,500, she is eligible for many of the benefits of a full-time employee — a common practice in co-oping. Her salary enables her to chip in $925 a semester for room and board at school — her parents contribute the $800-a-semester tuition — and still have some spending money.

23   Says she: "Working in the intense atmosphere at McDonnell Douglas has been a real confidence builder. I know it's going to pay off when I graduate." Right now Canavit, like so many other co-op students, feels like she's flying.

X
WHAT IS A GOOD EDUCATION?

The recent cries for radical education reform spotlight a question that all students and teachers need to answer for themselves — What is a good education? Is someone who reads Shakespeare better educated than someone who knows when to plant crops or prepare for a blizzard? Almost a century and a half ago, Ralph Waldo Emerson wrote that "The farm, the farm is the right school," and E. B. White's more modern essay reflects the same values. Today's advocates of "cultural literacy" emphasize verbal recognition of a broad range of items and ideas, including abstract and visual ones. Does living in society require a shared body of information? And if so, who decides what it should include, and how it is to be communicated?

Your experience reading in sections I through IX should help you enter the debate about what an educated person should be and know. Does such a person need to know the music of both Dvořák and Los Lobos? What should she or he know about the war in Vietnam? Should he or she be able to form opinions about nuclear power and euthanasia, or allow others to make decisions on such complex technological and ethical issues? Which of the authors in this section offers the most convincing definition of *educated*? Developing your own answers to these questions could change your approach to education during your remaining time at school.

WHAT IS A PRACTICAL EDUCATION?

Donald M. Murray

1 A university education is becoming more practical each semester. Our students are increasingly better prepared to go to work in a specific job the Monday after graduation — and that is just the problem. The better prepared they are for the Monday after graduation, the less prepared they may be for a lifetime of work in a society where change is the only certainty.

2   Few of us are doing the same job in the same way and in the same place that we were 10, five, or even two years ago. There is precious little security these days in being able to do a specific task for a particular organization. The successful survivors are those who can learn new jobs in a hurry. And the university has traditionally trained people who are prepared to learn and relearn as need or opportunity arises.

Donald M. Murray, "What Is a Practical Education?" *Foster's Daily Democrat* (Dover, New Hampshire), January 8, 1982.

3   In recent years, however, there has been an enormous, understandable pressure from employers, parents and students to deemphasize those courses of study in the liberal arts and theoretical sciences that appear theoretical, impractical, and frivolous and to emphasize those courses that are pragmatic and vocational.

4   This conflict between general or liberal education and more vocational courses of study has always existed within the state university. It is a natural condition of schools that originally taught the agricultural and mechanical arts before becoming universities. Both strands must exist within the land grant university, but increasingly the forces within universities across the country that speak out for specific education and oppose general education have become stronger. Last year there was discussion of a new general education proposal on the campus in Durham, and some of the academic debate ranged from acrimonious to just plain nasty. This spring the issue of general education will come before the university again.

5   I may seem a strange supporter of general education, since I teach "vocational" courses in journalism. I do think such courses belong in the university — in moderation. We do *not* have a journalism major. We think that the best prepared journalists are those who have a few skills courses and many general courses.

6   Students with a university education should have breadth. Our society is increasingly complex. Our students should be able to put their job, their evolving beliefs, their votes in context. We need university-educated leaders who can see their decisions as part of an historical, sociological, political, aesthetic, scientific, philosophical context.

7   A student with a university education needs not only skills but theory. The student needs to know *why* as much as *what*, the reasons that lie below the tasks of the daily job.

8   Above all, university students need to know how to deal with change. They must be educated so that they are not frightened by change, but capable of absorbing and making use of it. The university, if it provides a good general education, challenges the student and forces the student to think about uncomfortable ideas, unexpected concepts, frightening theories, puzzling problems. The university prepares the student for a life of productive discomfort in which the student can deal with ideas and points of view that are not the student's own.

9   The university must be an uncomfortable place, a threatening place, a challenging place, a place that does not prepare the student just for a specific job, but for the many different jobs the student does not expect to hold.

10   I went to the University of New Hampshire as a student, knowing I would never teach, and came back 15 years later as a professor. I have taught engineers who have become editors, journalists who have become judges, foresters who have become writers, reporters who have become real-estate developers. We must educate our students for the lives they do not expect to lead.

11   We in the university, and those of you outside the university, must make sure that our universities, in a time of economic stress, do not become so practical that our students are cheated of the education they will need in a society that will certainly change in ways we cannot predict. We must make sure our students are given the practical advantages of an impractical education.

BOOK LEARNING

E. B. White

1 Farmers are interested in science, in modern methods, and in theory, but they are not easily thrown off balance and they maintain a healthy suspicion of book learning and of the shenanigans of biologists, chemists, geneticists, and other late-rising students of farm practice and management. They are, I think, impressed by education, but they have seen too many examples of the helplessness and the impracticality of educated persons to be either envious or easily budged from their position.

2   I was looking at a neighbor's hens with him one time when he said something which expressed the feeling farmers have about colleges and books. He was complaining about the shape of the henhouse, but he wanted me to understand that it was all his own fault it had turned out badly. "I got the plan for it out of a book, fool-fashion," he said. And he gazed around at his surroundings in gentle disgust, with a half-humorous, half-disappointed look, as one might look back at any sort of youthful folly.

3   Scientific agriculture, however sound in principle, often seems strangely unrelated to, and unaware of, the vital, gruelling job of making a living by farming. Farmers sense this quality in it as they study their bulletins, just as a poor man senses in a rich man an incomprehension of his own problems. The farmer of today knows, for example, that manure loses some of its value when exposed to the weather; but he also knows how soon the sun goes down on all of us, and if there is a window handy at the cow's stern he pitches the dressing out into the yard and kisses the nitrogen good-bye. There is usually not time in one man's lifetime to do different. The farmer knows that early-cut hay is better feed than hay which has been left standing through the hot dry days of late July. He hasn't worked out the vitamin losses, but he knows just by looking at the grass that some of the good has gone out of it. But he knows also that to make hay he needs settled weather — better weather than you usually get in June.

4   I've always tried to cut my hay reasonably early, but this year I wasn't able to get a team until the middle of July. It turned out to be just as well. June was a miserable month of rains and fog mulls. The people who stuck to their theories and cut their hay in spite of the weather, took a beating. A few extremists, fearful of losing a single vitamin, mowed in June, choosing a day when the sun came out for a few minutes. Their hay lay in the wet fields and rotted day after day, while Rommel took Tobruk and careened eastward toward Alexandria.

5   The weather was unprecedented — weeks of damp and rain and fog. Everybody talked about it. One day during that spell I was holding forth to a practical farmer on the subject of hay. Full of book learning, I was explaining (rather too glibly) the advantages of cutting hay in June. I described in detail the vitamin loss incurred by letting hay stand in the field after it has matured, and how much greater the

E. B. White, "Book Learning," *One Man's Meat*, Harper, 1944.

feed value was per unit weight in early-cut hay, even though the quantity might be slightly less. The farmer was a quiet man, with big hands for curling around a scythe handle. He listened attentively. My words swirled around his head like summer flies. Finally, when I had exhausted my little store of learning and paused for a moment, he ventured a reply.

6   "The time to cut hay," he said firmly, "is in hayin' time."

EDUCATION

Ralph Waldo Emerson

September 14, 1839

1 An education in things is not. We all are involved in the condemnation of words, an age of words. We are shut up in schools and college recitation rooms for ten or fifteen years, and come out at last with a bellyful of words and do not know a thing. We cannot use our hands, or our legs, or our eyes, or our arms. We do not know an edible root in the woods. We cannot tell our course by the stars, nor the hour of the day by the sun. It is well if we can swim and skate. We are afraid of a horse, of a cow, of a dog, of a cat, of a spider. Far better was the Roman rule to teach a boy nothing that he could not learn standing. Now here are my wise young neighbors* who, instead of getting, like the woodmen, into a railroad-car, where they have not even the activity of holding the reins, have got into a boat which they have built with their own hands, with sails which they have contrived to serve as a tent by night, and gone up the Merrimack to live by their wits on the fish of the stream and the berries of the wood. My worthy neighbor Dr. Bartlett expressed a true parental instinct when he desired to send his boy with them to learn something. The farm, the farm, is the right school. The reason of my deep respect for the farmer is that he is a realist, and not a dictionary. The farm is a piece of the world, the school-house is not. The farm, by training the physical, rectifies and invigorates the metaphysical and moral nature.

2   Now so bad we are that the world is stripped of love and of terror. Here came the other night an Aurora [Borealis] so wonderful, a curtain of red and blue and silver glory, that in any other age or nation it would have moved the awe and wonder of men and mingled with the profoundest sentiments of religion and love, and we all saw it with cold, arithmetical eyes, we knew how many colors shone, how many degrees it extended, how many hours it lasted, and of this heavenly flower we beheld nothing more: a primrose by the brim of the river of time.

3   Shall we not wish back again the Seven Whistlers, the Flying Dutchman, the lucky and unlucky days, and the terrors of the Day of Doom?

---

*John and Henry Thoreau

Ralph Waldo Emerson, "Education," *Selections from Ralph Waldo Emerson*, ed. Stephen E. Whicher, Houghton Mifflin Company, 1960.

CREATING A "LEARNING SOCIETY"

Meg Greenfield

1 The best part of the report of the National Commission on Excellence in Education got the least attention in all the posturing and gloating and unconvincing lamentation that was set off by its publication. This was the report's suggestion that the value of learning is not contingent on any material public or private "payoff." The activity itself, pursued not just in school but rather throughout a lifetime, *is* the payoff. So the commission strongly implies, anyway, by its insistence that the principal object of our educational reform should be the creation of a "learning society," one devoted to the joys and rewards of continuous learning, as distinct from the one-shot passing of some exam or other.

2   True, this admirably uncommissionlike thought appears in the company of (no doubt justified) warnings about the perils we face as individuals and a nation by being such slobs about the quality of our schooling; and it may not be quite as unqualified as I would like and therefore have made it sound. But the thought is there. And — naturally — it was widely disregarded by the Axgrinders International when they took up the report. We were at once back to our usual national mode of discussing what is wanted from education: to keep ahead of the international competition, to maintain a strong defense, to get good jobs and keep them. We were also back in a cross fire of I-told-you-so's: the people who are against permissiveness felt vindicated, as, of course, did the people who are for the expenditure of more money, as did those (I am one) who do not find it inconsistent to hold both positions. In the melee, the part about the intrinsic value of learning got lost. It always does — when anyone is eccentric enough to bring it up at all, that is.

3   I realize that there is a sense in which we have a real emergency in the schools, that there are classrooms in various places full of teen-agers who can't read or write and teachers who aren't a whole lot better, that we are at an increasing competitive disadvantage in many areas and that some of what is being taught is so junky and unimportant that it's probably no tragedy that it is not being learned. All this, God knows, needs work. My complaint is that the values we bring to the effort to right the situation are precisely the ones that got us in trouble in the first place and are only likely to perpetuate our grief.

4   Education as an "investment," education as a way to beat the Russians and best the Japanese, education as a way to get ahead of the fellow down the street — it is true that generations of Americans have been brought together culturally by the great force of our public schools and that millions of them have rightly seen their schooling as a one-way ticket out of economic and social privation. But you really do not generate the educational values that count when you stress only these external, comparative advantages. People do not become educated or liberated so much as they become opportunistic in relation to such schooling. And anyway, on the great national-security issues, when was the last time you heard of a youngster doing his homework because he wanted to be better than the Russians in geometry?

Meg Greenfield, "Creating a 'Learning Society,'" *Newsweek*, May 16, 1983.

5   You give a child nothing, I think, when you give him this joyless, driven concept of the meaning of learning. But alas, there are plenty among us who think this is just fine. Following the great cackles of the political antipermissiveness crowd when this report was released, I was struck again by how much such people, who claim to be champions of education, implicitly view education as a disagreeable thing. It is invariably discussed by them — and with relish — as something between a medicine and a punishment that must be administered to its unwilling little subjects for their own good no matter how they howl. *It is not supposed to be fun,* they admonish, and children cannot be expected to like it — what ever happened to our moral fiber, and so forth.

6   Interestingly, this same conception of schooling as something essentially unpleasant that is ultimately vindicated by its benefits seems to animate our occasional bursts of enthusiasm for intellectual pursuits. It is all there in the historic news photos of the quiz contestant Charles Van Doren, earphoned up in his "isolation booth" back in the late '50s, before the program's scam was revealed. I remember thinking the revelation, when it came, was no cruel national disillusion (as the wisdom of the time ran), but rather the most useful thing that could have happened. For the real scam had been the game itself and the idolization of the contestant for trained-seal tricks of memory. It was a mockery of the life of the mind which it pretended to exalt, and the implication of all the adulatory comment was really: look how lucrative this boring, long-hair stuff can be. I was glad when the program and its "hero" crashed.

7   I am bound to say I sense something comparable in certain of those projects we hear about now for making infants preternaturally well informed — a physics instructor at seven months, an art critic at two, that sort of thing. Not all of it, but some of it strikes me as having nothing to do with teaching a child the joy of learning — of giving him that incomparable and invaluable gift. I see baby quiz-show winners, victims of the same fundamentally anti-intellectual values, people who want to acquire, to please, to show off — not to discover, to learn, to be surprised.

8   Schooling needs to be saved from these "friends" — the punishers, the opportunists and the exploiters who profess an undying devotion to the old-fashioned virtues and the life of the mind. But it will of course not be saved by the purveyors of "fun" whose idea of making education enjoyable is to gut it and teach things not worth knowing. There is a difference — night and day — between this kind of "fun" and the joy of learning, and everyone who has ever had one great teacher of a serious subject knows what it is. So do those kids in a handful of slum schools notoriously programmed to fail who instead thrive because they are in the care of people who know what teaching is about. If we could acquire, come to honor, this great value, if we could truly aspire to become a "learning society," the rest — the competitive and material benefits — would follow. But we keep trying to do it the other way around.

EDUCATION AND DISCIPLINE

Bertrand Russell

1 Any serious educational theory must consist of two parts: a conception of the ends of life, and a science of psychological dynamics, i.e., of the law of mental change. Two men who differ as to the end of life cannot hope to agree about education. The educational machine, throughout Western civilization, is dominated by two ethical theories: that of Christianity, and that of nationalism. These two, when taken seriously, are incompatible, as is becoming evident in Germany. For my part, I hold that, where they differ, Christianity is preferable, but where they agree, both are mistaken. The conception which I should substitute as the purpose of education is civilization, a term which, as I meant it, has a definition which is partly individual, partly social. It consists, in the individual, of both intellectual and moral qualities: intellectually, a certain minimum of general knowledge, technical skill in one's own profession, and a habit of forming opinions on evidence; morally, of impartiality; kindliness, and a modicum of self-control. I should add a quality which is neither moral nor intellectual, but perhaps physiological: zest and joy of life. In communities, civilization demands respect for law, justice as between man and man, purposes not involving permanent injury to any section of the human race, and intelligent adaptation of means to ends.

2   If these are to be the purpose of education, it is a question for the science of psychology to consider what can be done towards realizing them, and, in particular, what degree of freedom is likely to prove most effective.

3   On the question of freedom in education there are at present three main schools of thought, deriving partly from differences as to ends and partly from differences in psychological theory. There are those who say that children should be completely free, however bad they may be; there are those who say they should be completely subject to authority, however good they may be; and there are those who say they should be free, but in spite of freedom they should be always good. This last party is larger than it has any logical right to be; children, like adults, will not all be virtuous if they are all free. The belief that liberty will insure moral perfection is a relic of Rousseauism, and would not survive a study of animals and babies. Those who hold this belief think that education should have no positive purpose, but should merely offer an environment suitable for spontaneous development. I cannot agree with this school, which seems too individualistic, and unduly indifferent to the importance of knowledge. We live in communities which require cooperation, and it would be utopian to expect all the necessary cooperation to result from spontaneous impulse. The existence of a large population on a limited area is only possible owing to science and technique; education must, therefore, hand on the necessary minimum of these. The educators who allow most freedom are men whose success depends upon a degree of benevolence, self-control, and trained

Bertrand Russell, "Education and Discipline," from *In Praise of Idleness and Other Essays*, George Allen & Unwin, Ltd., 1935.

intelligence which can hardly be generated where every impulse is left unchecked; their merits, therefore, are not likely to be perpetuated if their methods are undiluted. Education, viewed from a social standpoint, must be something more positive than a mere opportunity for growth. It must, of course, provide this, but it must also provide a mental and moral equipment which children cannot acquire entirely for themselves.

4   The arguments in favor of a great degree of freedom in education are derived not from man's natural goodness, but from the effects of authority, both on those who suffer it and on those who exercise it. Those who are subject to authority become either submissive or rebellious, and each attitude has its drawbacks.

5   The submissive lose initiative, both in thought and action; moreover, the anger generated by the feeling of being thwarted tends to find an outlet in bullying those who are weaker. That is why tyrannical institutions are self-perpetuating: what a man has suffered from his father he inflicts upon his son, and the humiliations which he remembers having endured at his public school he passes on to "natives" when he becomes an empire-builder. Thus an unduly authoritative education turns the pupils into timid tyrants, incapable of either claiming or tolerating originality in word or deed. The effect upon the educators is even worse: they tend to become sadistic disciplinarians, glad to inspire terror, and content to inspire nothing else. As these men represent knowledge, the pupils acquire a horror of knowledge, which, among the English upper class, is supposed to be part of human nature, but is really part of the well-grounded hatred of the authoritarian pedagogue.

6   Rebels, on the otherhand, though they may be necessary, can hardly be just to what exists. Moreover, there are many ways of rebelling, and only a small minority of these are wise. Galileo was a rebel and was wise; believers in the flat-earth theory are equally rebels, but are foolish. There is a great danger in the tendency to suppose that opposition to authority is essentially meritorious and that unconventional opinions are bound to be correct: no useful purpose is served by smashing lamp-posts or maintaining Shakespeare to be no poet. Yet this excessive rebelliousness is often the effect that too much authority has on spirited pupils. And when rebels become educators, they sometimes encourage defiance in their pupils, for whom at the same time they are trying to produce a perfect environment, although these two aims are scarcely compatible.

7   What is wanted is neither submissiveness nor rebellion, but good nature, and general friendliness both to people and to new ideas. These qualities are due in part to physical causes, to which old-fashioned educators paid too little attention; but they are due still more to freedom from the feeling of baffled impotence which arises when vital impulses are thwarted. If the young are to grow into friendly adults, it is necessary, in most cases, that they should feel their environment friendly. This requires that there should be a certain sympathy with the child's important desires, and not merely an attempt to use him for some abstract end such as the glory of God or the greatness of one's country. And, in teaching every attempt should be made to cause the pupil to feel that it is worth his while to know what is being taught — at least when this is true. When the pupil cooperates willingly, he learns twice as fast and with half the fatigue. All these are valid reasons for a very great degree of freedom.

8   It is easy, however, to carry the argument too far. It is not desirable that children, in avoiding the vices of the slave, should acquire those of the aristocrat. Consideration for others, not only in great matters, but also in little everyday things, is an essential element in civilization, without which social life would be intolerable. I am not thinking of mere forms of politeness, such as saying "please" and "thank you": formal manners are most fully developed among barbarians, and diminish with every advance in culture. I am thinking rather of willingness to take a fair share of necessary work, to be obliging in small ways that save trouble on the balance. It is not desirable to give a child a sense of omnipotence, or a belief that adults exist only to minister to the pleasures of the young. And those who disapprove of the existence of the idle rich are hardly consistent if they bring up their children without any sense that work is necessary, and without the habits that make continuous application possible.

9   There is another consideration to which some advocates of freedom attach too little importance. In a community of children which is left without adult interference there is a tyranny of the stronger, which is likely to be far more brutal than most adult tyranny. If two children of two or three years old are left to play together, they will, after a few fights, discover which is bound to be the victor, and the other will then become a slave. Where the number of children is larger, one or two acquire complete mastery, and the others have far less liberty than they would have if the adults interfered to protect the weaker and less pugnacious. Consideration for others does not, with most children, arise spontaneously, but has to be taught, and can hardly be taught except by the exercise of authority. This is perhaps the most important argument against the abdication of the adults.

10   I do not think that educators have yet solved the problem of combining the desirable forms of freedom with the necessary minimum of moral training. The right solution, it must be admitted, is often made impossible by parents, before the child is brought to an enlightened school. Just as psychoanalysts, from their clinical experience, conclude that we are all mad, so the authorities in modern schools, from their contact with pupils whose parents have made them unmanageable, are disposed to conclude that all children are "difficult" and all parents utterly foolish. Children who have been driven wild by parental tyranny (which often takes the form of solicitous affection) may require a longer or shorter period of complete liberty before they can view any adult without suspicion. But children who have been sensibly handled at home can bear to be checked in minor ways, so long as they feel that they are being helped in the ways that they themselves regard as important. Adults who like children, and are not reduced to a condition of nervous exhaustion by their company, can achieve a great deal in the way of discipline without ceasing to be regarded with friendly feelings by their pupils.

11   I think modern educational theorists are inclined to attach too much importance to the negative virtue of not interfering with children, and too little to the positive merit of enjoying their company. If you have the sort of liking for children that many people have for horses or dogs, they will be apt to respond to your suggestions, and to accept prohibitions, perhaps with some good-humored grumbling, but without resentment. It is no use to have the sort of liking that consists in regarding them as a field for valuable social endeavor, or — what amounts to

the same thing — as an outlet for power-impulses. No child will be grateful for an interest in him that springs from the thought that he will have a vote to be secured for your party or a body to be sacrificed to king and country. The desirable sort of interest is that which consists in spontaneous pleasure in the presence of children, without any ulterior purpose. Teachers who have this quality will seldom need to interfere with children's freedom, but will be able to do so, when necessary, without causing psychological damage.

12   Unfortunately, it is utterly impossible for overworked teachers to preserve an instinctive liking for children; they are bound to come to feel towards them as the proverbial confectioner's apprentice does towards macaroons. I do not think that education ought to be any one's whole profession: it should be undertaken for at most two hours a day by people whose remaining hours are spent away from children. The society of the young is fatiguing, especially when strict discipline is avoided. Fatigue, in the end, produces irritation, which is likely to express itself somehow, whatever theories the harassed teacher may have taught himself or herself to believe. The necessary friendliness cannot be preserved by self-control alone. But where it exists, it should be unnecessary to have rules in advance as to how "naughty" children are to be treated, since impulse is likely to lead to the right decision, and almost any decision will be right if the child feels that you like him. No rules, however wise, are a substitute for affection and tact.

████████████

COMPUTER LITERACY IS NOT LITERACY
David Weinberger

1 I was the last person on my block to own a digital watch. In a typical liberal-arts way, I suppose, I resisted and resented everything about computers. Yet now I own a computer, have taught myself BASIC, am learning assembly-language programming, subscribe to computer magazines and find myself discussing baud rates more often that epistemology. I have, in short, become computer literate.

2   Having done so, I now see that despite the clamor for computer literacy from educators afraid their schools will be left behind in today's demanding educational marketplace, we certainly should not require our students to spend much more than, say, 45 minutes on it.

3   There is no denying that students should learn something about how computers work, just as we expect them at least to understand that the internal-combustion engine has something to do with burning fuel, expanding gases and pistons being driven. For people should have some basic idea of how the things that they use do what they do. Further, students might be helped by a course that considers the computer's impact on society. But that is not what is meant by computer

David Weinberger, "Computer Literacy Is Not Literacy," *The New York Times,* November 13, 1983.

literacy. For computer literacy is not a form of literacy; it is a trade skill that should not be taught as a liberal art.

4   Learning how to use a computer and learning how to program one are two distinct activities. A case might be made that the competent citizens of tomorrow should untether themselves from their fear of computers. But this is quite different from saying that all ought to know how to program one. Leave that to people who have chosen programming as a career. While programming can be lots of fun (I enjoy it immensely), and while our society needs some people who are experts at it, the same is true of auto repair and violin-making.

5   Learning how to use a computer is not that difficult, and it gets easier all the time as programs become more "user-friendly." I am composing this article on my Kaypro II using a word-processing program called WordStar, produced by MicroPro International. WordStar is not considered to be particularly easy to learn, yet with half an hour of instruction, one can be writing letters with it.

6   To learn all the complexities of WordStar might take another hour, and then it's just a matter of practicing until use of it becomes automatic. The newer word-processing programs, particularly on machines designed for them (such as the Epson QX-10) are even easier to learn. Learning to use WordStar, in other words, is a skill considerably easier to acquire than learning to drive with a stick shift.

7   Now, let us assume that in the future everyone is going to have to know how to use a computer to be a competent citizen. What does the phrase "learning to use a computer" mean? It sounds like "learning to drive a car"; that is, it sounds as if there is some set of definite skills that, once acquired, enable one to use a computer.

8   In fact, "learning to use a computer" is much more like "learning to play a game," but learning the rules of one game may not help you play a second game. So, when I first got my computer, before I knew anything about programming, I learned how to use it by learning the rules of WordStar. But those rules (e.g., type control-T to have it delete a word, control-QF to have it look for a word) are not transferrable. They will not work with ValDocs, or Perfect Writer, much less with a filing program, or a spreadsheet program.

9   There is no such thing as teaching someone how to use a computer. One can only teach people to use this or that program, and generally that is easily accomplished.

10   And we need not worry about helping our children over their fear of computers. What fear of computers? If they aren't using one at home, then they are at the corner arcade computing hostile aliens into glowing smithereens. This is a generation of Pactots and Intellivisinfants. Entire adolescences are being spent courting green-screened consoles. The last child who was afraid to use a computer is today Ricky Nelson's age.

11   Programming is a different matter. It cannot be taught in half an hour. Indeed, it is an open-ended, creative skill that many students will find enjoyable. But so is chess; it is not a liberal art we should be teaching in our schools.

12   Learning programming may have beneficial effects. To program, one must be able to analyze a problem into small steps. It requires a sort of analytic thinking,

and students ought to be trained in analytic thinking. Unfortunately, the nature of the steps is dictated by the programming language the student is learning.

13   For example, you want your programs to run as quickly as possible. This means they should have as few steps as possible. In S-BASIC (the version of BASIC I use, which is close to Pascal), there are varius sorts of commands (FOR . . . NEXT, REPEAT . . . UNTIL, WHILE . . . UNTIL) one could use. You will decide which one to use by analyzing your program in light of the options S-BASIC offers.

14   While this requires a desirable rigor of thought, it would be more useful for students to learn to analyze problems into terms other than those set by their progams. If we want students to learn analytic thinking, logic would be a better course to require than computer programming, for in logic they will discover the distinctions drawn by careful thought uninfluenced by the practical demand of having a machine respond properly.

15   Let them take philosophy where they will learn how to think in ways that respond to the needs of the time and of the subject matter, rather than learning how to analyze all problems into a series of computer commands.

16   A programming language in some ways is truly a language. I find myself at times thinking in S-BASIC. Perhaps it will be argued that it is beneficial for students to learn a new language. I agree. Let it be Latin. Let it be one that makes them more literate. That, after all, is the true goal of a liberal education.

CULTURAL LITERACY: A REVOLUTIONARY THEORY ABOUT WHAT WE NEED TO KNOW

Susan Tyler Hitchcock

1 Whenever E. D. Hirsch Jr. publishes a new book, idols shudder. In *Innocence and Experience* (1964) he contradicted prevailing assumptions about the poetry of William Blake. In *Validity in Interpretation* (1967) he stepped on the theoretical toes of literary critics in power. In *Philosophy of Composition* (1977) he drew fire from writing teachers, theorists and practitioners alike. And yet, once the dust settles in every case, Mr. Hirsch's work expresses a distinct message to which everyone in the field must pay heed.

2   And now he has done it again, with *Cultural Literacy: What Every American Needs to Know.* He has written a book that is extreme, controversial and urgent, a book that bluntly states that our educational system has been misguided for decades, and a book that proposes a way out of this mess.

3   "I am essentially taking on the dominant educational theory for the last 50 years," says Mr. Hirsch. He gestures, stops mid-sentence, looks out the window, looks back and grins. "Just because it was dominant doesn't mean it was right."

Susan Tyler Hitchcock, "Cultural Literacy: A Revolutionary Theory About What We Need to Know," *UVa Alumni News,* May/June 1987.

4   Mr. Hirsch believes that American schools, harking back to the ideas of John Dewey, have been teaching skills rather than information. As long as children learn to read and write words and manipulate numbers, they are literate, according to prevailing theories. As they progress in school, they are trained in more complex skills: how to recognize a figure of speech, how to summarize information, how to read a mathematics textbook, to quote from a list of skills Mr. Hirsch has generated from public school texts now in use.

5   But, Mr. Hirsch insists, a key component of literacy is missing from this gameplan: substantial information, a familiarity with facts, names and dates; idioms, stories and traditions; mottoes, symbols and concepts — the stuff of our culture. To grasp and remember such information is to attain cultural literacy. And cultural literacy is as necessary to becoming an educated, responsible adult as are the more basic skills of reading, writing, and arithmetic.

6   For example, Mr. Hirsch believes that a high school graduate ought to be familiar with titles, stories, characters, mottoes and speeches from Shakespeare's most famous plays. By saying this, though, he does not mean that every student needs to read every play by Shakespeare. "Let's say you are a teacher, and you've only got three weeks to teach Shakespeare. You can't have *Hamlet* and *Romeo and Juliet* both," says Mr. Hirsch. "If you're smart, you'll read *Romeo and Juliet*, because *Hamlet* is too hard for anyone under 30. But you had better teach the story of Hamlet and the 'To be or not to be' speech if you want your kids to be literate."

7   His case for an educational curriculum valuing cultural literacy is solidly and meticulously grounded in the scholarship of psychologists and linguists. Research indicates that reading comprehension requires not only direct word recognition but also recognition of schemata — that is, contextual background knowledge that fills in much more information about the meaning being conveyed. Mr. Hirsch says he began noticing the significance of background knowledge as he tested reading comprehension, seeking a way to define the most readable writing styles. What emerged in those experiments was that reading comprehension seemed as much a function of the reader's background knowledge as it was a function of how well the text was written. High school students who do not know who Ulysses S. Grant was (and there are many who don't, says Mr. Hirsch) could never fully understand a paragraph about Lee's surrender to him at Appomattox Court House.

8   The bulk of Mr. Hirsch's book is a disciplined, logical argument establishing background knowledge as essential to reading and establishing knowledge of a national culture as essential to responsible citizenship. What is drawing more attention and raising more hackles, however, is the book's appendix: "What Literate Americans Know," a list of some 5,000 items compiled by Mr. Hirsch and two other University faculty members, historian Joseph Kett and physicist James Trefil. From Abraham and Isaac to Zeus, Zola, and Zurich, the list represents a first concrete step toward making Mr. Hirsch's theories on cultural literacy educational realities.

9   "We consulted a lot of materials to get candidate items," says Mr. Hirsch. "The process was varied. I myself went through the *American Heritage Dictionary*, page by page. Joe Kett went through a number of history textbooks. Jim Trefil went to

the specific disciplines, asking what is the absolutely essential information in those fields. We followed different routes to get the candidate terms. The candidate terms that we reviewed must have numbered a hundred thousand. Obviously the thing to do is to get too many terms and then eliminate some that were too expert. I don't think we fully succeeded. I think there are some terms on the list that are still too expert."

10   As Hirsch, Kett, and Trefil refined the list, they devised a practical rule of thumb for making selections. "The main principle that we used was whether the word or phrase would appear without explanation in the front section of a newspaper like the *New York Times* or the *Washington Post*," says Mr. Hirsch. With that principle in mind, they were in fact generating a list of terms and concepts needed by Americans to read and respond as educated citizens.

11   "We kept the list of history terms sort of short, for example," says Joseph Kett. "It had to do with the extent to which individuals are remembered, not their importance in history. We tried to decide what people would assume you know. You would say that, in the 16th century, Charles V was much more important than Anne Boleyn, but she is on the list and he is not. People expect you to know something about her, but they would expect you to have to look up Charles V in the encyclopedia."

12   Although they didn't strive for equal thirds, their list roughly divides into three sections: humanities, social sciences and natural sciences. Because of the state of general science knowledge today, the science terms on the list represent a somewhat different criterion for inclusion. "In science there's a special problem, because the science education of the average adult has been sadly neglected in this country," says James Trefil, professor of physics and author of numerous science books written for the general public. "If we restricted our list to what people know in science, it would have been very short. The criteria became more normative. In a sense you could say that if you know the science terms on this list, you are not illiterate in science. That is saying something different from being literate in science."

13   Now that the list is compiled and published, Hirsch, Kett, and Trefil are at work on a dictionary of definitions for the thousands of entries on the list. While it will not replace encyclopedias, it may become a standard reference of associations and accepted meanings in our culture. "It's the sort of thing that somebody might buy to give a kid before he goes to college," says Mr. Kett. "It's really designed to make learning easier. We all assume that once they read about something in the dictionary, they will get interested in looking further for more information."

14   Mr. Hirsch has also organized a Cultural Literacy Foundation, which has two projects underway. First, it will market Cultural Literacy Tests, which draw systematically on the list and are meant to be administered at the 11th or 12th grade level, perhaps serving similarly to college entrance exams. Second, it will host a series of conferences at which the list of cultural contents will be divided according to learning levels.

15   Although an individual might pick up the list as a curiosity or, perhaps more diligently, a checklist for further readings, Mr. Hirsch feels that the most important

effect of the list will come when creators of textbooks and public school curricula take it seriously, producing reading materials that draw their substance from our cultural tradition. His research suggests that little if any of this sort of material is available for teachers. "I was at a conference and saw an elementary school textbook called *Odyssey*," recounts Mr. Hirsch. His hopes for a text that would expose young readers to the stories of Homer were dashed when he read the book. It was a collection of contemporary travel stories. "Nowhere in the book did they even explain the title," he says.

16   Mr. Hirsch doesn't mean for teachers to use the list as a vocabulary drill, but he won't be unhappy if that happens. "We all deplore vocabulary drills, but in fact they have been found to work. Young children love rote learning and memorization," says Mr. Hirsch. "Sure, I very much worry about these ideas being trivialized and misused, but the positive effects so outweigh the negative."

17   "It's a very revolutionary thing," says James Trefil of the list and the ideas behind it. "It's been a kind of gentleman's agreement up to now. You and I talk together, and we assume common knowledge. No one has ever actually written this down for someone who isn't in the club."

18   But revolutions — even intellectual ones — are rarely quiet, so Mr. Hirsch is bracing for the onslaught of arguments his book will raise. He has received praise from such powerful and diverse figures as U.S. Secretary of Education William Bennett, American Federation of Teachers President Albert Shanker, and California Public Instruction Superintendent Bill Honig. But he also has had to answer critics of the idea that cultural contents can be summed up in a list, especially a list compiled by three white males from the ivory tower.

19   "The ammunition is going to be hostile, political, ideological posturing," says Mr. Hirsch. "The ideas are going to be called fascist, undemocratic, and WASP. People are very upset by the fact that this sort of list would perpetuate the existing culture. But you can't get rid of tradition. Tradition takes you over. And this list might speed up change. There's no telling what literacy would do."

ON THE FINN SYNDROME

Robert Pattison

1   [*Cultural Literacy*] overlooks a crucial American reality, the Finn syndrome.

2   Huck took a passing interest in Moses till he found out he'd "been dead a considerable time; so then I didn't care no more about him; because I don't take stock in dead people." When cultural literacy impended, Huck lit out for the territory. Huck was as much a critic as a pupil, and there's no reason to think his descendants are any different.

Robert Pattison, from "On the Finn Syndrome and The Shakespeare Paradox," *The Nation*, May 30, 1987.

3   *Cultural Literacy* is built on the premise that urchins arrive at school like so many floppy discs fresh from the factory. There the teacher formats them for use in the economy and sends them on their way. Anyone who has tried to teach the apostrophe ought to know better. If, as Hirsch says, children are "storing facts in their minds every day with astonishing voracity," it is also true that they are selective. To claim that American students are ignorant because they are badly taught is a half-truth, the complement of which is that they are also ignorant by choice.

4   Hirsch himself provides ample evidence that the Finn syndrome lives on in postindustrial America. He quotes a Los Angeles man who wrote that in years of meeting with teen-agers he had yet to find one who could tell him when World War II was fought. Is it possible that one hundred California teen-agers have never heard the dates of World War II? If, as is more likely, some of them have run into the information, why didn't they store it "with astonishing voracity"? Here is the Finn syndrome alive and well. Students do not want to know the dates of World War II. They don't take stock in dead people. Hirsch is not likely to have any more success than the Widow Douglas in his attempt to "sivilize" the American people.

5   Hirsch includes a host of proverbs on his index: "Ignorance is bliss," "Easy come, easy go," "A little learning is a dangerous thing." He omits one that is particularly relevant to his enterprise: "History is bunk." Hirsch might make the young learn aphorisms of this kind, but what will he do if they believe them as well?

6   A culture may share information, but it lives by beliefs. Hirsch's book has nothing to say about these beliefs — and how could it, since many of them are antagonistic to the whole undertaking of *Cultural Literacy*. Hirsch recognizes that "even a descriptive list cannot be entirely neutral with respect to cultural politics." By politics he means the confrontations of the 1960s. Should Malcolm X and Betty Friedan be on the culture index? Hirsch includes both, and in this sense of politics, he is a liberal. But a culture index poses a fundamental political question: How far are the wishes of the people to be consulted in determining the nature of culture itself? And here Hirsch is a conservative: history, literature and science are enduring categories of human experience, and the inclination of the people to reject or reshape them must be resisted in the nation's best interests. Hirsch and his followers will have to find some way to quiet the not-so-still voice that says to the American whenever he is confronted by culture, "I been there before."

BOOKER T. AND W. E. B.
(BOOKER T. WASHINGTON AND W. E. B. DU BOIS)
Dudley Randall

1 "It seems to me," said Booker T.,
  "It shows a mighty lot of cheek

Dudley Randall, "Booker T. and W. E. B." *Cavalcade*, eds. Arthur P. Davis and Saunders Redding, Houghton Mifflin Company, 1971.

To study chemistry and Greek
When Mr. Charlie needs a hand
To hoe the cotton on his land,
And when Miss Ann looks for a cook,
Why stick your nose inside a book?''

2 "I don't agree," said W. E. B.
"If I should have the drive to seek
Knowledge of chemistry or Greek,
I'll do it. Charles and Miss can look
Another place for hand or cook.
Some men rejoice in skill of hand,
And some in cultivating land,
But there are others who maintain
The right to cultivate the brain."

3 "It seems to me," said Booker T.,
"That all you folks have missed the boat
Who shout about the right to vote,
And spend vain days and sleepless nights
In uproar over civil rights.
Just keep your mouths shut, do not grouse,
But work, and save, and buy a house."

4 "I don't agree," said W. E. B.
"For what can property avail
If dignity and justice fail?
Unless you help to make the laws,
They'll steal your house with trumped-up clause.
A rope's as tight, a fire as hot,
No matter how much cash you've got.
Speak soft, and try your little plan,
But as for me, I'll be a man."

5 "It seems to me," said Booker T. —

6 "I don't agree,"
Said W. E. B.

INDEX

Page numbers in italics refer to readings and authors of readings where mentioned in discussion; accompanying page numbers in Roman type refer to pages where the readings appear.